The Pain of Confinement

The Pain Of Confinement
Prison Diaries

Jimmy Boyle

CANONGATE
1984

First published in 1984
by Canongate Publishing Limited
17 Jeffrey Street,
Edinburgh, Scotland

British Library Cataloguing in Publication Data
Boyle, Jimmy
The pain of confinement.
1. Barlinnie Prison. *Special Unit*
2. Rehabilitation of criminals—Scotland
—Glasgow (Strathclyde)
I. Title
365′.66   HV347.G72B3

ISBN 0-86241-040-1

Typeset by Witwell Limited, Liverpool
Printed by the Pitman Press, Bath

*This book is
dedicated to my wife Sarah
who in giving so much of herself helped me
make it, and to my editor at Canongate
for her faith in me
and my work.*

1

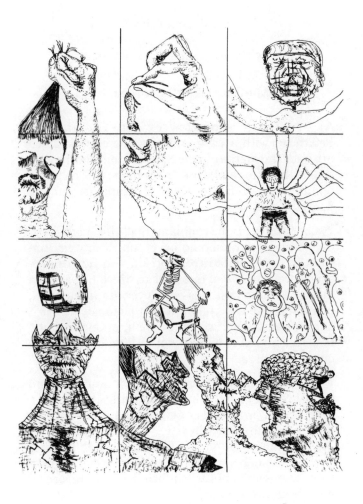

275/68 James Boyle Born 9.5.44
3.11.67 Glasgow High and Jury
Murder — Life Imprisonment

A report was submitted by the Governor of Peterhead with a view to having the above named prisoner transferred to the Special Unit, Barlinnie. I should like to emphasise two points which, in my opinion, make Boyle a prime candidate for the Special Unit.

I am firmly of the opinion that this man is so dangerous that he should never, under any circumstances, be liberated from prison and further, despite the assaults and incidents in which he has been involved in the past, he is still, even at this moment, planning further assaults and further incidents. He is liable at any time if given the slightest opportunity, to attack and kill anybody with whom he is liable to come in contact.

This may appear to be very melodramatic and highly coloured but I have studied this man over a long period and I am convinced that this report is purely factual. One alteration I would make from the recommendation of Peterhead, I think that Boyle should be trasferred to the Special Unit as soon as possible, not when the charges at Inverness have been disposed of.

GOVERNOR.

Unknown to me the preceding report had set into motion a series of decisions that were to have a profound effect on me. My last book, *A Sense of Freedom*, gave some insight into this but ended leaving many of its readers — if my mailbag is anything to go by — feeling angry at the state of our prison system; relief that I had survived the physical brutality of it; and wanting to know why the revolutionary concept of the Special Unit was being systematically undermined by politicians and prison authorities. *The Pain of Confinement* is meant to give a better understanding of this and is a personal account of the day to day struggle involved.

It would be presumptious to assume that people buying this book will have read the previous one and so for this reason I want to give a precis of the situation that led to the introduction of the Special Unit.

In 1967 I was one of a group of young men sentenced to long prison sentences in the wake of the abolition of Capital Punishment. I was sentenced to Life Imprisonment with a fifteen years recommended minimum. The media labelled me 'Scotland's Most Violent Man'. Like others I considered myself a young man with no hope or future. I was part of a group known as the living dead.

When such a devastating sentence is pronounced on a person it dramatically changes him or her. On the one hand I knew I didn't murder the man I was convicted of killing but on the other I was sensitive to cynical prison governors and policemen mimicking 'Every prisoner in prison proclaims his innocence'. This is their way of reinforcing — and perhaps living with — the system they represent. I was determined not to be seen to be bleating, complaining or showing weakness in the face of such people. If they wanted tough and ruthless opposition then they would get it. I had nothing to lose.

I found myself connecting with other prisoners who were in the same boat. We had a lot in common and built up personal relationships when in solitary through an archaic ventilator system that was linked to each cell. In this way we began to plan and co-ordinate our actions. We soon learned that the system which copes very well with individual troublemakers doesn't when these same individuals begin to organise and co-operate with each other.

In response to this the authorities became more reactionary and oppressive in their measures to contain us. After a succession of fights, riots and demonstrations five of us found ourselves held in the Cages in Inverness prison.

These were iron-barred cage fronts that sub-divided a prison cell; reminiscent of those used to hold animals in a travelling circus. We were, at times, kept naked and given one book per week to read. The decor and structure of the whole block was built for sensory deprivation. The rules — blatantly plastered on the wall — stated that no prisoner would be kept in the cages for less than two months or more than six. This was flagrantly abused.

Having taken us to the ultimate in official punishment the authorities had in fact played their last card. They were now helpless in the face of our rebellion. In a strange sort of way we had been set free. I was aware of having an unpretentious naked truth and dignity in that cage. The authorities would publicly portray us as monsters and animals, but privately we knew that the degree of brutal violence exerted on us by gangs of prison officers was no different to that for which we were convicted. It was condoned by people turning a blind eye to it and the public not wanting to know. In essence, it was an unconcious, unspoken collusion that was rooted in revenge. The underlying belief being that acts of physical violence have an instant 'cure' in the exercise of a more powerful physical violence. In fact, it made all of us worse.

The climax of this downward spiral took the form of a bloody riot in the Cages. Many prison officers and prisoners were injured. The doctors announced that I wasn't expected to last the night. Four of us were eventually charged with the attempted murder of six prison officers. It made no difference to any of us. I simply worked my body back to physical fitness in preparation for the next bloody occasion. I thought there was no alternative.

Behind the scenes, outwith our sphere of knowledge, the

authorities were stretched to the limit. A number of prison officers in Inverness resigned from the Service in the aftermath of the riot. Prison staff in other prisons were saying they wouldn't have the hard core of us back. The pressure was on to get the Special Unit opened.

It was a February morning in 1973, that two of my caged fellow prisoners were whisked off to an unknown destination. I arrived six weeks later. We found ourselves resident in the newly-opened Special Unit. It was a strangely disorientating experience. In earthly terms, it was as though we had landed in an unknown foreign country. Our suspicion, hostility and aggression clashed with the attitudes of the staff setting out to be warm and friendly. It was easier for us to cope with prison staff who were unhelpful, authoritarian and potentially violent.

My two fellow prisoners were as bewildered as me. Ben and I had come through so much together, starting with approved school then Borstal and continuing here in prison. Although from different cities (Ben was from Edinburgh) we had forged a strong, binding relationship in these institutions. Both of us had attempted to organise the Prisoners' Solidarity Movement and paid the consequences for doing so. Although he was the fifth prisoner in the cages he was not directly involved in the riot. His being the smallest sentence — seven years with small additional sentences for assaulting prison officers — we thought it best he refrain from participating.

Unlike the rest of us, Ben had a determinate sentence so knew when he would be released. His perspective of the Unit was different from that of all the others. Having been brutalised and given these additional sentences throughout the previous years he was not impressed by the fact that the authorities wanted to be considerate when he only had eighteen months of his sentence to serve. His anger and hostility towards them was at times uncontainable. The real dilemma for Ben was that his loyalty to me meant that he had to restrain himself in the Unit. He knew, the way things were going, that it was life or death for me. He hoped for my sake that this place was for real.

Along with Ben and I, the other prisoner, Larry, had come through approved school, borstal and prison. He was serving a life sentence for manslaughter. In addition he had incurred twenty years for riots and fights. In order to cope with this Larry demanded, and was given, drugs. Over the years this increased till eventually he was on a massive dosage. It was sad to see the transformation that took place in him as the daily dose began to take effect. He was extremely intelligent and witty but as the drugs took over he would become a rather pathetic, incomprehensible shadow of himself. He had been involved in the riot and was a co-accused, charged with six attempted murders.

Individually and collectively our reputations went before us. Ben and Larry informed me that the Prisons Department had resisted my transfer to the Unit. They considered that I would be a disruptive influence. Knowing that I had been kept in the cages alone — the two other co-accused rioters having been dispersed to Peterhead prison — and fearing what might happen to me there, these two had put pressure on the Unit staff to get me here. Both of them had been told that the Special Unit was a whole new ball game. They suggested that it should prove itself so by bringing me down.

There were two other prisoners in the Unit who had been transferred from other prisons. Rab was a very thin, shy young man with thick, greasy black hair. He wore heavily-framed spectacles which made his face seem thinner than it was. Sentenced to Her Majesty's Pleasure he had been inside since he was a boy of sixteen and was now twenty nine. He had been transferred from Saughton Prison, Edinburgh, more because he was an embarrassment to the system than because he was a troublemaker. The fact that he had been confined throughout some of the most formative years of his youth meant that he had been denied experiences and difficulties other youngsters have been through by the time they reach their late twenties. He found it very difficult to converse or communicate with anyone. He simply sat in front of the television all day. Emotionally he was still sixteen years old.

The remaining prisoner was a man called Ian. He was serving a life sentence for killing his girlfriend in a suicide pact that went wrong. He had served five years of his sentence. An obese man with very complex, personal problems, I marked him as someone not to be trusted. He was big, heavy and going bald and wore wire-rimmed spectacles with thick glass. He was thirty years old.

Out of all the staff in the Unit the one who stood out at this very early crucial period was Ken Murray. He was a principal nursing officer and also a member of the Executive Committee of the Scottish Prison Officers Association. A tall, striking man, he emanated an aura of sincerity and integrity, qualities that I seldom associated with a prison officer. He stood out above the others because he spoke his mind, often to the acute discomfort of his colleagues. He was also a very sensitive man and articulate with a keen interest in politics. He was a member of the working party that set up the Unit, playing a prominent part in its inception. Ken was the one person amongst the staff who was idealistic in viewing the true potential of the Special Unit as a meaningful alternative to the old penal system. Never at any time did I doubt his sincerity, but I had a lot of problems dealing with it.

In those first few days I took the opportunity to look around the Unit. Over the years I had been conditioned to think that I was only allowed to go where I was told. Here in the Unit there was access to all the nooks and crannies. It took some getting used to. Having come from solitary confinement I had the distorted perspective that the Unit was huge. In actual fact it was small and claustrophobic. It was originally used to hold female prisoners but had recently been made secure to hold us. Although a part of the main prison of Barlinnie, the Unit was completely segregated by a wall and barbed wire.

There was a small courtyard where we could exercise. Inside there was the reception/meeting room adjacent to which stood an open space where we envisaged putting a small pool table. Nearby was a hotplate and kitchen, the food being brought from the main prison. All of this was on the ground floor. Through a double-door entrance was the cell area. This was a slim double-tiered block with a wide corridor-type hall and five cells which looked over the hall. The cells had heavy oak panelled doors with steel lining. Each had a judas spyhole. One cell, No. 5, on the ground floor had an ominous double door, the one place to which we had no access. This was a punishment cell. There was an enclosed stair leading to the upper-level cells. This was where I was housed. The interior of this part of the building had four long windows that never seemed to let in any light. At the far end of each tier was a toilet area with some sinks for washing up. On the top floor there were two showers.

It was clear from the start that this prison was different from all others we had been in. We were told that we had the freedom to fill our days in whatever way we wanted. There were tools to use and this in itself was remarkable. We were given access to metal cutlery and other utensils that could be used as weapons. The attitude of the authorities was in giving trust instead of withholding it. This was established as soon as I entered the Unit with my personal possessions in a tied parcel. The prison officer, Ken Murray, gave me a pair of scissors to cut the string. Here I was, still awaiting trial for six attempted murders of prison staff and being given a weapon by one of their colleagues. It was mind-blowing.

What made the Unit unlike any other place was the way staff and prisoners were allowed and encouraged to sit down and talk together. This was the single most im-portant factor of the Unit. It allowed us to break down all the barriers of hostility between us. This was by no means easy. In conjunction with this there were built-in weekly meetings where we all sat down as a group and discussed the week's events and decided on domestic issues. There are a number of examples of how effective these groups were. In the preliminary discussions which the staff had be-fore the Unit opened they initiated some daft rules; being allowed one shower a week, and locking up the access to the shower taps. These were issues which we eventually tackled through these meetings. Another silly rule was that staff would make up our weekly wage on the basis of our daily attitude or dress tidiness etc. The wages in total were sixty pence. If our attitude was wrong one particular day they would recommend that two pence should be deducted. When we heard this we honestly thought the staff were a bunch of loonies. The origins of these rules could clearly be traced to the old prison tradition of 'good order and discipline'. This clearly clashed with our history of chaos and lack of discipline. The reality for Larry and I, because of the pending High Court trial was the prospect of a further twenty years each. How anyone could expect a two pence deduction to modify our behaviour was beyond me.

It was sheer coincidence that the Special Unit was conceived at a time when I was struggling with my own identity. In having a vague notion of where we were both going and what needed to be done I had to handle these realities even at this early stage. Ben and Larry were so full of hate and mistrust for the authorities that their behaviour constantly bordered on physical violence both to each other and to the staff. Being the recognised leader, I soon found my position was to support, and prevent them.

An example of this took place within a month of my arrival. I happened to be in one part of the Unit with Ben and some staff when Rab came running in, excited, saying that Larry was in trouble. We all ran through to the cell area to find Larry standing with a pair of scissors at the throat of a member of staff. I walked in and across to Larry and told him to give me the scissors. The atmosphere was very tense. The staff who had been following Ben and me stood there and let me do the talking. Larry reluctantly gave me the scissors and Ben moved in to separate Larry from the staff member. There was a whole series of on-the-spot decisions taken here that resolved the matter without physical injury. On seeing Larry threatening a colleague, the staff didn't go for their batons and rush in, but stopped, and allowed Ben and me to handle it. Had they drawn their batons then we would have turned on them as a group. By

9

doing what they did, they brought out the best in us.

Having defused the incident, we were left with how to deal with the aftermath, as there were a lot of high feelings buzzing around. In another prison Larry would have been locked up. It was decided that a staff/prisoner meeting should be held immediately, so everyone assembled in the meeting room. The Governor wasn't in but that seemed to be an advantage as it meant we could deal with the matter without the traditional 'official'. Feelings were still running high and though we didn't realise it at the time, this was the most crucial experience in deciding which way the Unit should go.

Larry was confronted by everyone asking him to explain his behaviour. The atmosphere was very heated. I was most vocal in taking him to task but Ben also spoke up leaving no doubt that he was angry at Larry. Rab and Ian said very little as they were out of their depth and possibly frightened. I could use hard words with Larry and get through to him. We were given the story as to why it had all started. Larry had been about to snip off his beard with the scissors when a member of staff intervened. Larry, like me, was awaiting trial for charges placed against us at Inverness and the rule is that accused persons are not allowed to alter their appearance before the trial. This rule applies mainly to people coming into prison on charges from the outside where identification is vital but once in prison it is unnecessary as the staff can identify prisoners with or without beards. When the staff member intervened, Larry thought he was trying to provoke him so he reacted violently. It was clear that Larry had been in the wrong and so in my view had to be taken to task, as should a member of staff had he been wrong. He admitted that he shouldn't have gone for the staff member and apologised. There followed from this a general discussion on staff/prisoner relationships and it was agreed by everyone that there should be no restrictions placed on disagreements being aired verbally but that physical violence must be forbidden in this Unit. The tension within the room was so thick, it could have been cut with a knife.

After the meeting, both Larry and the staff member went to his cell and sat there for almost two hours discussing the whole thing. They came to an amicable understanding, shook hands and left the matter like that.

We had redefined 'punishment' as we knew it. Had Larry been locked up in a punishment cell, he would have lain there and reinforced his anger, and his belief that all staff were bastards. Had he been beaten up, it would, to him, have justified what he had done and made him determined to do it again to show that he wasn't afraid of them. It came to me than that the issue of punishment as practised in the normal penal system is counter-productive and can only make matters worse. However, having experienced this meeting, I could understand why people want to lock the offender up — it is easier. The very fact that we had to sit with Larry, expressing our views on what he did, meant that we were committing ourselves to the Unit and, beyond this, accepting responsibility for our own and other people's behaviour. But it wasn't easy, as some of those people present saw Larry as a very frightening character, and the fact that they were openly reprimanding him was in itself scary as we were still not sure of these meetings or their possible repercussions. It let us see, however, that there is a lot to be learned from incidents such as this one and that through confrontation we could come to understand why people behave in an anti-social manner. In fact, all of us were being taken to higher levels of sensitivity. We were learning to learn from experience.

Although this may sound as though the matter was concluded to everyone's satisfaction and that we were all happy, this was far from the truth. It affected all of us in different ways. Some of the staff felt vulnerable with Larry still walking around amongst them. They were worried that they might be attacked. The fact that I had disarmed Larry, and that Ben had also played a positive part, receded into the background. Ben, Larry and I were too closely associated with violence and with each other, and when one of us did something, the other two were seen to be his allies. It was difficult for the staff to see any of us as

11

individuals. I distinctly remember, while blasting Larry at the meeting, thinking that my whole world had been turned upside-down. The thought of my having a go at another prisoner in this way for going at a prison officer would previously have been unthinkable. I felt quite treacherous. That night, locked in my cell, I went through intense periods of torment at the thought of 'selling out'.

No sooner had this incident cooled when all hell erupted between Ben and another staff member. It started with a heated exchange but Ben left and stewed it over and the whole thing started to build up inside him. He was intent on beating up the staff member and I had virtually to hold him down in his cell till his rage and anger had subsided. These things happened outside the knowledge of the staff. Ben had been good in dealing with Larry's anger, but in dealing with his own he wasn't so adept. These incidents confronted us with parts of ourselves that we just didn't know about and couldn't handle. In these tense moments both Ben and Larry would ask me why I stopped them going ahead, reminding me what bastards staff were. I would agree but my thoughts were on the potential of the Unit not the hatred I felt for staff and this was the difference. They were both going round constantly watching staff, taking their every word as being against them. Sometimes they were right and other times they were wrong. The damaging part was the obsessive nature of their attitudes. In spite of the fact that my sympathies lay with my friends I could also see the good things staff were doing and I did not want to ignore them or see them as part of a 'con game'. Ben and Larry were making me question myself. Maybe I was falling for a 'con game'? There were moments when I would look with penetrating clarity at my life sentence, my treatment in prison, the brutality, the further prison sentences and now another High Court trial overshadowing me. Maybe I was being too naive.

Ironically, it was a group of prison officers who helped dispel my doubts about the place. It was impressive to see them push forward radical steps for the development of a more humanitarian regime. An example of this was when we debated the abolition of the punishment cell. This was a lengthy discussion on an emotive issue. When winning the vote by an overwhelming majority, a group of us — prisoners and prison staff — armed with hammers and chisels went through to dismantle it. We immediately transformed it into a weight-lifting room. 'Punishment of another kind', remarked the obese Ian. It was a powerfully symbolic moment for all of us. Having no punishment cell meant that if things went wrong and a prisoner became violent there would be nowhere to punish him or keep him out of harm's way. Trust would become paramount.

Three months after the Special Unit opened we were taken to trial and, as expected there was elaborate security with armed police and a helicopter buzzing overhead. I didn't know why this was, for no-one was going to attempt to get me or the others out as we had no money and didn't know any people who would be willing to help. It was like a circus and though we were the main performers it was stage-managed beyond our control. In my view this whole procedure tends to be nothing more than a deliberate propaganda exercise initiated by the police. It is effective in prejudicing a jury. Knowing this I set out to counter the propaganda by replying to the judge when asked to plead to the charges that I didn't understand them. On being asked what I didn't understand, I replied that on the night in question I had almost died and yet no-one had been charged with attempting to murder me. This captured the headlines the following day.

At this point Larry and I didn't really care what we received as we both felt that our lives were finished anyway, so whether it was two or twenty years hardly mattered. I was more interested in exposing the conditions of the Cages and the whole penal system and so arranged my defence around this. The evidence unfolded with prison staff saying that the prisoners had made an unprovoked attack on them while attempting to escape. Despite the seriousness of the occasion there were moments when we were all dumbfounded or doubled-up with laughter during the telling of the tale. One prison officer told of finding a transistor radio in a chamber pot. Another told of finding a twenty foot makeshift rope in a cage. Almost all the prison officers denied using their batons although there was extensive medical evidence that our injuries bore traces of their use. The medical evidence also showed that I wasn't expected to last the night as a result of my injuries.

The four of us, aided by Ben, had our turn in the witness box. Even amidst this massive security the court refused to take the handcuffs off us. Our defence was that we held a peaceful demonstration but when the prison officers attacked us with the batons, violence erupted. We made it clear that our protest was about the brutality and the conditions we were kept in. We highlighted the fact that our human rights were being seriously abused. The attempted murder charges were reduced to assault, of which we were found guilty and given six years. The attempted escape charge was dropped. Larry and I were returned to the Special Unit and the other two accused, to Peterhead Prison.

There was considerable publicity surrounding the trial and the conditions we had been kept in. The point was made that if human beings are kept in such conditions, it is little wonder they react like animals. What interested me was that the Cages had been implemented without public knowledge. It was clear that most politicians were unaware of their existence. Even more intriguing, many prison officers didn't know about them. The Departmental Working Party set up to look into the treatment of long term prisoners (whose findings recommended the setting up of the Special Unit) noted in their report that the Cages, in fact, made some prisoners more violent. It was good news that they weren't to be used again. We took the opportunity to suggest that the solitary block be converted to a Special Unit type block. The fact that we had been given an additional six years meant little to us in our no-hope situation.

Having it all out of the way was also of considerable relief to our families who were another crucial aspect of the

Unit. They were initially allowed to visit us on Saturday and Sunday afternoons in the meeting room. We would sit around tables in a relaxed atmosphere, one prison officer sitting nearby. In the normal prison system, the visiting arrangements were that long-term prisoners would be granted nine hours per year, and usually that was in a small cubicle with glass and wire barriers separating visitor from prisoner. We could now sit around an open table with coffee, chat and even touch if we wanted to.

Although I could never openly admit it at the time, there were a number of problems attached to this new visiting situation. Over the years in prison I had almost become a stranger to my family and was very apprehensive about their coming to see me. I didn't know what I would be able to talk about for this length of time. I was dreading those moments of long, drawn out silences when we were all lost for words. Although the prison system had done nothing to help matters over the years the blame could not be laid entirely at its feet. I was suddenly faced with the fact that never in my life had I really sat down and had an interesting conversation with my family. We were all inarticulate, and didn't know about such things as politics, or other matters that dominated our lives. I would simply have to get to know my family all over again. However, the overwhelming advantage of the visits was the humanising effect it had on us. Larry was a different man with his mother and family. I would glow when my old relatives visited me bringing my two children with them. We embraced each other with tremendous warmth and comfort. Sadly, some of the others had few visitors. The good thing about the Unit was that these guys got to know our families so in this way they also felt connected to outsiders. In recognising the value of allowing families to become closely associated with the Unit the visiting situation was allowed to develop so that visitors could have free access to the place during its opening hours. Prisoners were soon allowed to have their visits in their cells without supervision.

Another development of the visiting was to encourage interested members of the public to come in and see how the place worked, to discuss crime and punishment, law and order or any other topic of interest. One early visitor was Joyce Laing, an art therapist, and she started coming in every week. One day she brought in a small bag of clay for us to fool around with. I know it sounds corny but I did feel something magical happening to me while fingering this clay. I did a portrait of Ben. This was the first time I had ever done anything creative. I could feel the adrenalin pumping; I could feel my insides soaring with pleasure; I could feel the elation of seeing the finished object. Within a short space of time I was involved in sculpture to a serious degree. I was soon working with hammer and chisel on large blocks of stone.

As the months progressed, some of us were beginning to get deeply involved in what we were doing; others were drawing back and beginning to feel threatened by it all. It became apparent that some of the staff didn't want to continue in the Unit as they felt they were losing their authority. On one occasion when Joyce Laing was sitting with us, a senior member of staff stood up and made a startling outburst. He wanted to get out as he didn't like calling prisoners by their first names, and that as a result of working here, he and his family were on tranquilisers. Most of us were surprised at this as he had been making positive suggestions. The truth of the matter was that he, like one or two others, was under considerable pressure from colleagues in the main prison with whom they socialised who were opposed to the Unit.

You see at first, when Ben, Larry and I were brought into the Unit, there was a sigh of relief throughout the prison service that we had been taken out of their hair. But the rumour amongst staff was that the place would only last a few weeks before we got fed up with it and rioted and stabbed staff willy-nilly. However, as time wore on and they saw that this wasn't happening, they then accused the staff of being afraid to say no to anything we asked for. Rumour followed counter-rumour and soon it was being said by outside staff that we were getting breakfast in bed and that the staff were serving us. This resulted in tremendous hostility from prison staff throughout Scotland. The pressures on Unit staff were considerable. They would, for instance, be openly heckled by their colleagues coming through the main gate on their way in. Most stayed in prison quarters within the shadow of the prison walls and the hostility became so intense that as well as the men being given the 'silent treatment', their families were also. On the one hand, this brought the staff and prisoners closer together within the Unit, but on the other hand meant that those who were undecided would say little at our meetings if a progressive suggestion was made.

Despite all of this, progress was being made. Rab was now allowed out on escorted paroles. Ian and Ben were also allowed out under the same conditions. Ben was very much ill-at-ease taking prison officers to his home. After his second visit he refused to take any more. Ian and Rab developed theirs so that they were soon going out on a daily basis. These outings were invaluable to all of us. In giving the prisoners contact with the changing world outside it would eventually assist their readjustment when finally realeased.

One problem we had was with the Governor, who up until now had remained in the background. He was a man that most of us knew from the old system. He was a Governor Class 4, the most junior rank, working in a place where the Community meeting — staff and prisoners — discussed the day to day events and made decisions on them, a situation far different from that in any other prison. As a result he found himself in a sort of no-man's land. He seemed to find it difficult to become a part of the group, so kept himself distant from all of us. He was certainly uneasy in his present position and made no secret of this. He was putting pressure on his superiors to define his role more clearly. But then most of us at times longed for a more black and white situation when we found the going tough in this new place. We all tended to long for the world we knew rather than grasp this new concept and make something of it. The Governor's hesitancy to become a part of what was happening contributed to the split in the staff. Those who were career-minded and who could see the Governor as being influential in this respect, tended to play the game according to him when he was present, and to the rest of us when he wasn't. This was something that we, a nucleus of staff and prisoners, couldn't tolerate. It was my view that in accepting the Unit, one had to be loyal to the concept and the philosophy of it, and not to any one individual. If the staff were being loyal to the Governor, who appeared to be opposed to the Community decision-making process, then it would be damaging. Equally, if the loyalty of any of the prisoners had been to Larry during the scissors incident, it would have killed off the Unit then and there.

Out of all the people who visited the Unit in those early months it is well worth mentioning Alick Buchanan-Smith, Under Secretary of State for Scotland for the Tory Government. His arrival was a big occasion. It was important that this guy, the first politician to come and see us, should know that what was happening here was unique and indeed was showing the way forward for the entire penal system. He came in surrounded by civil servants and other officials. We made it clear to him that he would get an honest account and not a whitewash, and he said he appreciated this, acknowledging that this sort of things goes on with people in his position. We made what we thought was a solid case for expanding the concept of the Unit. He agreed but said that he had to play his cards right due to the public attitude over these issues. He felt sure that it would expand. He made it clear that he was hanging his political hat on this place and had great hopes for it and that if we were experiencing any problems we should not hesitate to get in touch with him direct. I was impressed with him. When a minister makes a visit such as this to a prison, he has to inform the local M.P. and this was Hugh Brown who expressed a willingness to come too. He was a Labour M.P. and also a man who made a good impression on us. He became a strong and loyal defender of the Special Unit.

Peter Whatmore was the Consultant Psychiatrist to the Unit. A tall, handsome man with a benign manner, he moved around almost like a shadow without real presence. Knowing our hostility towards his profession this low profile was wise. After the initial settling-in period he had a chat with me saying that after a while he would like to do a sort of case history on me. He had approached the others with the same proposition. I told him I didn't want to know and he accepted this. However, we did have interesting discussions about the Unit and he said he would be quite happy to be made redundant from the place if it meant that people had no need of him. He visited us on a three sessions a week basis. I found that his views were similar to those of Ken Murray and myself. So in Peter I found an ally. It was important for me to be able to connect to people who were like-minded as they would help me to keep my thoughts clear on what we were doing.

While we were having these discussions, Peter Whatmore frequently suggested that I should keep a personal diary of what was going on within me and the Unit. This struck a chord in me.

Within the Unit hierarchy itself, the official second-in-command was Chief Nursing Officer Walter Davidson. He had twenty odd years service behind him and had missed the beginning of the Unit because of a serious car accident. He had joined us almost four months after the place opened and was a real asset. Most of us had known him for years in Peterhead prison where he was looked on as an old traditionalist. It was interesting to watch a man of his service and rigidity try to break into the way of the Unit. Some mornings, he would come on duty looking be-draggled after a long night tossing and turning. All of us could identify with it but in him it was most noticeable and touching.

I was beginning to recognise that the Unit could be a golden opportunity to create a new model for the penal system and would be an important springboard for radical changes throughout. In order for this to happen we had to formulate a realistic and practical concept that could prove its worth. This meant for me having to make a superhuman effort not to succumb to either group but to remain loyal to myself and what I felt to be right. There was much to learn from the past experiences that all of us had had and this could be used to gain knowledge and understanding of the whole law and order issue. I got tremendous support from Ken and Peter Whatmore at this point, but they were going home each night and having time off whereas I was constantly in it, there was no break for me or the other prisoners. I could not allow my problems of adjustment to effect others. Sometimes I was successful, other times I wasn't. In short, it was bloody hell.

In contrast to me, Ben was more at a disadvantage as he would fluctuate from the relaxed to the tense. We would occasionally sit in his cell where he would lie on his bed all day, full of anger. We tried to talk through what it was that was bothering him but he was so mixed up that he didn't know himself. I was very close to him, but always wondered why he had so much anger bottled up inside him. He felt that he had lost most of his remission, had been given further sentences, had been brutalised by staff and that in putting him to this place they were trying to palm him off, and the truth was that he just didn't want to know. He simply said that he wanted to go back to the world he knew best, the old penal system.

During the process of my coming to grips with the Unit, I began to structure my own day with a series of activities that would help me to survive a very long period of incarceration. Rather than lie passively and wish my life away, I decided that I would continue the fight to stay alive; this time, my tools would be used in a creative and constructive manner.

I got up every morning at 6 am and did some jogging round the small outside yard, then inside to do my weightlifting, yoga and other exercises. I had a punishing routine that gave me strength, stamina and suppleness. I would spend the latter part of the morning on my studies — sociology and psychology. In the afternoon I would do some sculpting and reserve the evening for writing or visitors. When the doors were locked I would do creative writing into the early hours. I was reversing the prison routine by not having enough time on my hands to get the day's activities done. I became a workaholic — this was my drug. Although I tried to keep to my set routine, life in the Unit was such that unforeseen incidents would arise and get priority. Added to this was the fact that we were getting many visitors and as I played a prominent role in the place I would take them around or be deeply involved in the discussions with them.

In March 1974, thirteen months after the Unit had opened, there was a change of government, with Edward Heath being replaced by Harold Wilson. There was jubilation amongst us as we were all sympathetic to the recent miners' cause, and against the three-day working week. But there were also mixed feelings about Alick Buchanan-Smith leaving as he was a genuine person and in regard to the Unit we were sad to see him go. But overall we felt that we were onto a winner with Labour taking over. Normally, it doesn't make much difference who is in power as far as prisons go, simply because politicians tend to shy off them as they are low priority in any government's policy. It was our naive view that the Labour Government would recognise the value and importance of the Unit and use it as a wedge to make inroads for change in the penal system as a whole. At a junior ministerial level within the Scottish Office we had Hugh Brown MP in charge of the prisons, along with agriculture and fisheries. God knows what they had in common but there you are. We were glad to see that it was someone we knew who had the post and who had been in the Unit. I'm sure it was important for Alex Stephen to have as his boss an under-secretary who was sympathetic to what we were doing.

There was no doubt that Alex Stephen was doing all he could to promote the Special Unit. As one of the Unit's founders, his most encouraging innovation was to take one of the large halls in Peterhead Prison and model it along lines similar to the Unit. Clearly he had support of the Governor there. What made this particular experiment so bold was that Peterhead Prison was believed, by both prisoners and staff, to be a place of no hope. A young, energetic Governor was put in charge. It was meeting lots of opposition, just as the Unit was, but was moving along in the right direction.

In addition to this he was planning the new semi-Open Prison, Dungavel, in a similar way. This meant that there would be a larger model of the Special Unit standing on its own. When it did open, he placed in charge the young energetic Governor from Peterhead Prison. It was very exciting as it meant that others were benefitting from the work we had been doing. The Unit concept was given a further shot in the arm when Alex Stephen informed us that his opposite number in the Home Office was flying up from London to see what we were doing. It seems they were looking for ways to resolve the quite complex problems they were having. They were contemplating an isolation system similar to the Cages in Inverness. Alex advised against it, recommending that they visit the Special Unit. We were told to expect then as their flight was booked. It was cancelled at the last minute. Apparently this was because of inter-departmental wrangles. The Home Office went ahead to implement Control Units which were based on sensory deprivation.

In the midst of all this Alex Stephen put it to us that he was thinking of bringing members of the media into the Unit to see what we were doing and he asked our opinion. We felt that it would be a good idea and an ideal opportunity to put our case to the general public. There was a great deal of discussion on this with varying opinions being expressed. The Department suggested that we should speak to some representatives of the Scottish Information Office. This was the first I had heard of this group but it was explained to us that they are the official Government body who deal with the media for all Governmental departments. They asked if we could help them write up an official press hand-out which we did.

Concrete moves were made to prepare the way for a Press open-day and we were trying to ease them in by doing some P.R. first. There was lots of discussion on this matter.

We were protective of the Unit and would have hated to see it torn apart by journalists who had no idea what we were trying to do. We invited the editors of the Scottish press in and although only two came, we made the most of this.

The relationship between the Department and ourselves was good and things were moving along smoothly. We still had regular visits from the various departments within the Prisons Division and even the Parole Secretary had asked me to help him work out a new booklet that they were intending to circulate round the prison system. This sort of thing was indicative of the relationships we were establishing. Knowing that these were the people who really made the recommendations and decisions I missed no opportunity in bringing home to them the plight and conditions in the main system.

This was an important reason for inviting more and more outside visitors to the place. We were actively working to break down the myths that ordinary people tend to believe concerning prisons and the people incarcerated in them. Hugh Brown MP, now Under Secretary of State in charge of prisons was exceptionally good on this as he wrote saying that although he had now become a Minister, he would like to keep in touch and come in on an informal basis to visit us. He was a very earthy speaker who liked a good argument and we enjoyed his company. He was a man of the people who was concerned about social issues. Another MP who was less sympathetic to us was Teddy Taylor, also from Glasgow, who was loud in his hardline views on the issue of Law and Order. Many people said he believed in what he preached though I was never convinced of this. I see him as no more than a 'political illusionist', pretending that there are simple answers to this very complex issue. A wily politician, he seems to cover his underlying thirst for revenge behind a facade of crusading zeal for the public safety.

Another person I was introduced to at this point who would be important to my life was Richard Demarco, the Gallery Director from Edinburgh. He was a small man with a strong personality and a tremendous amount of energy, a one-man tornado. Coming in he moved around, never standing still, always talking. Joyce Laing, Alex Stephen and another departmental official Tom Melville brought him in. Ricky then took over. He walked around my sculptures that were on display, examined and discussed them using words that I was ignorant of. He said, there and then, that he would like to put my work on show at his gallery during the Edinburgh Festival. I was quite happy about this and it was arranged that Larry, who was doing poetry, should have his work displayed alongside it. An exhibition of my works was something that I hadn't thought about, though I was excited by it. I had been doing these sculptures and putting them on shelves in the Unit and now had a good collection. The next logical step was an exhibition but as it was all new to me there hadn't seemed to be a next step, until now.

On the day of the Press Open Day, we all made the necessary arrangements, including the making of tea and sandwiches. We were told that there were so many they would have to be split into two groups, one in the morning, the other in the afternoon. Some of the younger representatives of the Scottish Information Office were present and they seemed very nervous, more than we were. In the morning group, we split then up and everyone helped to take them round, while the SIO stayed hot on our tails, listening to every word and in a constant state of agitation. We then sat down to have a question and answer session. We had agreed to be as open and honest as we could and try not to hide anything, even the warts. We felt proud of what we were achieving here and were quite prepared to talk about it and stand up for it. During the discussion one journalist asked what was the most serious issue we had had to face to date and I began to tell him about the scissors incident and how we had handled it. I happened, at this point, to catch sight of one of the SIO representatives and he looked as though he was going to have a fit. He was shaking his head from side to side so blatantly that all of us were sure that the journalists must see it. The fact was that the SIO wanted us to play a nice safe game and not give the

24

media anything they could get their teeth into. I believe that they wanted the media to get as little information as possible and that they disapproved of this type of session.

On this occasion I think that the journalists, on the whole, reciprocated our honesty. One of them made the point, in reference to my sculpture and the brief chat we had, that he found it hard to accept that I possessed anything other than violence. Another, who had attended most of my trials, thought that nothing could be done with guys like me. One of them said that he had just completed a pre-recorded TV programme in which he had put across the view that no murderer could be rehabilitated, but during our discussion he had come to realise how wrong he was and he now retracted all he had said. The one newspaper that didn't come in was *The Scotsman* and an SIO guy told us that they had refused on principle because they would not submit their articles to the SIO for vetting prior to publication. This certainly endeared me to this newspaper as in my view the interference of the SIO is an infringement on the freedom of the press. It was through examples such as this that I was gaining more and more insight into the subtle controls that exist in our so-called 'free society'. After the question and answer scene, I was interviewed by journalists, as were Larry and the other prisoners.

In the afternoon, we had a similar situation to the morning. One journalist remarked that he was totally against gangsters and the like but since speaking to me, if he could, he would take me to his home that night. It was all good stuff and somehow we felt we had made a breakthrough. That night, exhausted, I lay in bed. The reports wouldn't be out till the following week as they had to be given a going over by the SIO who said they would keep us in touch with what the articles were like, as they received them. Throughout the next week, the SIO guys called in giving us the latest. By now all their nervousness was gone as they were over the moon at the quality of the reports even from the 'gutter press'.

The newspaper reports came out and were unanimous in

applauding the Unit, saying what a good experiment it was. The SIO phoned, with a big sigh of relief, to say how pleased they were. In conversation we were told by them that they had to advise the newspapers to drop one of two things from their copy, on the grounds of security. The same representative remarked that on the whole the press were self-regulatory, knowing what the SIO expected of them. It seems that this subtle censorship on prisons is adopted because the media as a whole are dependent on them for a mass of government information. On this occasion it worked to our benefit but I was made aware that this was a case of the tail wagging the dog.

With all this going on, I was told in confidence that the present Governor would be getting transferred shortly and that we would be getting a new one. I think this was welcome news to both him and us as it just wasn't working out. Although it was becoming quite an emotional issue amongst us all, we felt that a parting of the ways was best for all concerned. It was soon after this that our new Governor arrived.

Just before the Festival exhibition, the BBC and ITV television companies were given permission to come in and do documentaries on the Unit. The directors came to see us and explained exactly what their thoughts were, and asked us for ours. Because of the recent publicity, the Department was being inundated with requests from overseas, from journalists and television people, to come in and see the Unit. Within the next four weeks, three different television programmes were made. But the climax to this whole period came when I was told that I would be allowed to visit the Edinburgh Festival to see my work on show. I just couldn't believe it. The psychological jump that was needed to leap from being a no-hope person to someone walking the streets for a day was too much to accept.

On the morning of the 15th August '74, I labelled all my sculpture, crated it, and with the help of two members of staff, put it in the van and we drove it through to Edinburgh prison where the Final selection was to be made. We off-loaded it and then went into the City. The elation I felt at my feet touching the first street pavement in many years was a shock. Here I was walking along the street, almost as though I was in a dream. I had lain awake all night expecting someone to shout through my cell door that it had been cancelled, but no. Just simply seeing people and being with them outside the walls of the prison was wonderful. I watched cars passing by, people going about their everyday things, unaware that I was looking at them enviously. We walked along to the Demarco Gallery where we met all the artists I had been introduced to from there. The reception was fantastic. All of us went to the well-known Henderson's Restaurant for a meal and then to a pub for a beer but I went outside and stood there alone at the doorway as I wanted to watch all these everyday things. I stood there, alone with my thoughts, letting my mind think over the past eight years and what I had been through in prison, and yet here I was, standing in a busy street, alone, but knowing I was returning to prison in the evening. It was a strange experience but much as I abhorred prison, there was no way that I would have done anything impetuous or silly to harm the Unit or the future which I now felt I had. If anything, my standing there in the street with these thoughts was proving the success of the Special Unit.

Later in the day, I went with a girl to the Private View of the Paul Klee exhibition in Edinburgh's Botanical Gardens. While there, I was introduced to many other artists. We then walked through the gardens to see the Henry Moore sculpture, *Reclining Figure*.This was the first sculpture that I had really seen and I let my hands run over it, caress it, putting the upper part of my body inside it. We returned to meet the two staff members and drove back through the busy streets of Edinburgh on our way to Glasgow and prison.

That night, I lay in bed afraid to go to sleep and blot out the events of the day. I was so alive within myself that every fibre of my whole body seemed to be tingling. All that had happened was now a kaleidoscope of images in my head. On two occasions during this Edinburgh Festival period I was allowed out on the same basis. It was a fantastic morale boost for me. There was now real hope injected into my life again.

Alex Stephen told us that Larry's poems were being favourably commented on at the Festival and that a publishing company had approached him about the possibility of publishing them. Larry was asked what he felt and he said he was interested so it was arranged that the publishers be brought in. This was a tremendous boost for Larry. He was making an effort to come off his drugs and the fact that he was gaining recognition as a writer came at the right time. All of this was bringing him to the point of trusting the people around him.

On the subject of publishing material, I spoke to Alex saying that I would like to write about my life, thinking along the lines of an autobiography. He informed me that the Department were looking into this and encouraged me to continue in the hope that something might come of it.

Within the Unit, generally speaking, there was a sense of achievement amongst everyone. The morale of the staff was very high as they felt the work they were doing had some purpose, they were seeing an end product. This was very rare within the penal system. Their recommendations were very progressive. They put forward a proposal which was accepted, that prisoners could have access to the phone. They took the view that as visiting conditions were open and most of the prisoners were going out on daily paroles the natural extension of this should be the availability of the telephone. Each of these freedoms that we were given had to be used responsibly. If we abused any of them then the matter would be reviewed and curtailed. In doing this they were throwing the responsibility onto us.

One day the Governor told me that the SIO were on to him as the local press were making enquiries asking if I had been out at the Edinburgh Festival two weeks before. I spoke to Tom Melville, the Departmental official, on the phone and he told me not to worry or lose sleep over it as it would be okay. There were small factual pieces on the front page of two daily newspapers. A few days later it was followed up in another paper with Teddy Taylor quoted as saying he was writing to the Secretary of State for Scotland about this. I shouldn't have been shocked but I was. What did they want? Here I was, still in prison, but behaving responsibly. Is this not what people should be looking for from people like me? No-one had thought to say how well behaved I was when out. I was left feeling that all people like Teddy Taylor wanted to do was to crush me into some sort of merciless submission. In addition to this Joyce Laing told us that two people from the press had approached her, offered her money, and tried to get her to say that sexual orgies and drinking parties took place in the Unit. One of them asked if it was true that I had given a social worker a child. Teddy Taylor had written a letter to the Secretary of State alleging that he was receiving alarming rumours from a source saying that girls were coming in and out of here as well as the allegation that a social worker was pregnant. In the letter he only made a brief reference to my being allowed out on parole.

It was at this point that a major row broke out among the Executive Committee of the Scottish Prison Officer's Association of which Ken was a member. The Committee issued a statement to the media saying that prisoners in other prisons were assaulting staff to precipitate their transfer to the Special Unit. Ken told them that this just wasn't true and asked if they had been to the Department for the official figures of assaults since the Unit opened. The General Secretary of the Scottish Prison Officer's Association hadn't been but he insisted on publishing the statement just the same. Ken said he was disassociating himself from it and said that he would like to make a public statement to this effect and they agreed to this. The result was that both Ken and John Renton appeared on television to be interviewed on the matter. Ken had the official figures which showed that the amount of assaults on staff had greatly decreased since the opening of the Unit. There was tremendous anger against Ken from some of his colleagues for showing disloyalty to his Executuve Committee colleagues and as a result of this, he was expelled from the

Committee. Ken is a born negotiator and thinker and it was crystal clear that in expelling him, the prison staff had cut off their noses to spite their faces. No-one amongst them could equal him. Ken himself was deeply hurt by this and very bitter at having been treated in this manner. He wanted the Committee to be a leading force in advancing public thinking away from the usual sterile arguments surrounding crime and punishment. From our own selfish point of view, we knew we were now without a voice in this important policy-making body.

Added to this, Tom Melville appeared in the Unit and announced that Alex Stephen was to be transferred to another department in the Civil Service to take over the Scottish Devolution issue at Dover House in Whitehall. His successor was to be Mr John Keely who was coming from Planning — Roads Division, with no experience of prisons whatsoever. This was quite a stunning blow to us but at this point we didn't realise just how much it would affect us. Tom offered some reassurances by saying that he was to be promoted to Senior Executive Officer and that he would have the ear of the Director, but this wasn't much of a consolation to any of us. The only touch of humour at this point was my receiving a letter from a crank, addressed to Babyface Boyle, and she offered to come and sing for us.

We were informed that the man taking over Alex Stephen's position, John Keely would not be directly responsible for the Unit but that this would be handed over to Mr John Oliver. Now Oliver was a man who had come from the prison service as a basic grade officer, and worked himself up to Governor and now found himself in a very powerful position. For obvious reasons the post Alex Stephen held was to be divided in two, with John Keely as Controller of Administration, and John Oliver as Controller of Operations. The fact that someone who was steeped in prison tradition was now responsible for us left us in a state of more than a little trepidation for the future operating of the Unit. I had come to know Oliver over the years in prison. He was Inspector of Prisons when I had been kept inordinately long periods in the Inverness punishment wing.

We arranged a farewell lunch party for Alex Stephen, inviting some guests in. It was a moment of false gaiety for us as we felt as though some giant force was manipulating the wind of change against us from behind the scenes. After lunch Alex spoke to the prisoners individually and he came to my cell to have a talk. He said that a lot of responsibility would weigh heavily upon me. I asked him what was on hand for me. He went on to say that my escorted paroles would continue. He mentioned that there had been some controversy over them and that David McNee, Chief Constable of Glasgow and later Commissioner of the Metropolitan Police in London, had been on to the Department about it but had been told, diplomatically, to stick to his job and let the Department get on with theirs. He then revealed to me that he had seen me in Inverness, looked at me through the spy-hole into the Cage lying there unconcious, shortly after the riot. He felt ashamed of what they had turned me into. It was an emotional scene between us. In each of us was the unspoken question — what was going on? The Community was seeing first hand the very civilised way in which the System disposes of its radicals.

Alex pointed out things that I should bear in mind. I took them seriously. He said that the Unit and its future was pretty secure as we had a number of influential visitors who supported the place and we had had very wide, successful press coverage. He said, wisely, that only the prisoners could blow it, or provide the ammunition. I took this very much to heart. In telling me this Alex Stephen was warning me of the opposition we would meet when he moved on. I made sure his words and advice were taken seriously.

Most of the prisoners were having plenty of personal visitors as well as outsiders coming to see the Unit. I had my family, and most of my other visitors were from the art world. I had more or less lost contact with the people I used to go around with on the outside. I was moving into new spheres of understanding and so was rapidly changing. On the other hand, both Larry and J.C. had friends up to visit them that they had made in prison which meant that some of the local criminals from Glasgow started coming in and I was apprehensive about this. During my spell in the Unit I could have had a great number of guys like these in to see me and in fact had refused quite a lot who had asked. It's not that I didn't like them but simply that the emphasis of my life had changed. There was also the fact that I knew the Glasgow scene and how if the police got to know, and no doubt they would, then they would automatically assume that they were bringing other things with them. These guys could have made problems had this been the case, but it would have been more from sympathy and misguided loyalty than badness.

Larry and J.C. found themselves getting into this scene but felt they were out of their depth as they didn't know how to talk to the guys on this level and so they approached me to speak to them. I had to explain that the Unit was a different scene and that it wasn't on to abuse the trust we'd been shown. The amazing thing is that the guys respected it and this to me was heartening. It would be silly to say that none of us ever had a drink in the Unit as that would be a lie, but it had to be discreet and not too often. It had to be done in such a way that the staff didn't know. My own view was that if I was asking prisoners, who were in prison and had been for many years, to exert self-discipline and try to accept responsibility, then I shouldn't expect them to be superhuman.

On writing this I feel trepidation knowing that those hypocritical sections of our society interested in sensationalism will make meat of this revelation to justify their allegations of drinking parties and orgies in the Unit. But such was not the case. Comparatively speaking, the Unit was a model of restraint and good sense when put beside the abuses that exist in the main penal system. There, drugs, drink and sexual exploitation play a considerable part in day to day activities.

Rab, by now, was going out every day to do 'community

32

work' in the Citizen's Theatre. Ian was breeding budgies and still going out on paroles but on the whole he was a loner. He would go into deep depressions and lie in his cell for days on end. He should have been getting help in a psychiatrically orientated hospital setting. J.C. was still going out daily and had been home to his mother's house in the Shetlands. Both he and Rab were awaiting decisions from the Parole Board. The strain of this was apparent in them.

I was heavily involved in my sculpture and had a boost on hearing that the Director of the ICA in London had seen my work and was keen to exhibit it. I hadn't really thought of other exhibitions so this was a pleasant surprise. There was also a request for me to speak to a group from the Howard League for Penal Reform and the Governor said he would support this.

When my case for getting out was put to the Department on 1st October '74, they were hesitant, saying that I wouldn't get a day out until the following summer as the Chief Constable (David McNee) had sent them a letter and they had to be careful. They accepted totally that there was no problem in terms of security and knew I wouldn't do anything silly, but they would like to have a 'cooling off' period. I found it difficult to comprehend that the Chief Constable could influence the Prisons Department to this extent. It was something that Alex Stephen had told me had been sorted out.

Whatever happened at that fateful meeting between Wattie, the Governor and the Department people, it certainly wasn't to our good. There was a distinct feeling within the Community that our activities were being looked on as subversive in some way. There was a wind of change in the air, and no mistake about it. Information started to seep through the grapevine that Alex Stephen had been doing things without informing the Department. We found this very hard to accept. In certain circles of the hierarchy, the new trend seemed to be that anything that Alex Stephen touched stank. The flow of visitors from the Department swiftly dried up and communication with them became somewhat restricted.

As though to reflect the changes at the top, things began to fragment within. There was a bad scene between the Governor and those members of staff committed to the Unit. The Governor was having difficulty accepting that Ken was their recognised leader. He said he was too involved with the prisoners and that staff couldn't trust him. It was clear than Ken had become a target. Word was shifting through to us from the Department that we had moved too fast too soon, that prisoners had too much say in the running of the place, and too much freedom. The Governor was in the unfortunate position of being the man in the middle, which wasn't a problem when Alex Stephen had been keeping regular contact with the Community, but now this was gone, a more cautious regime was there and the emphasis had clearly shifted.

Until the point that I entered the Special Unit I was considered a product of a failed social and penal system. From the age of twelve I had been in and out of institutions, some of which were considered the harshest and toughest in the country. Since that age I had spent twelve and a half months on the outside, never sustaining freedom for more than three months at any one time. On looking around me I could see many others with similar backgrounds. Institutions as they exist at the moment are a danger to the community. They simply harden attitudes and make prisoners more dependent by taking away all responsibility. When locked behind the walls prisoners are forced to depend on each other. They will band together to beat the system, sometimes for the most commendable reasons: to help someone smuggle out a personal letter to a wife, for instance, when their marriage is under considerable pressure. They share books, magazines and tobacco. By the same token they will share techniques in crime and make new contacts. When feeling the pain of their confinement at its deepest level they have to listen to politicians, the media, and public, calling for tougher sentences and prison regimes. However, when being

34

critical of this traditional system one must be able to offer a constructive alternative and in this I will nail my colours to the mast at the outset of this book.

Penal reform does not mean an easier time for prisoners and I hope the following pages make this point quite clear. There can be no punishment more severe than the loss of one's freedom. If we work from this premise then we should be gearing our system to making offenders more responsible people so that on release they will be capable of playing a useful role in society. How do we do this? First, we have to accept that some individuals, because of their irresponsible behaviour and danger to others, have to be taken out of society for a period of time. Once they are inside we must try to understand why they resorted to, say, violent behaviour; from the understandable though unacceptable domestic murder to the more complex sadistic killing. Our learning from such incidents will be invaluable in building up knowledge and perhaps preventing similar ones. At this and other levels the prison system would be making a valuable contribution towards crime prevention.

We should make our prisons more accessible so that members of the public could go inside and discuss crime with prisoners. It may be that they would want to confront them directly as a result of offences in which they have been the victim. Prisoners who never really see the effects of their offences would be made to think more deeply about it. They should have more access to their families: a wife having to cope with a family and household responsibilities would allow the prisoner to share the emotional trauma that his irresponsible behaviour had left her with. The full burden of the offence would be brought home to the offender. In doing so it would introduce an outside perspective into the heart of the institution.

We should ensure that the day-to-day running of the system is geared to making people more socially responsible. How do we go about it? We should be building up people's confidence in small things: cooking, how to budget and manage the small finances they will have to live on, how to articulate and discuss their needs and problems without resorting to violence. We should be teaching people how to drink in moderation which would mean having supervised access to alcohol. They should be allowed to have sex, and to share their feelings with a partner at an intimate level. The prison authorities should be making every effort to link the prisoner to a group of people making a positive contribution in the area he is returning to. This would mean the prison system running along lines parallel to society, the dividing line being the wall that surrounds the institution.

As for the more complex cases, and it should be remembered that these make up a very small percentage, there should be Special Units for them. They need a highly skilled and specialised regime; one that can help unravel their deep needs and problems. In saying that their crimes are bizarre and often outrageous, I am quick to add that they are human beings, and much as we are revolted by their misdeeds we still – for the sake of humanity – must learn from them. What made them do what they did? Only they can tell us, or can they? At least we should be attempting to find out. In removing people from our society we should bear in mind that we are exercising a powerful punishment. The least we can do is ensure that all of us learn from it.

I began to keep a detailed diary of what was going on in the Unit. In the process I took copious notes of daily events. Publishing the diary seemed the best way of telling the story, since it is a record of my thoughts and reactions to each day, not judged with hindsight and distorted through time. All of this has shaped my past and present experience into a vision of what the penal system should be.

2

Speak not so loudly
For I am in pain
your voice's sharpened edges
Are cutting my brain

Larry Winters

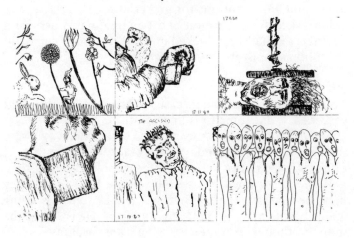

28th SEPTEMBER '74

Rab went out with a staff member today and had a good day. Larry isn't sleeping too good and had to get his drugs increased. He is on a lot of drugs and I'd like to see him reduce them...

3rd OCTOBER '74

This morning I went straight into my studio/cell and cast the two pieces I was working on. I was in there till 4pm.

Rab went out to work at the Cits [Citizens Theatre] today and J.C. went out for groceries.

Ian asked for a Petition and is intending to ask for a transfer. He had been locked up all day though came out for food as he is obviously depressed.

5th OCTOBER '74

Took my sculpture from its cast — 'Struggle'. It turned out very well. I did some finishing off on it.

David Scott (BBC) came in with a colleague. David said the Unit film is okay and will be a cracker. He is putting it off for a few months due to the internal politics of the BBC.

World In Action sent us £100 for the Unit fund. They have been okay. James Lindsay (new prisoner) is going about bewildered and is trying to adjust. He is lost at the moment though everyone is trying to assist him.

6th OCTOBER '74

Did some more finishing on my latest piece 'Struggle'. Also took 'Mantrap' from its cast and it looks good. Spoke to James Lindsay quite a bit today. He is still very much at a loss and will take a bit to settle. He stands about not knowing what to do.

Larry is doing fine but is in a bit of a drugged state. I told him he should reduce them and he says he will. He had a visitor today and I sat in with him.

7th OCTOBER '74

Did my usual exercise routine this morning. 7.45am — something made me go over to close Larry's cell door as I was about to punch the heavy bag, but peeping in, I found him lying naked and unconcious on the floor behind the door. There was hardened mucus around his nose and mouth. I pulled and slapped him but he wouldn't move and was very cold. I lifted him onto the bed and ran for the medical staff. The doctor came in and examined him, taking blood pressure etc. He was rushed out to hospital.

I felt terrible at seeing Larry in this condition. He is now in the Intensive Care Unit and it still unconcious. Everyone is very depressed and feeling lousy. At 4.30 the Governor returned from the hospital saying that Larry may not recover.

Ken came in later in the evening saying that Larry had recovered consciousness and that the doctors said that he had taken a massive overdose. It is thought that he was keeping drugs back from his official dosage and took them all at once.

8pm: Larry reacted violently and started a fight with those around him and pulled the tube from his nose. Another member of staff was detailed to go to hospital, making three in all.

I went into my studio/cell and did some sculpting until 6.30, working in a frenzy, under a cloud of total depression, thinking, after the Governor's statement at 4.30, that Larry would die. I created my first tender piece of sculpture. It was a weight lifted from my shoulders when Larry regained consciousness.

For some reason, Ian seems to be jealous of the attention being given to Larry as he told me his is going to do the same. I gave him a telling off and he got embarrassed.

8th OCTOBER '74
It was a case of waiting all morning to hear any latest developments concerning Larry. He had a peaceful night and was to be brought back at 2.30pm. His mother came with him in the ambulance.

The Governor called me from the Community meeting to say that everyone was relying on me to help Larry as I was closest to him. Mrs Winters, her husband, and one of her sons came in, with Larry on a stretcher. Mrs Winters fainted, obviously she had been through a harrowing experience.

Larry, still a bit dozey, embraced me...

9th OCTOBER '74
Did some casting this morning and sat speaking to Larry. He said, 'Trying to die isn't easy.' We discussed suicide and he admitted doing it and said he wrote a note of some sort.

I discussed this with the Governor and Ken, as Larry may try it again. Ken was saying that Mrs Winters told him that Larry was very depressed because I was allowed out to the Festival and he wasn't.

Today Larry said that the screws beat him up in the hospital. It's clear to me that Larry's mind is very disturbed and that he is crying out for help. He is also acting strange in the presence of J.C. I think he is playing out the brain damage bit. I could be wrong as he may be bad but he is always okay in my presence. One of the staff on his way into the Unit was told by one of the main prison staff that Larry had been to hospital. The Unit staff member asked "Is he bad?" He was told, "He can't be as he's still breathing."

James Lindsay is helping to prepare the lunch today though is still a bit lost but settling in okay.

2nd NOVEMBER '74
Larry and I discussed the 'silent scream' — that moment when one is alone in the locked cell facing the full horror of confinement. Those of us who have experienced long periods of confinement immediately recognise the torturous 'silent scream', but rarely talk about it. Larry said that in finding himself in one of these moments, the futility of his position crept up on him and he felt that continuing was a waste of time. Prior to Alex Stephen leaving, Larry was reduced from 'A' to 'B' category. He was so suspicious of the System that he looked on the reduction to 'B' category as just another ploy, part of the whole psychological game of the Unit. He still hadn't come

to accept that we could work positively to change the system. My relationship with Larry was still linked to our old prison life but always I was trying to use our new life in the Unit to get him to see the potential. He often made it clear that what he didn't like about it was that it took away the only weapon he had had in the old system, the power that he could wield through the use of fear. He would, on occasions, revert to this in the Unit, using words and almost theatrical-like gestures, but this was acceptable as it was a big improvement and a step forward from actual physical violence. Time would be the only thing that would completely eliminate this. Obviously, the important ingredient was his being in a place that wouldn't give credence to his suspicions. The difficulty was in getting Larry to have some belief in his own talents as he was an exceptionally intelligent man and a gifted poet and a musician.

2nd DECEMBER '74
This morning I went into the joinery room and built a cage and dolls house. I was in there nearly all day.

Ken came back from holiday. Peter Whatmore also returned from a month in Broadmoor. Arthur Dooley, the sculptor, called me to say he will visit me this Sunday.

Larry and J.C. were in a fight in Larry's cell. I was sitting in my cell with Ken and Bob Riddell (staff member) discussing the next issue of our magazine *The Key*. There was a rumpus and a staff member ran past my door downstairs. He got to Larry's door, saw the fight and was about to go for assistance when I went in and broke it up. A meeting was called. Larry said it was his fault. After a discussion the Community accepted their explanation and let it end there.

It's very good to notice that the Community is maturing and keeping such incidents in perspective.

Tom Melville phoned through and is perturbed about two articles in the forthcoming issue of the magazine. One is Gerry Ryan's (staff member) poetry. He feels if Gerry is identified it could ruin or effect his career. Gerry wrote a poem about prison life in the main system and it was very good. The other article is by Prof. Shelly Killen, a visiting art historian, who has been equally blunt.

4th DECEMBER '74
I went into my studio/cell early this morning and cast two pieces. David's head and a two figure form. I was in there till 4pm and am dead beat tonight.

The Governor said that he has been asked for a Parole dossier on me. This is normal procedure after seven years of a life sentence. There is a lot of narkiness amongst the prisoners, me included, and this seems to come in cycles. I think it happens as we get fed up looking at each other. Jim Gillespie (staff member) approached me today saying he would give the prisoners £1 every week to eat lunch with us! We agreed to this.

9th DECEMBER '74
Ken, Larry and I put up the Christmas decorations today. Larry stripped the wallpaper from his cell and Rab is papering it.

The Governor gave me my Parole representation for my 1st Review. He remarked that he didn't think I would want to fill it in. I told him I would. My Representations are:

> That this paper is an exercise in futility as will be the ones following it, for a good number of years. Being in the Special Unit has given me the proper atmosphere to reflect on the past and I realise the futility of it equals that of this paper. The inner change of an individual may be seen on a superficial level but can never be measured in depth. Therein lies your problem, one that will be with you for many years.
>
> This representation has some value in that it allows me to record that on three occasions this year I have been permitted to make, with an escort, visits to Edinburgh on an educational basis. It should be noted that on these occasions I mingled freely with members of the public and acted responsibly at all times.
>
> I was, and am, aware that parole by your Board is a long way off but must emphasise that I found

tremendous value in the educational/social aspects of these days out and at no time did they delude me into thinking I would get an early release. I fully understand my situation and am aware of the position. However, I re-emphasise these trips did much for me as a human being. Having reciprocated the trust shown in me by the Unit Community and the Prisons Department I certainly hope this practice will continue.

19th DECEMBER '74
This morning I lost my cool with Walter and gave him a blasting. It was my fault and completely uncalled for. It was over the daily papers that hadn't come in but I was fed up anyway when I got out of bed. After falling out with Walter I went to my studio to work on the casts. Later I went round to apologise and both of us aired our points of view. Dr Neil Smith was in touch with the consultant who can't take me into hospital (for my cartilage operation) till 6th January. The police have to be informed and two staff have to be with me at all times. John Oliver says he can appreciate the Unit's feeling in only wanting one staff at the hospital with me but they have to watch in case of political repercussions if this got out.

25th DECEMBER '74
Sat up till twelve listening to carols last night. The first time I have done this as I usually get to sleep as soon as possible. Felt very emotional.

This morning Larry brought me breakfast in bed. J.C. went to Aberdeen for the day.

Ian stayed in his cell all day as he was feeling bad about Christmas. Rab was the same, though he came out, but took no part in activities. I put a face on today but was emotionally disturbed, so much so that I was surprised at the strength of it. Wanted away on my own to think things out but couldn't as everyone was hanging around.

4th JANUARY '75
Larry came in with a magazine, *Bananas*, published by

Emma Tennant. One of his poems is published in it. He is delighted.

A senior policeman phoned Ken about my going to hospital. Ken told him they don't want an escort but was merely informing them. The policeman asked what was wrong with me and when told replied, 'It should have been his fucking neck'. Larry didn't get his visit today.

6th JANUARY '75
Larry was on his pills heavy last night and is really down at the moment. I spoke to him about it but he slung me a deafy. He had a mild clash with Wattie prior to my leaving the Unit.

I am writing this in hospital, left the Unit at 9.40am with Bob Riddell and Bob Malcolm who will do a twelve hour shift throughout the day being relieved by two other staff at night.

We stopped at my cousin's shop and I collected some fruit and then went for a coffee at the restaurant across from the hospital. I sat there amongst all those people like any one of them and yet not so long ago I was, and still am sometimes, labelled by the media 'Scotland's Most Violent Man'. It somehow makes nonsense of the whole thing.

I sit here speaking to other patients around me and though they see the two Bobs with me they don't fully comprehend yet, and as we are so friendly to each other they wouldn't imagine we were jailer and jailed. My leg was shaved and I was told to go to the bathroom and have a bath. During my absence a nurse approached Bob to tell him to keep an eye on me as I may not go for a bath (meaning that I may go out of the window). Bob told her it was okay and just sat where he was.

After lunch I was given a change of bed and screens were put around me. This isolated the three of us from the rest of the ward. I asked Bob R. to speak to the sister about this but he took fright saying they usually run their wards with an iron hand. I jumped out of bed and approached the tall, formidable lady and asked her if it was necessary as it made me feel like a black guy in the Deep South. She gave the okay for it to come down, much to my relief. Lying in this bed I feel very much the prisoner with two staff at my side. Patients around me are casting furtive glances when they think I'm not looking. I don't like this sort of treatment but I intend facing up to it.

Invisible chains are holding me.

7th JANUARY '75

Didn't sleep last night as the ward was very noisy and the mattress too soft.

J.C. and Bill Allen came down to visit and said Larry is acting up in the Unit and is on the verge of ruining the place. Wattie, Ken, the Governor and changes in the shifts also confirmed fears about Larry. It was agreed between the two Bobs, Ken and myself that I sign myself out of hospital if Larry doesn't improve.

I had had my operation by this time and was in great pain but it went okay.

It seems to me that everyone is terrified. Apparently a meeting was called and Larry asked to be sent away. Davy (staff member) and some others agreed to it. Larry tore out a page in the Minute book and took a sort of brainstorm, apparently grabbing the Governor by the tie.

Ken said that Larry should stay and Davy cracked up, shouting at Ken, swearing at him and calling him a lot of names, insisting that Larry be put to Carstairs or Peterhead. A decision was made — staff and prisoners agreed that Larry be put away. There was complete panic in the place.

Wattie came down telling me that I mustn't sign myself out of hospital as things were okay.

8th JANUARY '75

Spent a restless night which resulted in the nurse giving me an injection to kill the pain. The Governor came in to see me today and we discussed Larry saying that he might need to lock him up (solitary). I told him that I thought this would make matters worse and he agreed. I still feel that he would have carried it out though.

I am getting physiotherapy treatment and my leg is much better for it.

10th JANUARY '75
Had a good few hours sleep last night and felt better for it. Did exercises this morning and managed to lift my leg off the bed. David Scott (BBC) came up and we had a good chat. We discussed the Unit and the latest crisis so he will go up this morning and talk to Larry.

The Governor came down but was quite evasive. Later Bob told me that apparently a kitchen knife in the Unit is missing and there is a lot of suspicion going around. It seems a staff member has taken it but no-one knows his motives.

The police called the hospital to ask if I was still in, then asked the nurse to keep them informed.

11th JANUARY '75
The Sister came round this morning and told Bob M. that there was a piece in the *Daily Record* about me. I was dreading this. The newspaper article was front page and says that a patient's family is concerned about my being in the same ward as him. I feel terrible lying here having to face these people, almost as though I am some alien from another planet.

Once the newspapers circulated the ward, there was a strong reaction from the patients who were angry at the *Record*. 'Cheap journalism' is what they called it. The reports were taken up by television and radio and our 'dial-a-quote' MP, Teddy Taylor, was reported as saying that I should be locked away in a room, separated from ordinary patients. This had the patients fuming and they all signed a petition which was sent to the newspapers. The spoke to Radio Clyde stating how they are being used and going on to say that I had a first class relationship with everyone in the ward. I am so glad of this as it once again shows me how papers like this have no hesitation of exploiting situations like this.

David Scott came in saying that he had been to see Larry

and told him I was disappointed in him. David heard most of the story from Wattie as he drove him home, about Larry grabbing the Governor by the tie and spitting in a staff member's face. David is going to try to get to know Larry better as he recognises that he is lonely.

13th JANUARY '75
There was a radio comment on my being in hospital and the controversy. It mentioned the patients writing a petition and all of them signing it stating that the *Daily Record* article was untrue. The comment was accurate which is all I ask for. The Glasgow Herald printed the content of the patient's petition and also presented the article factually. It lets people see that there is another side to the story. The doctor came round this morning and saw me. I told him I was feeling fine and he said I could go.

There was relief at my entering the Unit, from everyone present, and as I didn't show much warmth to Larry, he went off to his cell. I went in after him.

We had a tense confrontation, with me pointing out that he had gone a long way to damaging the Unit and I asked him why? He said that he didn't know why and at one point he thought he was mental as he couldn't control himself. I told him that the position is that he is the one big question mark in this place and that no-one can trust him, that the days of frightening people are over. He sat there accepting it, offering no excuses. I think he is really disgusted with himself.

I called a Community meeting concerning Larry's transfer and how it was a waste of time as no other prison would take him and that in fact he had now thought about it and didn't want to leave the Unit. The staff and prisoners pointed out that in agreeing with his transfer, they had simply responded to the position Larry had put them in.

14th JANUARY '75
Larry burst in on Wattie asking for his pills because there were no letters for him. He was expecting one from his girl-friend. I met him coming out of his cell. He was chalk-white

and so we went back into his cell where he stood shaking like a leaf.'Jimmy, I'm cracking up, I feel it, they'll [staff] see me and put me away,' he said, breaking down and crying. I comforted him. He told me he can't cope with this new experience. He has no confidence or drive and thinks he is mentally abnormal.

We sat there till 6.30pm when the pills took effect and he was drugged and began speaking about himself. Ken came up afterwards and sat speaking to Larry for a long time and then came in to my cell and we talked. Ken looked worn and drawn. He is taking too much on himself.

27th JANUARY '75

Slithering, sliding through the darkness in search of shadows that flit in and out of my life like seconds in the minute. Creeping, crawling along the passage in search of that which is non-existent as though I am certain of finding it. Feeling, groping, trying to assess what really is. All in the vague hope of surviving. There is a touch of reality about this fantasy so that if one tries hard enough the dream will exist...

11th FEBRUARY '75

John Oliver and Tom Melville came this afternoon. We had a discussion on the transfer issue. John Oliver said that the transfers were for the good of both prisoners. Everyone disagreed with this except the Governor. It became clearer as the discussion went on that the Department were acting on the Governor's recommendation. After a prolonged, and at times heated, discussion they agreed to let both remain.

Ken brought up the issue of civilian clothing for staff saying they were still keen to wear it. Previously they had been refused permission because it might stir up trouble amongst the main prison staff. Mr Oliver said he would reconsider this.

Bob Riddell asked him to consider my paroles being continued on an educational basis. Other staff joined in to support this. John Oliver eventually agreed that I could go out for a constructive reason. The Governor surprised us all by stating that I was aware that I could go out on an important sculptural event.

We debated the whole penal system, trying to persuade him to implement what had been learned from the Unit into other prisons. He asked how it could be done and we explained that it could start with the 'A' category men in Peterhead prison, a group that are already segregated to an extent and who are all doing long sentences. He voiced the opinion that if this were done then it would make the other prisoners jealous. We pointed out to him that in most prisons, 'A' category men were already deprived of football, night classes and many other things and that the authorities always seemed to be sensitive to jealousies when it was a case of being more humane, but when responding in a less humane manner there didn't seem to be any problem. We suggested that it should only start with this small group and then most certainly expand it to other prisoners with less trepidation when they didn't need such careful watching.

J.C. had to leave hurriedly to attend his father's funeral in Aberdeen. We, at least, have some good news for him on return.

12th FEBRUARY '75
On the day of our second anniversary we held a lunch, inviting the Director of Prisons and other Department officials. Only Tom Melville appeared besides some outside visitors. The first overt sign of the Department's thinking came when the meal ended. Tom Melville informed the Governor that J.C. and Rab were to be transferred to Saughton prison in Edinburgh in two weeks time. This was a bombshell and against everything that we were supposed to be doing in the Unit. All of us within the Community believed that if we were to be meaningful at all, in terms of preparing prisoners for release, then we should be able to release them direct from the Unit. J.C. and Rab were visibly shaken at this decision and the remainder of us were astounded at the stupidity of it.

It meant that they would be stopped from going outside on day paroles and that any visitors going to see them in Edinburgh prison would revert to speaking through a glass and wire barrier. It meant that they would be restricted to censored mail and entitled to one letter a week, nine hours visiting time per year, prison uniforms and all the other degrading and humiliating aspects that are a part of that system. They wouldn't be able to speak to the majority of staff in anything other than a subservient way and they'd be constantly ordered about. All responsibility would be taken away from them. If all of this would be an ordeal for J.C. it would be even worse for Rab who had progressed so well in the Unit and we had doubts about his ability to cope with this sort of regime after having been encouraged to adapt to living and working in the outside community. Anyone from the Unit going to a normal prison would find himself subjected to a great deal of hostility because of the attitudes of staff to the place. We felt that it was grossly unfair to subject both these men to this. In addition to this, they were both under 'review' by the Parole Board, hopefully, for a provisional release date which was usually two years in advance. We assumed that when the time came the Community would be consulted on this issue at which point oint we would ask that they both be released from here. But the Department had taken the bull by the horns and recommended that they be transferred. The Community in turn demanded to see Mr. Oliver.

24th MARCH '75
I was with Ken when he phoned Alex Stephen (Dover House, London) about my manuscript A Sense of Freedom. Alex said that we should give it straight to the Director and that the Director would get on to a Mr Ford who is a specialist on these matters. He said he feels strongly that prisoners should be able to publish their own material. Alex feels that we should by-pass Mr Oliver and everyone inbetween and go straight to the Director.

6th APRIL '75
I am in good form, keeping the moments of despondency away by keeping busy.

There are times when I get the urge to move along to the empty cell a few doors away. A big part of me doesn't want to get too dependent on the materialism of this place. I am thinking constantly of this and try never to forget the past. I have to keep re-opening old wounds in order to stabilise myself here. If temptation comes my way, yesterday's memories keep me from succumbing. In many ways my revenge against the system will be in making this place a success. I know this will hurt every pig who took a liberty with me. There are times when I feel my existence seems to be motivated by hatred. I keep having flashbacks of sitting on the bare floor of my previous cells in other prisons where the stench of urine was mixed with everything. There are times when I would like to rest from my physical exercises but I can't. They are a part of my survival kit.

8th APRIL '75
The Governor said that the Unit came in for heavy criticism at the recent Governor's Conference. He said that his colleagues objected to the recent *World in Action* film, and the Unit magazine *The Key*. The editorial in the latter was described as 'Jimmy's editorial'. It was pointed out that the editorial isn't mine but that of the editorial committee. The Governor stated that the message coming across was that the magazine was undoing a lot of the other Governor's work, taking the feet away from the training they are doing. Everyone laughed at this.

He went on to say he was dreading the forthcoming BBC film, and that in his opinion the press publicity and TV programmes were the worst thing to happen to the Unit...

9th APRIL '75
A social worker and the assistant governor from Polmont Borstal came in and we sat speaking to them. I enjoyed the talk as they asked some penetrating questions. They asked the old question that most visitors do: 'Do you ever get fed

up talking to people like us about prisons or the Unit?' I replied that we never weary simply because we realise that there are guys living in abominable conditions in the main prison system and we must talk for them. Tonight the Governor came in and asked to see me. On going into his office he had a piece of paper in front of him. He told me that Mr Oliver had a copy of a manuscript purported to have been written by me and the Department had a copy of it. How many copies were there? I conceded that there were two, one that I sent to Alex Stephen and another that my family had. He asked how Alex Stephen got hold of one. I told him I posted it through a friend. The Governor said he had no objection to it being printed but he would like to see it before going to the Department on Friday. I told him I couldn't get it for him tonight but would tomorrow. He replied that it would be his day-off but to give it to Wattie and he would deliver it.

I intend making sure that I photocopy the manuscript before giving it to the Governor.

24th APRIL '75
Moods that come and go, fluctuating from bad to good. Going off people without really knowing why. Getting irritated with small things that are really of no consequence. Feeling smothered by the surrounding walls that stand so firm and menacing, feeling so powerful at times that one mighty blow could destroy the walls, and then so weak that I cringe with fear as they overpower me. There is no escape, only confrontation. It is here and now, this very second that is now the past. Why am I locked in? Venus and Mars are at work tonight, each has moments of domination, each taking its toll.

It's 10.30pm and I've spent the whole evening trying to rid myself of something. It seems as though I've wasted a lot of time sitting here, doing nothing, but the truth is I couldn't concentrate on anything else as I must try to understand what is going on inside me. There is something in there pushing like fuck as I remain trapped in this concrete cube, restlessly trying to console the bubbling energy.

My thoughts aren't concentrating on the one thing; they move from one subject to the next. I'm sure I could pull the locked door off its hinges if I really tried. I really should do some meditation to rid myself of this restlessness but there is a perverse side of me that wants to examine it, to find out more about it, that wants to sit here and type it out. I am really speaking to myself at this moment, putting it down on paper, all the time realising it's a load of crap. Be that as it may, I still have to face it. I cast an eye to the window and notice the sky is darkening. Saturday night in prison is this: sitting locked up with one's thoughts — reason enough for going stark crazy.

The thin veneer of the outward appearance means nothing — it's what goes on within that counts. Take for instance the screw that goes round every now and again to peep into the judas hole to see if I'm alright. He does this and sees me sitting here typing and says to himself that all is well. He cannot see inside my head, that my thoughts are 'the next time he comes round I'm going to pull out my cock and flash it at him'. It's all so superficial. 'Last night I had a dream, you were in it, I was in it with you. . .' so goes the song. Reawakens some beautiful memories that song, takes me to a time when I was out of here for a few hours — hours so beautiful that I cherish them. It's now 11.05pm and the night is dark so I may as well go to bed, put the light out and lie thinking what this has been all about. . .

Thoughts brought to life.

25th APRIL '75
My mind is working overtime on the problem of the book. I asked the Governor this morning for a petition and sent it off to the Secretary of State. In reality it goes to someone in the Prisons Department.

> *Dear Sir,*
> *The Prisons Department have two copies of an auto-biographical manuscript written by me and I would like to know if I could have permission to have it published?*

I would like you to know that the prime motivation for my writing the book is to illustrate – using my own life experience – how a child can go from a normal life to become enmeshed in a life of crime. It will be apparent to you that the main theme of the document is the waste of human life and how there is nothing glamorous about the criminal way of life. I don't think I've excused myself in it, nor anyone else, but I feel that this is important in order to help the worsening crime situation.

I do hope you appreciate that the copies the Prisons Department have are rough and untouched for libel etc. I did feel it only right that you see it in this condition. I would, if you agree to publication, be pleased to accept your advice and assistance on this matter.

Yours sincerely

26th APRIL '75
This morning Ken and I were sitting outside in the yard when Peter Whatmore came in. I asked him about this Crime Council he is on as they are recommending Stop and Search powers etc. to the police. He tried to give excuses then bolted into his office.

The Governor came in at 10.15am. Ken and he went into his office. Some minutes later Ken came out fuming and told me he is being transferred. I was as stunned as he was. He was given a letter from the Department saying that he is to be transferred to Saughton Prison, Edinburgh. I sat with some of the staff when the Governor came in and joined us. One of them expressed his fears that his prediction made some weeks ago that the Department are intent in 'changing the place' is coming true. The Governor denied this. I told him my opinion is that Ken's transfer is part of a calculated attempt to control the place and that he, along with the Department, are intent on wiping out all that Alex Stephen has achieved. The Governor stood there saying nothing. I feel so utterly sick being near the man as he is so subversive. He hung about all morning trying to ensure that no-one started blaming him. It was all in vain for he is being blamed.

My heart went out to Ken as he has done so much for the Unit and lots of us in here. Who could ever imagine that I would be thinking like this about a screw. They seem bent on destroying him. What chance have we of improving the penal system when people resort to strokes such as this?

The Governor came in this afternoon for an hour and stood about not saying a word and looking very much like Judas.

Over lunch I spoke to James Lindsay, Larry and J.C. saying that we must stand by Ken right to the end. They all felt this anyway. Larry wanted to give the Governor an ultimatum but I felt we must wait till Ken says all is ended as we don't want to jeopardise his case at this stage. Whatmore, in speaking to Larry, told him that he is relying on him and me to pull the Unit through this period. There is a lot of suspicion that Whatmore knew about it but that is a matter for debate.

What do we do from here? It is obvious that the Unit is going to be staffed by what the Department call 'more reliable staff'. I must come to a decision as to whether I want to continue in the Unit the way things are going. It seems to me that the Governor and the Department will continue catering for Larry and me. There are indications that the other prisoners will be transferred shortly. At the moment Larry and I are still fresh in the minds of the prison staff in the main system so the pressure on the Department will be bad if there is any talk of moving us back. At the same time I don't want to continue here in a watered-down version of the real thing.

Rumours unofficially circulating say that Jim Gillespie and Bob Riddell are being persuaded to move on to the Nursing Course. They are two decent staff. If this is true then we are in even more trouble.

27th APRIL '75
This morning Ken came in to my cell. He described how his wife woke him up in the early hours crying about his trans-

fer and the diabolical way he is being treated. There is no doubt that everyone is livid at the way Ken is being stabbed in the back. It is not a move to help his career in any way but one to sweep him under the carpet because of his outspoken views. The Governor had a personality clash with him and rather than work it out he made the necessary moves to get rid of him.

Larry had a good visit from his brother. James Lindsay had a visit from his mother. I had my aunt Peggy, aunt Maggie and the kids in. J.C. was in at my visit, playing with the kids. I thoroughly enjoyed it and haven't laughed so much in a long time. Peggy is a real funny person.

Rab had a visit from a couple he met.

Ian sat with the Governor (spew!!!).

The staff are peculiar people. Not long after expressing their disgust about Ken's transfer they were all sitting together discussing who would get promotion and who would take over his duties. They are insensitive people with little loyalty to anyone. I've no doubt that some of them will support Ken a hundred per cent but most of them couldn't care less as they all look to see how it will improve their position.

The Governor came in this afternoon for two hours as Ken had to go of and give a talk to the Penal Reform meeting. He came upstairs with mail for me. I was so involved with my visitors that he took me by surprise. I began to introduce him to my aunties but stopped dead and left him standing there.

29th APRIL '75
This morning I tried to do my Open University but could feel things building up about the forthcoming meeting. Larry was the same as he was in and out of my cell all morning.

At the meeting Kay Carmichael and Dr Keith Wardrop came in. It opened with me saying that the issue with Ken is the only thing I want to discuss. There then developed a lengthy and heated discussion about the whole affair. I blew up telling the Governor that he had been instrumental in putting this into action and that he is a filthy rotten bastard and one of the most dangerous men I know. He has been set on destroying the Unit because he has this personality clash with Ken and that any staff who build up a relationship with prisoners are given the heave. Larry was also heated in his remarks. Ken also expressed the view that the Governor has played a dirty trick.

The Governor gave the impression that he was sorry that Ken was going but that he was subject to transfer just as he himself was. This is absolute rot. Ken asked the Governor to resist his transfer. He said no. The Governor said he felt that a gun was being held at his head. In other words he was saying that Larry and I were threatening to be violent if Ken's transfer wasn't stopped and he wasn't going to act under duress. I told him that I had not threatened violence under these circumstances as I wouldn't be violent in the Unit. Larry rose and walked towards the Governor in a gesture of sheer frustration. Lots of others had their say, unanimously opposing the transfer. The Community stated that they wanted a meeting with John Oliver to discuss the issue with us. I don't want to give an opinion on what effect the meeting or its intensity had on the Governor. I will be watching him like hell.

After the meeting he came up to me and said I am doing him wrong in judging him on this and was about to tell me how he has fought hard for all of us. Bill Allen (staff member) standing next to me called him a dictator getting rid of him and Ken as he thought they were opposition. Bill told him he was fooling no-one. The Governor then went to Larry to speak to him but Larry isn't wearing it.

30th APRIL '75
I went downstairs and saw the Governor making coffee. I challenged him about ruining the whole Community. He said I must believe him, that he wants the Unit to go on and that if he thought the Department was going to close it he would put his resignation in tomorrow. I told him I thought they weren't going to close it but that they were going to make life in here so intolerable that trouble would

break out and it would inevitably close — that is how they work. I told him that the staff getting transferred were not intimidated by rank but were working in the best way for the Unit and that was why they were 'moving' on or being shanghied. I said that he is the one holding the gun at our heads by threatening to remove staff who oppose him. I walked out and left him sitting there.

Murray Stewart (staff member) caught hold of me and asked if I had words with the Governor. I told him I did. He told me that the Governor will be underestimating the rest of the staff if he thinks that Larry and I are the only ones who will react to the transfer. He candidly expressed that some of them aren't go-getters or for that matter very vocal but they want the Unit to go on the way it has been.

I understand that Kay Carmichael has heard a whisper that I am to be transferred. I am not putting too much on this. Anyway, I am inwardly prepared for it and have been since talk of Ken's transfer. In many respects moving me would be tantamount to murdering me as I know what prison staff in other prisons feel about me.

The fact is, I have never been so fulfilled since I became caught up in the work I have been doing here. I have been using my past experience to help the situation but I have always kept myself aware of the possibility of the whole thing falling through. I knew that if it did then it would be the fault of the authorities.

2nd MAY '75
The Governor came into my studio with a signed letter from Tom Melville saying that the request by the Community to get permission for me to go out to the Demarco Gallery exhibition has been refused. He told me the Department are concerned that my being allowed out could attract publicity and that this would put pressure onto the Ministers.

5th MAY '75
This morning I was loathe to get up as it was back to the grind of the bad atmosphere and being faced with false

59

people. I sat outside with Larry trying to do my Open University but couldn't concentrate on it. We sat in the sun as it was a beautiful day. The feelings were very tense inside both of us.

I am being extremely watchful of everything and already see small signs of deterioration creeping in. Larry and I are staying close to each other. The staff are keeping very close to each other too and already they are starting to prepare, a noticeable feature being their going back to carrying their batons. This is the start and from here on in, unless something dramatic happens, it will go from bad to worse.

Malky (staff member) put his resignation in but let me see it before doing so. He explained his reasons, saying that it is due to the Prisons Department and the Governor. He told me has too much respect for me and would never work under circumstances that would mean screwing me down. Both of us discussed this later and Malky said that only the staff can do it by putting in a block resignation paper to the Department. He says someone approached him to say he is next on the Department list for shanghai. All our outside support is making moves to Harry Ewing, the Labour minister with responsibility for the Unit.

Larry's mother came in this afternoon and told us both not to resort to violence as this is what we are being provoked to do. She says she can't understand why for two and a half years they've allowed this to go on and are now turning back.

6th MAY '75
I had a long talk with Wattie about the situation and asked him to be more forward on this issue as he only has two years to go till he retires on pension. He replied that after twenty seven years in the Prison Service he is finding it difficult to question the Governor and the Department due to conditioned loyalties.

We had our meeting in the yard as the weather was so good. Wattie told the Community that the Governor is off sick for two weeks. This confirms a staff member's comments on some Governors having the ability to

Houdini in order to get themselves out of a tight situation. Wattie then told us that John Oliver will come down next week.

I pointed out to the Community that things were reaching a dangerous level and that the two groups, staff and prisoners, have stopped talking to each other and that staff are now carrying their batons. There was a general reluctance at first, by staff, to discuss this. They made excuses, one saying that it is part of the dress. Other staff denounced this. Gerry said he was carrying his because he has been feeling very insecure. Bob admitted that the present situation has made him start carrying his. This was reiterated by others. It was good that we aired all of this.

7th MAY '75
This morning while eating my breakfast in the T.V. room Ian came in and told me that when he and a staff member were out buying groceries yesterday they bumped into the Governor...

9th MAY '75
I am thirty one today and received some nice cards. It may be taken as a sign of old age but I did feel mellow this morning. It has felt like a birthday and that sure is saying something in the light of our present problems.

Everyone is very talkative and open in discussing the Governor. It seems that Wattie was on the phone to him and they had a blow-out. Wattie was questioning the fact that the Governor had the staff in the main prison standing-by with riot batons and hadn't informed him or any of the Unit staff. The Governor replied that he had told a Unit staff member. Wattie asked for the name. The Governor said he couldn't remember as he has had them on stand-by a number of times.

10th MAY '75
I sat speaking to Ken for some time this morning. Wattie phoned saying that he now knows where he stands for the first time in two years. He said that for the first time in

weeks he had a good night's sleep, saying he took some tranquilisers. Wattie now seems to be on the trail of the righteous.

Ian had his parents up today. This is the first time he has seen them since being in here. It went very well and he seemed pretty relaxed with them. The atmosphere in the place is really quite good. I hope this continues for Oliver coming.

11th MAY '75

This morning Wattie came in at 7.30 looking terrible. This is his weekend off and it shocked the staff to see him in this condition. They felt he was on the verge of a breakdown. Ken took him out of the prison and they walked arm in arm round nearby Hogganfield Loch. Wattie told Ken that he isn't sleeping. He said he has been rotten to the Community and to Ken in particular as he had supported the Governor in doing things that were pretty devious. He said that he had discussed Ken's transfer with the Governor six weeks ago. The Governor made it plain that Ken would have to go and changes would have to be made. Wattie said he told the Governor that he would have to watch what he was doing and at this point quickly left the office — this, he says, is where he lost out and withdrew from the Community.

I had a visit from Harry, Margaret and my kids. They are looking great. We had a good visit.

12th MAY '75

This morning, after advice that he should take the day/week off, Wattie came in. He looked euphoric and this remained throughout the day. He caught hold of me in front of staff saying that he is going to tell 'everyone' in the Community the truth. This is the day he will start being truthful. Ken was worried and phoned for some medical assistance.

Wattie called a Community meeting and told everyone what he had told us. Most people gave him support and sympathy. The bad feelings towards the Governor intensified. Wattie explained that it all started when he went with the Governor to the Prisons Department last year. The intention was to discuss Unit policy and the external programmes for individual prisoners. Wattie said that the Governor opened up the meeting by telling Oliver that the place is out of control and it would take him six months to get it into line. Wattie told us there was next to no policy discussed.

I can't help thinking of the past and present staff problems and saying to myself, 'These are the people responsible for controlling my life'. What is despairing is that I have to rely on them to assess, and put in reports on me. Thank fuck I'm against arse-licking otherwise I'd have succumbed to being controlled by them and found myself completely fucked up. No wonder injustices are perpetrated with this calibre of person being in complete control over another.

14th MAY '75

This morning I phoned Anne, Ricky Demarco's assistant, and discussed the ICA exhibition. Also had a letter from Denis Rice who is organising the Leicester exhibition. Wattie has been pretty bad today and I sat with him for five hours. He didn't want to leave me all day. He told me his life story, how he was a staunch Boy's Brigade fanatic, how he met his wife, married and settled down. He sees the meeting with Oliver as being the panacea for the problem. The meeting tomorrow will in fact be an anti-climax for us all but I'm sure that it will be good for Wattie as it's to them that he supported the Governor, therefore, it's to them that his biggest trial of honesty will have to be.

Wattie was saying that while on the phone to Tom Melville the other day talking about my manuscript, Tom said there is no chance of me getting it published. It will be interesting to see how they respond to my petition. Wattie said that when I gave the Governor my copy of the manuscript to read he went to the Department taking the copy with him. They compared them to see if they matched. He returned to tell Wattie that there are more copies as the two didn't match. It seems that if they had I would have been told that the two copies would have to be confiscated. Now they suspect that there are other copies, they will play me along. Wattie said they are frightened of it getting published as it is too near the mark for comfort.

I have been keeping check on the number of hours the Governor has been in the Unit. Between 8th April and 5th May he has been here a total of sixty six hours. He has been off ill since then.

15th MAY '75
At the big meeting John Oliver started by saying that the Unit was not going to shut and that the Department were learning from it. The staff then came in asking why the Department changed in attitude, giving my parole outings as one example. Melville answered this by saying that the Department had information that the *Daily Record* and *Evening News* were waiting for me at the exhibition and that was why I was knocked back. We rejected this. We referred to the transfer of staff and asked why they were being pulled out and they replied that all of them, Oliver included, were subject to transfer at any time. Staff came in heavy on this saying they would be contesting the moves via the SPOA. We referred to the prisoners' individual external programmes that they shelved when the Governor gave them last November. They expressed surprise saying they had never received them. Oliver was asked if he thought the prisoners had too much say in the running of the Unit and he replied that he didn't. Dr Keith Wardrop, Ian, Wattie and the prisoners had lunch together. Wattie dominated the scene telling Keith to fucking shut up. It was all taken in good spirits.

This afternoon Dr Neil Smith from the main prison came in and stood about very suspiciously speaking to me as I chiselled my sculpture. It was as though he was examining me and the others he spoke to. I never felt like this before with him.

16th MAY '75

This morning I slept in till 7.30am, then got up to do my exercises. It's been a very quiet morning with Wattie off for the day.

Dr Smith came in again and spoke to me as I chiselled. Again, I felt he was examining Larry and me when we spoke to him. I found out later that Oliver was so concerned that he called a top doctor in the Department and got him to speak to Dr Smith in the main prison to have a look at Wattie in particular but also everyone else. This will continue for a week.

17th MAY '75

This morning I lay in quite late before getting up to go outside and work in the sun as the day was beautiful.

I really got into the carving of this latest piece enjoying it immensely. I lost myself completely with the feeling, for the first time, of knowing the tools. I spent the whole day at it working patiently and very relaxed. When I parted from it at five o'clock I placed it so that when in my cell that night I could look out my window at it. This seemed very important to do and so far I've looked at it several times.

I've been thinking over the publication of my book and have decided to give permission to publish. There is no doubt that when I look at the possible backlash to the Unit I hesitate, but yesterday I was told a pal of mine in Peterhead prison is lying in the solitary block — brutalised. Jim is doing four years for trying to help me in the Inverness trial — he sent a bomb to one of the staff there — and as a result is paying for it. When I hear things like this it brings me back to earth, to the realities of the situation. It is okay for the Department to say that the Unit is changing the penal system and point to the new wing in Peterhead but there is the real side of it which continues unabated — brutality, and how does one fucking change that! I feel all the old hatred welling up in me for the bastards. Ian was speaking to me this afternoon. He is getting worried about going to Edinburgh prison. It is clear that he is having second thoughts. He is going to ask for a date for his transfer next Tuesday so he can get away as soon as possible. . .

19th MAY '75
This morning after my exercises I went out to the yard and
worked on my piece of stone, making good progress. I sat
there for a part of the morning but Wattie came in wearing
civvy clothes and dark glasses. He seemed okay at first but
then started pulling me into the kitchen to make him coffee
and toast which I did. He had some phone calls to make
and wanted me present. The short time he was in the Unit
was spent beside me.

There is a lot of activity over Ken's transfer as it seems
that someone at the Department doesn't want him to get
his interview with the Director. He had a letter asking his
reasons for an interview with him. Ken said he was non-
commital in his reply.

14th JUNE '75
This morning I spoke to Barry Barker from the ICA in
London. He was saying that my exhibition and the work is
being complimented by people visiting. There have been a
few offers to buy pieces but he hasn't had time to sort this
out yet. He is taking photographs of the exhibition for me
and will send them on. He said that there is a strong need in
viewers to touch the work. I thought that was fine.

Ken came in this morning to see if there was any mail
about his transfer situation. He is very concerned and
looks under tremendous pressure but is keeping his cool.
Both of us sat in the Governor's office and he described a
wierd dream he had last night.

He was in the Unit with lots of new staff, all had tanned
faces as though they had been lying in the sun. They were
telling him they were behind him in what he was trying to
do. He couldn't identify who they were. He left the Unit
with two of them and when he returned he noticed a change
in the place. Prisoners he didn't know were on their knees
scraping the floor and on a nearby table sat all our belongings. The staff were sitting on the floor in a drunken
manner celebrating their victory over the Unit. Ken then

recognised that we were lying in our cells manacled and naked. Ken tried to get the drunken, victorious staff out by the scruff of the neck. He made no impression. They told him they were a new tactical squad sent in to change the Unit. Ken said that at this point the door opened and I came in with a big knife and they all started screaming and running away. Ken shouted after them, 'Go on you bastards, let's see how victorious and hard you are now'. End of dream. I know little about dream interpretation but it certainly shows the depth of Ken's anxiety about what is happening to us.

15th JUNE '75
This afternoon I had a visit from aunt Peggy and Maggie, Pat and my kids. It was a good visit though Pat is looking bad with the booze. Patricia wasn't too well and fell asleep on my bed holding onto me. Larry, J.C. and James Lindsay had visits today.

Ian is back on sleeping tablets — Seconal — as he is all tensed up with his pending transfer. He is now saying that his visit yesterday — to his aunts — has made him think a bit more as they want him to stay here rather than go to Edinburgh on the terms offered.

16th JUNE '75
I didn't get to sleep till after 3am. Thoughts were flashing through my mind about my position here. There is no doubt that I am going through a crisis point with myself. Freedom is a balanced diet of the mental and physical, and though mentally I feel I'm as free as I'll ever be, the fact is that I am physically restricted. This is a telling factor in my present problems. I went out a few times last year and some this year for physiotherapy after my operation. I thought that because I had played my part in acting responsibly it would be an on-going thing. I was wrong.

I spent the whole day from early morning till late afternoon working on the piece of stone in the yard. Every hit of the hammer on the chisel was full of violence; so much so that I lost count of all time. I was so absorbed in my thoughts and the piece before me. Tired and worn I went to my bed at 4pm and lay till this evening.

17th JUNE '75
This morning I awoke fresh and feeling much better.

Received a letter from Paul Overy, *The Times* art critic, saying he stumbled over my exhibition by accident and what a find he said. He has put a short piece in *The Times* and it is a good review. I was pleased.

Wattie came bck to work this morning looking very well but still not far from breaking point. We sat in my cell speaking. He feels that his conscience is his problem now due to the fact that he connived with the Governor. We spoke on this for some time and I'm sure he is the better for it.

Tom Melville came in this morning and we both chatted. It was a superficial discussion as Tom doesn't want to know about profound talk on the Unit and this is why I hate speaking to him.

At the meeting today there was a general discussion on three Peterhead prisoners nominated for the Unit. Peter Whatmore, Ken and Bob gave their views on the interviews they had with the three. After discussing each case it was decided that Mathers and Bathgate should come but that there was no place for the third. It was decided that Mathers was an emergency case and should be brought first, then Bathgate.

A group of social workers came up today. During our discussion with them they described a lecture they had with a senior prison official on the platform. After his talk he was asked about the Special Unit. Without naming names he stated that Larry and I are getting on okay here simply because it's an easy time. He said that if either of us were released we would cut the first person's throat we met. He went on to describe how evil we were and put the Unit down. I was bloody mad at this but not really surprised. This official comes in here and makes out he is one hundred per cent behind the place but I can tell he hates the idea.

18th JUNE '75

This morning after my exercises I went outside and started sculpting, getting lost in the piece and making great progress with it. I truly love carving as it really gets into the soul. For the first time I felt as though the hammer and chisel were extensions of my arms. The rain came down but it was nice to stand there in the middle of it and get soaked. This is what sculpting is all about. The piece is taking on a masculine form but underneath and inside there is something feminine about it. I would like to carve something large, a full-sized figure.

Ian went out for the weekly groceries and got on okay. He is still upset about going to Edinburgh and I feel that if he is kept hanging on much longer he will crack in some way.

There is a lot of sick leave by staff and really the tension with the limbo situation between Ken, the Governor and the Department is out of order. I discussed the matter with Wattie and Peter Whatmore who agree that the Department are treating us harshly on this matter.

24th JUNE '75

Ian went to Edinburgh prison this morning. He shook hands with everyone before leaving. Murray (staff member) returned saying, as they got nearer and nearer to Edinburgh Ian got higher and higher. Murray took him for a meal and a walk round Edinburgh before going into the prison. Murray said, as they entered the prison a screw said, 'Oh, another one from the Special Unit.' Ian was thrust into a 'dog box' — a small cubicle where the depersonalisation process begins. God knows how Ian will get on.

27th JUNE '75

I heard information that the Cages in Inverness have been repainted and it looks as though they may be re-opened. At our last meeting Tom Melville declared to us that when the last riot was over the Department gave an assurance to the staff there that certain classifications of prisoners would be kept out of Inverness and the Department were now regretting this.

Tom McGrath, director of The Third Eye Centre came in with another guy. Shelly brought them in and so I took them round. Tom is wanting to do a show of my work and is away back to the Third Eye to look at dates and will send me an official request.

Davy Mathers, the new prisoner, seems to be quite settled and getting on alright. He is getting through the overpowering parts of the Unit though he is full of the old prison culture.

29th JUNE '75
While speaking to Davy Mathers this afternoon all he talked about was the quality of the programmes on the TV. It's clear that on just coming straight from solitary to here he sees everything as great. He is completely bewildered by this whole place. He whispered to me that we should watch these bastards — the screws — but there is no sense me plunging in and telling him about the situation here as it will have to come with time and experience.

3rd JULY '75
Wattie was telling me that Brian Coyle (a social worker) received a reply from Harry Ewing, Under-Secretary of State, saying that due to sickness Ken won't be transferred at this stage. However, he could be transferred some time. It looks as though the Department have taken this way out and are feeling the effects brought to bear on them by outside parties. It looks as though we have reversed the decision but Ken won't be satisfied with this reply. We should now talk very seriously about plugging this gap by getting serious negotiations going about staff transfers. The emphasis should be on staff who do want to be moved but can't.

4th JULY '75
Mr Aithie, from the Department phoned to say Ken's transfer was cancelled. Ken was standing beside me as

Wattie talked on the phone. It was terrific as the weight literally lifted from his shoulders there and then. The news was sweeping through the Unit and the prisoners had glowing faces.

10th JULY '75

I had words with J.C. and James Lindsay at the table during lunch as I notice that the new prisoner Davy is doing both of their cleaning tasks in the morning — they having sunk into retirement. I told them that they had better not be taking liberties with him and they denied this. Both of them know that Davy is a big easy going guy who will do anything anyone asks. All this week I have seen him either scrubbing out the kitchen or the hall area. I really was pissed off at this as both James L. and J.C. said they would do their bit when this was raised two weeks ago. Even Larry who is heavily drugged every night gets up to do his bit along with me. James L. has taken the huff due to my giving him a pull. J.C. and I are having bad vibes too. He puts on a face that is near to tears and really does mean what he says at such times but his resolutions fall away within a short period of time. We will wait and see what happens but really I can see that J.L. and J.C. both dislike me but that's the way it goes. There is no doubt that at such times I feel rotten and very much like a screw which isn't very nice. I often wonder if I am being too forceful.

There was a meeting today to discuss the case of the new prisoner Bathgate coming to the Unit. There are rumours that Ian is in some trouble in Edinburgh prison so with this in mind we decided to postpone bringing Bathgate down till we had more knowledge of Ian's situation.

14th JULY '75

I had a very strange night late on, a powerful one, and I thought about something that has been coming to my mind on and off for some time. I lay listening to music — classical — till the early hours, full of emotion. I wasn't sure whether it was a mood or something that is very deep within me. Doing away with myself raises its head in moments of solitary despair. This is the 'silent scream'. I wonder if I made a decision some years ago and am living it out. I don't know. No one seems to be taking an active part in consolidating the Unit's position now that we are welding together again. I put this to Ken, Wattie and some of the other staff.

I intend to hold a sculpture exhibition in the Unit court-yard over a period of five days/evenings from 6.30pm — 8.30pm. I would like to select a group of people to visit each night to view the work and the Unit. It will mean using the exhibition to get people here to see the Unit and what we are doing. I have been talking to others about it and they seem to think it is a good idea. I will bring it up at tomorrow's meeting.

Wattie was looking very drained when I saw him talking on the phone and I sat speaking to him for some time. He said he badly needed someone to talk to. He said he felt like getting up and walking out earlier this afternoon but felt much better after sitting speaking to me.

17th JULY '75
The Governor had a day off today. We were surprised when Wattie returned from the main prison, very angry, to tell us that the Chief Officer there told him that our Governor has taken an office in the main prison. I had to calm Wattie down as he was concerned at the Governor making this move without telling him. The whole scene is getting more bizarre every day. David Scott and Bill Hook who made the film for the BBC brought it in on video for us to have a preview. David did very well and I think it was okay. The only sticky bit, as I see it, is when Alex Stephen, summing up on each of our futures, states that Larry, as he says himself, has no hope of release.

22nd JULY '75
This morning I went into my studio after doing my exercises. I worked on 'Censorship' and made good progress.

While some visitors were in, J.C. approached Larry who

72

has been feeling very depressed these past few days. As he was going out he asked Larry if he needed anything. Larry told him to fuck off. He did this in front of the visitors. J.C. told me he is afraid of Larry as he is injecting himself with Codeine and this is why he is down. Ken says that Larry has approached him saying he wants away from the Unit. He told Ken that he is going to die in prison and wants to do so in the old system. We came to an agreement that we should work together to pull Larry out of his depression. Peter told me to warn Larry of the dangers of injecting but I told him Larry was well aware of this.

I spoke to Larry after lock up and he was saying that he thinks he has hepatitis and they are going to take tests. He said that Dr Smith was in and looked for puncture marks on his arm. He had fooled him and he showed me his ankle and four puncture marks on it. Larry told me that he had given up injecting but feels he needs this danger element as he knows that every time he injects himself he could kill himself with an overdose or air bubble. He said when lying in pain the other night he wanted to die.

23rd JULY '75
The Governor came in this morning but kept to his office. At the Community meeting the Governor attended with Tom Melville and a Tom Donoghue, also from the Department.

Ken brought out and read the paper he was asked to write for the Community concerning the Negotiating Board which will represent the Community when dealing with the Department, so as not to be at the mercy of one person's opinions of the place. The Governor asked if he could have more time to think it over. Ken replied yes but went on to ask the views of everyone else. It was approved unanimously.

1st AUGUST '75
This morning during the early hours I was awakened by Larry getting more pills from the night-shift — the sound of his door opening wakened me. It really disturbs me as

Larry isn't seeing that this is killing him. This morning at 6am I found him in the toilet area with his chamber pot over him as he lay on the ground; urine covered the floor. He had fallen as he was heavily drugged. He came down to help me with the daily cleaning task but I told him to leave it to me.

I pulled Ken aside this morning and told him that unless he and Peter Whatmore were prepared to sort out Larry's drug situation I was going to bring it up at the meeting as I was seeing that they were helping Larry to kill himself. Larry told me that he had nineteen seconal since eight o'clock last night which is incredible. I pulled Peter Whatmore and told him to do something. We spoke in the hall area and he kept looking up towards Larry's cell in case he was listening.

4th AUGUST '75
Last night Larry went on his bell and was given two extra tablets to put him to sleep. I had a very bad night as things seemed to build up in me. Eventually I went to sleep but it was restless and I awoke in the early hours. When I wakened this morning it was as though I hadn't slept a wink. Every inch of my exercises was torture but afterwards it was good as I relaxed through Yoga.

The Governor came in and walked past Larry who spat at his feet. He repeated this some time later as he passed again. I wasn't there but heard about it much later.

Sometime this morning the Governor sent for Wattie. He told him that I am running the Unit and what are they going to do about it. He came on very strong against me but Wattie said he refused to be drawn into this. He told the Governor to take it up with the Community.

Peter Whatmore came in this afternoon and I cornered him about the Governor having a go at me via Wattie, about me running the place. I reminded Peter of the deal he made with me when the Unit was fragmented, about his defining my role to the Department. He explained that if someone tells him I am running the Unit, he admits this, saying I'm making a good job of it. Afterwards Peter had a

74

session with Larry. Larry came to me saying that Peter wanted him to have shock treatment. I don't know whether the truth is that Larry has asked for this.

By this time I had heard about the spitting incident. I told him that this was bloody stupid and that he is giving the Governor ammunition to use against us. Larry said he knew it but couldn't restrain himself. We then talked about the bad time he is going through at the moment and I told him I am finding things difficult also. I told him about last night but Larry doesn't want to know this. I switched topics and told him he is frightening staff by pushing things too far. I think he is glad of straight talk as he seemed much better afterwards.

Staff are getting frightened of my going back into hospital soon and some are suggesting this is the reason for Larry's present behaviour. I don't agree with this.

12th AUGUST '75
This morning I felt terrible and went to get my chisels and begin a new piece. I started work before nine o'clock and worked straight through till four. The anger in me is really bad and I kept thinking of sculptors from the past wondering if they worked with such torment. I took an untouched piece of stone and nearly completed the sculpture by the time I stopped. I didn't have the remotest idea what I was going to do when I started and it's turned out great. There is no way that the feeling of working while angry can be measured but I am very tired and weary and have to get out of this fucking place or I will go crazy. Prison is killing me.

Arthur Dooley the sculptor said in a letter today that a friend of his who runs a gallery wants to put an exhibition of my work on. There was also a nice letter from Mike Meyers, the artist from Kansas City with a photo-slide of one of his works titled 'The Egyptian Sideways Blues for Jimmy Boyle'. It is hanging in his Chicago exhibition.

21st AUGUST '75
At lunch today Davy made a nice meal for us. I was kidding him on that his cooking was terrible and we were laughing

at this. Larry was joining in. The whole thing was very funny and Davy was laughing heartily. However, for a few brief seconds Larry and him were joking then out of the blue Larry stood up and threw a cup of hot tea in Davy's face before any of us knew what was happening. I flew up and shoved Larry away and Davy just stood there. Absolute rage came right up in me and I turned to Larry calling him a dirty fucking coward and that he had taken a liberty. I called him every name under the sun and he sat rigid in his seat. By this time I was over him and have never come so close to punching him on the jaw. I was totally disgusted with Larry. He sat for a few moments then got up and left and we haven't said a word to each other since. I am not giving a fuck as I can't stomach the bastard at the moment. Both J.C. and Davy were very frightened at what happened, and by any standards it was out of order. Davy wasn't burned though his face was red.

Alex Skade brought Laurence Demarco who runs Panmuir House in Edinburgh, a place for kids in trouble. We had a good talk. He seems okay and is intending to do good things.

J.C. and I walked up and down the yard tonight talking. He was saying that he thinks Larry is crazy, also that it's a case of him either being at your feet or your throat.

23rd AUGUST '75
I have just emerged from a period of sitting in the darkness with earphones playing Vivaldi's *Four Seasons* to blot out the prison sounds around me. I have to think. I have to go inside myself and find out what it is that is bothering me. While sitting I look at the closed/bolted/locked door and recognise it is this, the fact that I am in here and in torment. What am I to do? An assortment of solutions come to the fore, each as silly as the next. There is this feeling of absolute aliveness in me and it's hard to control because the physical reality is that of a cripple within this tomb. My whole heart and soul aches with the pain of being here. I know that I've reached the stage where freedom must be given to me. I feel they may take me beyond the brink and

in a way that even I can't tell, destroy a great deal of what's within.

It mostly comes on a Saturday night simply because that is the night I am locked up from 5pm till the following morning and the diversions for the mind are severely restricted. Self-confrontation does no good as I've gone over it all before; it's the freedom thing and nothing can solve it. Minute by minute I am faced with it. The will to live again is tremendously strong within me. I want to see life and in many ways for the first time as I have never lived. . .

The curtains are closed to shut out the light from the dying day, to blot out of sight that there is an outside. Earphones and darkness keep away the reality, and are measures taken to help me through the night as tomorrow the day will bring new hope.

It's at moments like this that I love classical music, it somehow seems to match my mood and go to the core of my pain and caress it. The key to everything is patience and that is a very painful process, as I am experiencing. Thousands of us are locked up in similar boxes thinking/dreaming of the same thing. Beyond the wall lies our dream and beyond that lies another dream. . .

Tomorrow the Edinburgh Festival opens and I have some sculptures on exhibition at Ricky's. In a way part of me is outside as I put tremendous feeling into the pieces on show.

It seems to help when I write out my thoughts like this, as though I am ridding myself of them.

It's 8.45pm and the night has a long way ahead. I want to get up and pace the floor and not think about anything. I want to run away from what's inside me. The walls stand firm and the locked door becomes an intimidating enemy. I am locked in with myself. I see me — too much. I hate to be confronted with the fact that others have this terrible amount of control over me. I am not bad. I AM NOT BAD! The fantasy of taking them inside my soul to show them all is well will remain a dream.

Someone said to me — again — that if I had given the Governor his position and crawled to him then I would be out on paroles today. Is this what they really want? Is this what they want me to become? Deep within I know that the person who said this is speaking the truth. I cannot have freedom at that price. I don't want to know.

26th AUGUST '75
Ken and I talked about the Unit and the advantages it has for the whole of society in its success. I really love getting into this sort of dialogue with Ken as it brings me to life...

29th AUGUST '75
Apparently the Governor came in and asked Gus (staff member) to show me a letter from the Department:

> *Dear*
> *I refer to a note sent to the Department some time ago about a proposed external programme for J. Boyle.*
> *The requests that he be allowed to visit the Kandinsky Exhibition at the Scottish National Gallery on 3rd Sept. and attend a tutorial at Langside College for Open University students in November are not approved.*
> *Yours Sincerely*
> *T. Melville*

31st AUGUST '75
Larry, James L. and I are still not speaking to each other. Otherwise things are going smoothly enough. I am quite content with things as they are, simply because I feel that by not speaking it's the lesser of the two evils as Larry and J.L. have never contributed more than they presently are and by this I mean in their relationships with others in the Unit. Both are being considerate to others.

Ken has to write up a log every day and was trying to find out if the Governor had been in this morning and no-one could say. What a crazy situation.

78

1st SEPTEMBER '75

This morning I went about getting things prepared for the Unit exhibition tonight.

It was a bad start with Mr Scrimgeour, Director of Prisons, sending a brief letter saying he wasn't coming. It was word for word what Mr Keely the Controller's letter said. It's disappointing as the whole thing was meant to encourage these people to come in.

I started getting everything together and sorted out in the yard and it looked really good. The work gave the area a different feel. I thought it was looking great.

Around thirty people came in, staff and their wives, Governors and their wives, and others. The atmosphere was good and everyone tucked into the food we had prepared. Gus took photos of the whole thing. All in all the night went very well and I'm sure the show did wonders for the Unit. I think the four other nights will be even better. Afterwards all of us remarked on how well it went. We were full of enthusiasm for it.

6th SEPTEMBER '75

Murray Stewart (staff member) was telling me that three young teenagers who stole a car and crashed against three screw's cars from Barlinnie in the staff housing quarters were given a terrible beating by the screws. A senior cop came on the scene as they were attacking the kids. He turned a blind eye to what was happening. The kids were given bail straight from the Royal Infirmary. This really upset me.

2nd OCTOBER '75

Tonight I spoke to Gerry (staff member) and he was telling me that three weeks past Monday he went to the Shooting Club that another staff member attends and while there the Governor, who is a member, 'happened' to drop in. He told him that he will be leaving the Unit by the end of October. He expressed his dislike for certain members of staff, particularly Ken. He said he is being transferred to the Department but not on promotion. He advised the staff member to get out in six months time but he said he was staying. Gerry then asked him why he isn't coming into the Unit. The Governor said he wasn't going to allow himself to be 'broken'.

Rab and J.C. were given their liberation dates. Rab was told he will go to Edinburgh prison, then Peninghame Open Prison and then Training For Freedom (TFF) and will be released in February 1977.

Rab came in from his work in the Citizens Theatre tonight and was informed. He was sick as he thought he would have been given better than this. It's terrible as Rab has to wait another two years for freedom and more to the point, give up a good job and go back into a prison situation. It is an indictment on the Home and Health Department.

4th OCTOBER '75
The Governor was in the prison this afternoon. He told the staff that he wants J.C. transferred to Edinburgh prison on Wednesday. He stated that the Governor of that prison wanted J.C. transferred in the way of other prisoners as Ian's going through with a member of staff from here made it more difficult for him to settle and adjust to Saughton.

I am really sick at the way J.C. and Rab are being put back as it is cruel.

10th OCTOBER '75
Ma is dead forty six months tonight and I said prayers for her and miss her terribly — she is well remembered.

I went up to read my mail when Ken called me saying there was a meeting. When I came in he was sitting in a furious mood. He read out a letter from Tom Melville saying that Davy (the new prisoner) had sent a letter to a Mrs Morrison at St Andrews House, asking her to send another enclosed letter to the head man, Mr Fraser. In the second letter he said the Unit is doing nothing for him and that he wanted transferred, asking him to contact Oliver and Melville on his behalf. In it Davy referred to the falseness of the Unit in pretending to do something for him.

80

Ken then threw the subject open to the community. There was pure anger directed at Davy by me and everyone else. He was visibly shaken by it. This is the his first experience of the hot seat and the first I've seen in some time. It was pointed out to Davy that at this stage we are beginning to make up some ground that we lost due to the Governor's setting us back and here he is doing something blatantly stupid. Melville said in his letter that it may be that Davy's mail will have to be censored by one of the senior staff. Davy tried to squirm out of it but eventually admitted it was stupid and he apologised. We discussed the situation and Ken proposed that Davy have his mail censored from here on in — incoming and out-going. Staff — Gus and Bob, proposed that his use of the phone be terminated but this wasn't accepted as his mother phones him and as she is in bad health this restriction would affect her.

24th OCTOBER '75
J.C. is gone. I will miss him as he was okay and had many loveable qualities. I am sure that one bloomer has been made, that he's been prematurely transferred from here. He had a lot to learn from this place and was taken away at a time when he was ripe for it. He says he will go to Edinburgh and put on a front and build barriers to keep them at a distance in order to get through the anticipated provocation. I think of him as I write this knowing he will be in a cell with two others. In the morning he will wake to the sounds of the old system, scraping keys in locks, chamber pots being emptied...

25th OCTOBER '75
This afternoon we all had visits... I had a lovely time with my daughter Patricia. We both went off to sit in the weight-lifting room. We sat for a good while speaking. She seems to be getting on very well.

30th OCTOBER (a.m.) '75
It's the early hours of the morning and I have been lying listening to Larry, in a drugged state, fall all over his cell

making tremendous crashing noises. I went to my cell door and shouted through asking him to go to bed. I asked again. In the end I shouted, 'You fucking idiot, get to your fucking bed'. This had no effect whatsoever — he is too drugged. I ended up shouting to him as I type this, 'I hope you break your fucking neck'. The pain of having to listen to this is unbearable. It takes me back to Inverness and the Cages when they were loading him up with drugs. The bangs of him falling could be heard all through the night as he crashed against the Cage front. I know all of this scene off by heart and want to fuck away from it. He is doing this by choice in here but it shouldn't be, it just shouldn't be. . .

31st OCTOBER '75

This morning I went through my usual routine then got into my OU studies and made good progress.

There was some talk about Duncy (new prisoner) coming and it was relayed to us that he had destroyed his transistor radio as some screw in Peterhead told him that he wouldn't be allowed his radio in the Unit. Also that he had been given a dose of drugs on leaving prison.

I greeted him when he came in, a small oily skinned man with shifty eyes, and Larry welcomed him with a cooked meal. The staff escorting him said he sat silent throughout the journey. This guy is really steeped in prison culture, probably more than any other in here apart from Davy. Duncy began by trying to impress me, saying that he was going to attack a screw, that he did make an attempt but failed to connect, almost as though I wanted to hear this. Probably in the past I would have and that's the way it goes in that culture but it's alien to me now. He came straight from solitary where he had been kept for a few weeks though he says four months which isn't true. This isn't to say he didn't have a hard time.

Larry was incapable of walking at lock-up time tonight so I had to help him to his cell with Murray Stewart. The drugs had really worked. He had his emergency dosage this afternoon and a full whack tonight. What a state he was in. He seemed apprehensive about Duncy coming down and has been on about his religious bigotry. This showed when Duncy was speaking to us. Larry sat there very quiet before getting up and walking away.

10th NOVEMBER '75
A social worker from Saughton prison phoned the Unit. In conversation she mentioned to Ken that J.C. is having a hard time. He is in a pretty depressive state because staff there are picking on him. It seems that even the two prisoners sharing his cell are getting a bad time since J.C. joined them...

10th DECEMBER '75
Tom Melville was on the phone saying that the Governor looks as though he is going to put a sick line in every week till he is transferred. He was saying that a Departmental circular of Governor's moves will probably be issued at the end of this week or the beginning of next. We know our new Governor — unofficially.

Wattie quizzed Tom about J.C. who is lying in solitary and refusing to shave or anything. He suggested that J.C. be returned to the Unit but Melville replied no. Apparently they are thinking if he has to go anywhere then it will be Peterhead. It really is rough. The Department don't seem to have learned anything.

25th DECEMBER
This morning we all had breakfast together, except for Rab. The meal was good. A short time later Ken called me aside to say that Rab had been violently sick in his cell, that last night he had taken an overdose of pills. This came as a great shock to me. Ken called a Community meeting and told everyone. One of the staff had spoken to Rab who told him that he had left farewell letters in the homes of his family. On going back to speak to Rab in his cell Ken found the door barricaded. He wouldn't let anyone in. I went to his door telling him that I didn't want him to open the door but to let me know he was okay. He said he was but wanted to be left alone. I reckon he has made an attempt on his life

and having failed is now ashamed to face anyone. The Community agreed to call Dr Whatmore and the Governor. Bill Allen (staff member) went to Rab's family and retrieved the letters. They were worried and at a loss what to do.

The whole day had a gloom cast over it. The fact is we can't pick and choose when to have crises and this is what the Unit is all about. Bill Allen did a wonderful job with Rab's family, he is an exceptional person. He went off duty to take his family out for Christmas lunch but afterwards returned to see how Rab was. These are the things that matter, not the superficial tinsel of Xmas. Later I sat speaking to Rab. He apologised for causing us trouble and ruining the day but I told him not to worry, that our priorities were about people and not the day. He said that he was sick with this girlfriend falling out with him and not being allowed home for five days.

Moira (Unit visitor) went to Davy's mother's house last night in time to save her taking an overdose. She was in the house, cold lonely and with nothing to eat. Moira detected something in her voice over the phone and went to find her in a terrible condition. The doctor had to be called and the old woman taken to hospital with pain from a heart condition. She told Moira that she wants to die and would only for Davy who needed her. Ken has kept this from Davy till tomorrow. There is no doubt that we will get a reaction from this. Tomorrow is the Governor's last day, Hoooorraaaaaayyy!

26th DECEMBER '75
I spoke to Rab and he was up walking about but not very talkative. He says he is feeling much better.

The staff aren't paying too much attention to anything that is going on except for Ken and Gus. This is the second day we have only had two staff on duty and the place seems to run more smoothly. I am going to make a note of the times we are working with one or two staff on duty for lengthy periods. Although they won't say officially that they work best with less staff they all agree that they do.

84

The Governor was in and made farewells to one or two staff. He didn't come near any of the prisoners. I'm glad he didn't come near me. Thank fuck he has left.

27th DECEMBER
Duncy seemed upset this morning due to his pills being reduced. Wattie was on to Peter Whatmore and it looks as though Duncy will be put back on his pills. He tried to stop his wife visiting today but she came anyway. They had a good visit.

29th DECEMBER '75
This morning I was very tired and wakened full of pressure and tension. I found it very difficult to get up and on finally doing so it was hard to do anything. I dragged myself through my exercise routine knowing that I had to complete it.

The place is getting to me; the pressure from the Governor experience was all coming down on me. My whole body is listless and aching with tiredness. My right eye had a sort of tick to it. I completed my exercises then came to my cell and lay in solitude. Ken and Wattie came up and I told them I was tense. Wattie said he felt the same.

Tonight I had a long talk with Rab. He said the visit from his girl yesterday brought a lot of things home to him. He now realises she had nothing to do with it but that he brought it all on himself. There is no doubt that Rab has grown out of this and is already seeing things he hadn't seen before. This doesn't mean it will be smooth for him as it won't. He said the fact that he has to leave here is getting to him. I feel proud when I speak to Rab at times like this as he has matured a lot since coming to the Unit. Thank Christ this latest lapse happened here and not the conventional prison, otherwise they would have put him on Strict Observation. He is looking forward to returning to work tomorrow.

30th DECEMBER '75
'Masked Violence' is what I am experiencing at the

moment. There is no physical bruising for the eye to see. Who can measure the scars on a person's soul? Who can measure the pain? Do I really want to become a part of this? What am I striving for?

I am sick of tiny minded bureaucrats who violate my person with impunity. I realise they have me in a position where they can and are doing what they want. I have to live with myself. Am I going to sit in this cold storage and let them rub my face in the shit? Jimmy, what the fuck are you allowing to happen? When the ultimate coyote rejection was taking place and you lay animalised in your cage you were able to see life in society for what it was. Why pretend it is different now? Why climb the mountain to fall down the other side? Between the past and the future lies the pain of today. The height of impotence — being violent with a typewriter.

Who soothes the heart that beats in agony? Who kisses the soul that writhes in torment? Who mends the shattered self?

2nd JANUARY '76
It's an exciting time for me at the age of thirty one as I am finding out a great deal about myself. I am making new relationships and living in a world totally unknown to me. I love it yet there are times when I hate it. I am torn between two worlds — alienated from the old one and a stranger in this new one.

I love it as I feel the inside of my head blossoming like a flower and realise I am changing into something else but with this comes many insecurities. I have to work on a level that is different in style. Who could possibly begin to understand what I am experiencing? With this change comes the fear that in adapting to their way, those 'respectable' enemies will do as they want. As I am now accepting their ways they will expect me to retaliate similarly but they will be in a position to manipulate the scene. I do feel they have the upper hand and what I find difficult is the thought of continually losing to people who hate me.

Even though I am in prison, these are the finest years I've

ever known. There are times when I am not in prison, when I have transcended this and feel free. There is one thing that I am sure of, that I have been in a personal prison all my life until these past few years.

There are times when I think I do too much thinking.

There are also times when I am really in a prison and I think this is due to the fact that I am freer in the mind and realise that mental freedom is not enough, it's at these moments I feel the walls smothering me. I feel more a machine, getting up at the same time each day, doing exercises, working, being locked up. Although all of this comes and goes I have come to terms with it and realise that I am going through a phase that will last a short spell. I'd love to see my children more and get even closer to them but I can't surmount the fact that we only see each other a few hours a month.

Sporadic thoughts made in the night for reasons I don't know. I do feel pretty good and have all through this writing. Some day I'll look back and wonder why I sat typing this.

3rd JANUARY '76

At lunch time I spoke to J.L., Davy and Duncy as we ate. I told them that this is a crucial year for us and that we should help the Unit as much as possible. I told them to treat people in the Unit with the respect they are due. If Larry abuses a member of staff they don't have to side with him. Davy told me Moira is going to see his mother in hospital. He was saying his mother is getting out. I was pleased to hear this.

Duncy had a visit from his wife this afternoon. She told me that she couldn't manage to bring the kids as her social security money didn't arrive on time. Duncy has saved £2 and he gave it to his wife for her birthday and their anniversary.

4th JANUARY '76

Davy came down with another letter and told John (staff member) that Moira had better not see his mother as she has been sneaking behind his back to tell Ken and Wattie things, that she had ransacked his mother's house and told tales about his mother not having any food in the house. He threatened to stab Moira if she visited the Unit. He said he was suing her and getting a court order to stop her seeing his mother... Ken reminded Davy that Moira had virtually saved his mother's life. Larry came in strong against Davy as did everyone in the Community. He was verbally abused for threatening visitors to the Unit who had done us a lot of good. Davy is definitely sick and I told him so. He asked to be put back to Peterhead prison. He has gone on long enough within the prison system without help; he needs treatment. It may be that the Unit has served the useful function in Davy's problems being seen whereas elsewhere they were ignored. I don't think there is anything more we can do for him.

8th JANUARY '76
Wattie and I had a chat with Moira when she came in this morning. We informed her of the meeting with Davy. We suggested that a Community meeting be called and she agreed.

The meeting opened with all the same old things being regurgitated and Davy jumping from excuse to excuse. Moira grew in stature as the meeting went on. She handled it magnificently. The meeting was one of the best I have attended and of a high standard. Lots of earthy facts were put to Davy, as well as compassion. He sat agreeing with everything. It always seems to me as though what is being said shoots over his head. A decision had to be made as to whether Moira should continue to involve herself with his mother by bringing her to visit Davy. Moira said she initially got involved at the request of Davy. She did so hoping it would help him get more involved with the Community but this didn't seem to be working so she thought she should leave it for a spell. Davy thought this right but was clearly shaken.

After lunch Joyce came in. She had a newspaper clipping from *The Scotsman*, it quoted Nicholas Fairbairn Q.C.

(now on a Tory platform). 'The treatment of prisoners on life sentences should be known to be different from other prisoners. It should be more rigorous more like a detention centre than like the Special Unit at Barlinnie, which is an art shop.'

9th JANUARY '76
Tom McGrath came up and we had a long talk over the exhibition. He has taken it to the Arts Council and told them that he is putting it on and that it may arouse controversy. He went into detail and they backed him. Tom and I discussed the whole thing and he took my material away to use at his discretion. He is doing another exhibition in the Third Eye early next year about various forms of violence and has asked me to contribute. He is holding an open night on the second week of the exhibition inviting members of the Establishment along as well as other people. He is intending to do a good catalogue. My knee collapsed this morning.

12th JANUARY '76
Peter Whatmore has received a letter saying that Anthony Lester Q.C. (Roy Jenkins' advisor at the Home Office) was wanting to meet him on 11th February. Peter showed Ken the letter he received from Keely and Meikle (Dept.) saying that they want to meet him on Monday. They are doing an in-depth study of the Unit (I imagine for the Home Office) as they want to see Alex Stephen. Things are beginning to move. The hypocrisy of the Department people is diabolical as they know they are going to be asked questions so are now scurrying like rats to get all the information they can at the last minute. It will be interesting to see if they come into the Unit. They have arranged to meet Ken and Wattie separately — outside the Unit.

Between 5-6.30pm lock-up Davy came to speak to me and went into the whole situation about his carry on. We had a good discussion about everything and I would like to believe that we have come out of it with something, but time will tell.

Larry came and told me he feels Duncy is being snide to him and is now introducing his Orange Order talk into discussions. I advised him to speak to Duncy now rather than wait till it gets worse. He did. James L. is growing one of those funny beards but seems much better than he has been lately.

14th JANUARY '76
This morning I did my exercises and then helped get things prepared for the Department reps coming in. Ken brought in the mail and with it a copy of the Department Whitley Council Minutes held in the Conference room at Government Buildings, Broomhouse Drive, Edinburgh.
The Official representatives were: Scrimgeour (Chairman) Oliver, Keely, Aithie, Collinson, Burnett, Frisby, Hendry, Peerless, Beveridge.
The Staff were: Adams (Chairman) Donaldson, Lawrie.
6. *Barlinnie Special Unit*
   The Staff Side referred to recent correspondence regarding the shortfall of volunteers for the Special Unit, and since they were anxious that the experiment should continue they would welcome a discussion of that matter.
   The Staff Side expressed concern about the regime in the Unit. It had been suggested that because of the extra pressure on staff the incidence of sick leave is higher in the Special Unit than elsewhere, although this has been refuted by Personnel Branch. The Staff Side felt that a fresh look should be taken at the Unit and that a limit should be set on the length of time officers serve there. It was further suggested that Barlinnie was the wrong place for the Unit.
   The Official Side reported that recently Mr Oliver had met with the staff of the Unit in two groups at the College. The discussions had proved useful and informative for all concerned and it was generally agreed that the Unit had moved too fast too soon and prisoners given too much latitude. The situation now is that the staff have been asked to draw up guidelines for the

90

running of the Unit. It is hoped in future it will be possible to meet annually with the staff.

While the Official Side agreed that Barlinnie might not be the ideal site for the Unit, it was the only place available. Whether or not a time limit could be set for service in the Unit would depend on there being a constant flow of volunteers to replace officers due to move.

The Staff Side were glad to hear that things are changing and asked how this could be conveyed to the staff.

The Official Side said that this might be done during courses etc., and of course the minutes of this meeting would give some indication.

Ken was very angry at this as were other staff who feel that the two-day conference has been completely distorted by Oliver. Ken and Wattie who were waiting to meet Keely and Meikle intended bringing this up with them. I am very suspicious of what is being said here as I am being told the exact opposite by staff and Department whenever we see them.

After their respective meetings they came into the Unit. I took them both round. I explained that the weightlifting room used to be our punishment cell. Keely joked that it still was a punishment cell (meaning the weights). I took them to the cells and into mine explaining to them how we have our visits here. Meikle enquired about my children. He asked how I was and I said okay except for my knee. He asked how hard it was for prisoners to settle into the Unit. I replied that it was very difficult for staff and prisoners. I was as enthusiastic about the Unit as I could be without going overboard. Meikle asked how long I had been in and I replied that I was into my ninth year. I told them that we hadn't seen them recently and they said they didn't want to be seen breathing down our necks.

We then went into the meeting room for a coffee and general chat. All the staff were there. The discussion went into how the Unit should expand. Meikle replied that there was a financial crisis but we hit him with how it costs nothing to encourage staff and prisoners to make relationships. Bill Allen (staff member) said that the feeling in the Unit is that the Department are not doing much to encourage staff to take up working here. This was supported by the rest of us. Meikle went on about how the Department have a lot more than the Unit to contend with. He said that if the Department wanted they could have halted the experiment any time during the last three years just as this could happen any time during the next three years. Keely sat not saying much, just listening. I think it is clear that the Department presence within the Unit in future will be very limited. I explained to them that the cost of the staff training was going to waste as the staff were being put back into ordinary working places where their experience could not be put to good use. He said the staff would be rubbing it off on other less experienced staff.

16th JANUARY '76
Larry was making a terrible noise last night. He didn't sleep a wink and when I saw him first thing he was still heavily drugged. He was falling about. Ken had a word with him about it but Larry is saying that he feels hostility directed towards him from everyone in the Unit at the moment.

He came in and spoke to me later saying he is depressed but won't say why, that is if he knows.

28th JANUARY '76
This morning I wakened very early but wasn't feeling right so did a part of my exercise routine that included running round the yard, rowing, sit-ups and yoga. I did the right thing as I am weary and needing a rest and felt better for the light exercise period. Some people who work in Panmure House came in from Edinburgh. I showed them around and they put some pertinent questions and we had a good session going. In the meeting room we had a lively debate on corporal punishment.

I had to leave them as Tom McGrath phoned asking me to write another paragraph for the catalogue, along the lines of what I'd do if I suddenly found myself released tomorrow. Tom said he has a small play going at the Traverse Theatre just now but would like to do one on violence and asked me to write it with him. He said that he would split the profits right down the middle with me. He went on to say if I did want to write it myself then he would have no objections. I told him the phone isn't the best of places to discuss the matter so we should do so when we meet. He will be up shortly.

29th JANUARY '76
Ben was pouring his heart out as he is having serious problems adjusting to life outside. He said that after a full year out he should really be well, whereas he is finding that this isn't the case and is only now encountering the problems and there is no-one to talk to about it. He said it was when under this black cloud that he left a pub under the influence when a young cop approached him, gave him a push and told him to get on. Ben realised that if he punched him it would make matters worse but the pressure was on him and he did. He said that he can best describe it as the alcoholic who takes a drink knowing he isn't going to stop.

10th FEBRUARY '76
Anthony Lester Q.C. (Home Office) and Tony Pearson (Governor grade) came here at 11.20. Before they arrived, a message was sent by Lester saying he didn't want a staff meeting but just to enter and speak to people informally. When they came in the new Governor was highly excited — all of us were remarking on it. On taking them round we were trailed by Meikle and the new Governor. What was pleasing to me was Anthony Lester saying that the place wasn't as luxurious or expensive as had been made out. Afterwards they left for the Garfield Hotel for lunch.

They returned to take part in a Community meeting. Ken chaired it and after the Minutes had been read we concentrated on general business. After the normal meeting we broke for coffee then re-assembled. Anthony Lester told us that he was here at the request of Roy Jenkins to look the place over as the Home Secretary had heard so much about it. We then had an extremely long and interesting discussion on the Unit. Anthony asked us about privileges and we told him about the use of the phone, uncensored mail, unsupervised visits, community meetings and being allowed to express ourselves freely. We did say that though these weren't looked on as privileges they were what made the Unit conditions better. The meeting went on till after 6pm.

There were lots of things said that I haven't mentioned here as I can't remember them all. Anthony will return tomorrow morning. The day was very rewarding and most informative.

I spoke to Tom McGrath and he said that over a thousand people had visited my exhibition on the first day and half.

12th FEBRUARY '76
The Barlinnie Governor Bob Hendry, Dr Neil Smith, Giles Havergill and Joyce Laing came in for our third anniversary lunch and we had a very enjoyable meal. The new Governor gave a good speech thanking the guests for coming. Kay replied with a speech that hit us all.

Wattie mentioned to me that Tom Melville phoned him saying Harry Ewing (Labour Minister) wanted to know who was paying for the Unit anniversary meal. Wattie told him the prisoners and staff had paid for it. Most of us don't believe that Harry Ewing wants to know, we think it is the Director.

They are probably on about the expense but we question the public money being spent to take Anthony Lester and the gang of them to the Garfield Hotel when we could have fed him.

10th MARCH '76
This morning I did my exercises then started cleaning the floor as usual. While putting the polish down I heard a bang coming from the hall area and looked to Davy who was preparing the vegetables. He looked then went back to work.

94

JUST DROPPED INTO THIS PLANET TO DAY, WHAT A STRANGE PLACE IT IS. I AM GLAD TO BE AN ALIEN - THERE IS NO WAY I WANT TO BECOME A PART OF THEM. THEY ARE WHAT I WOULD CALL NITPICKERS, PLUCKING AWAY WITH THEIR MICROSCOPIC EYES, DELVING INTO EACH NOOK AND CRANNY. THE DRONE OF THEIR DRIVELLING VOICES IS LIKE A SOPHISTICATED PIECE OF REPRESSIVE TECHNOLOGY GEARED FOR SENDING ONE INTO A DEEP CATATONIC STATE. THEY HAVE PLACED ME IN THIS SMALL CELL WITH ITS SPECKLED WALLS. THE WINDOW LOOKS ON TO LUSH GREEN HILLS, PAST THE WIRE FENCE AND WALLS THAT IS. THIS THEY SAY, IS PROGRESS. THEY ARE MOVING ME THROUGH WHAT THEY CALL "THE SYSTEM". THERE ARE A NUMBER OF MYTHS AND RUMOURS ABOUT THIS. THE OFFICIAL STATE — AND THIS IS A LIE THAT I AM MERELY FOLLOWING THE HELL TROD-DEN ROUTE OF "THE SYSTEM". OTHERS, INDIVIDUAL STAFF AND SOME PRISONERS SUGGEST THAT IT IS TO JUSTIFY THE SYSTEM AS A WHOLE AND NOT ONLY THAT OF THE SPECIAL UNIT. THEY ARE ENGINEERING THE SITUATION TO PRODUCE COMPARISONS BETWEEN THE SPECIAL UNIT AND THE TRADITIONAL SYSTEM. PUTTING ME IN HERE THEY LOCK ME UP IN A CATCH 22 SITUATION. SO, I'M IN HERE DRESSED IN THEIR UNIFORM WHICH FEELS, LOOKS, SMELLS HORRIBLE. THIS EXPERIENCE IS FELT MUCH MORE DEEPER THAN THE WEARING OF THE CLOTHES ITS WHAT IT DOES TO ONE FAR BEYOND THIS. THE APPALLING ACT OF STRIPPING ONE OF HIS OWN CLOTHING AND FORCING HIM TO WEAR AN ILL-FITTING UNIFORM THAT HAS BEEN WORN BY GOD KNOWS WHO BEFORE, TO PULL ON SOCKS THAT SMELL OF ANOTHER PERSON, TO SNIFF THE SWEATY FEET OF ANOTHER IN THE SHOES THAT ARE WRINKLED WITH USE. IN THE COURSE OF THIS NEW CELL THEY'VE PUT ME IN LIE A PAIR OF SMELLY SLIPPERS. I STILL CAN'T BRING MYSELF TO LIFT THEM AND TOSS

THOUGHTS CONTINUE TO RACE THROUGH MY HEAD AS I SIT HERE IN MY EARLY EVENING. I CAN SEE THE CITY LIGHTS FROM MY CONFINEMENT, CARS AND BUSES FILLED WITH PEOPLE
THEM OUT. NEVER MIND WEAR THEM. LAST NIGHT PRIOR TO COMING HERE - NEW YEARS THAT ALL THE DOCTORS WERE OPEN OR TEA - PRISON TEA WHICH WAS THE NORMAL PRACTICE IS THAT GUYS CAN USE HOT WATER FROM A TAP TO MAKE COFFEE OR TEA AS THIS IS BETTER. THEY WEREN'T AMUSED. SOME WERE BLUNTLY TOLD TO "FUCK OFF". MOST GUYS WORK TO BECOME A PART OF THIS, TO TOUGHEN THEMSELVES UP SO THAT THEY CAN BE LOOKED UP TO AS "WIDEO'S". ITS THIS WORLD I WANT TO STAY AWAY FROM IN. REALITY, IT IS A HOUSE OF HEARTBREAK, OF HUMAN TRAGEDY. PRISONS ARE MONUMENTS TO HUMAN MISERY. BEING IN HERE AMONGST THESE GUYS, I DON'T SEE THIS AS THE EVIL PEOPLE SECTIONS OF OUR AND PUBLIC PORTRAY THEM AS. WHY IS IT THAT RESPONSIBLE SECTIONS OF OUR SOCIETY CAN MISLEAD THE REST IN THIS WAY? I AM NOT ABSOLVING ANYONE IN HERE, MYSELF INCLUDED, TO AVOID OUR OWN PERSONAL RESPONSIBILITY. BUT IN THE SAME BREATH I HAVE TO POINT OUT THAT THESE SO-CALLED RESPONSIBLE SECTIONS OF SOCIETY DON'T APPRECIATE OR UNDERSTAND THAT OTHER SECTIONS OF SOCIETY — FROM WHICH 99.99 OF THE PRISON POPULATION COME FROM HAVE VALUES WHICH CONDONE DEVIANT BEHAVIOUR. RESEARCH HAS SHOWN THAT A LARGE PER-CENTAGE OF KIDS IN THESE AREAS ARE "BORN TO FAIL". WE CAST ON THE ONE HAND LIVE IN A SCIENTIFIC AGE, ACCUMULATING SCIENTIFIC KNOW-LEDGE THAT IS GOING TO INCREASE AND EXPAND OUR ECONOMIC OUR MATERIALISTIC POSSESSIONS AND COMFORTS AND IGNORE EQUALLY VALUED KNOWLEDGE OF HUMAN HISTORY WITH-OUT BUILDING OF LONG TERM RADIUM FOR OURSELVES. IN DOING SO WE ARE CREATING AN IMBALANCE GOING AT THE PRESENT RATE THERE IS GOING TO BE A LARGE AMOUNT OF THIS POPULATION WHO WILL HAVE EXPERIENCED PRISON - A LARGE PROPORTION WHO WILL BE VERY MUCH ANTI-AUTHORITY AS A RESULT OF THIS.

RUSH BY MY WINDOW. HOUSEHOLDERS HAVE ARRIVED IN THEIR HOUSES UNAWARE THAT I LOOK FROM AFAR. I VIEW THE WORLD IN OBLIVION NOW I HATE IT. I LUST FOR LIFE ON THE OUTSIDE. I SIT HERE TRYING TO INSTILL PATIENCE IN MYSELF, THINKING THAT IT WILL COME. IT IS HARD, IT IS VERY HARD BUT IT MUST BE DONE. LESS THAN TWO YEARS TO GO BUT I TELL MYSELF LOOK AT THEM OTHERS AROUND HE WHO HAVE A LONG TIME TO GO. I DON'T FIND MY HUGE SOURCE IN THIS AS I AM IN IS VERY TRYING TIME. I AM SICK OF LOCKED AND CLOSED DOORS, SICK TO THE TEETH OF THEM, OF LIVING IN A WORLD WHERE OTHERS DOMINATE MY EVERY ACTION. I NEED SO MUCH TO BE FREE. I WANT MY FREEDOM! I HAVE FOUGHT FOR 15 YEARS TO RESIST BECOMING A PART OF THIS WORLD. I HAVE OPENLY FOUGHT ITS CLINGING DISEASE OF BEING INSTITUTIONALISED AND OF THE VERY FACT OF LIVING IN SUCH A PLACE MAKES I AM CONTAMINATED BY IT. I TAKE SOLACE FROM THE FACT THAT MOST PEOPLE ARE ALSO CONTAMINATED BY THE INSTITUTIONALISING RUT OF THEIR DAILY LIVES. I SUPPOSE PART OF ME LIKE A HARDCORE AND YOUNG WAS RESISTING THIS TO THE OTS IN AND WILL CONTINUE TO WHEN I AM OUT. AT THE MOMENT ITS BEEN THE STRUGGLE OF THRU INSTITUTIONAL LIFE THAT HAD DOMINATED ME. I HAVE BEEN RESISTING THIS IN ALL ITS FACETS FORMS AND DIFFERENT LAYERS REFUSING TO BECOME ITS WILLING SUBSERVIENT. THERE ARE MOMENTS WHEN I HONESTLY DOUBT IF ULTIMATELY I KNOW I WON'T SUBMIT OR LET IT HAVE ITS WAY. DEEP IN ME I KNOW THAT WHEN I LEAVE THIS PRISON I WILL STRUGGLE, CONTINUE MY STRUGGLE IN WHATEVER FORM HOW-EVER I MAY BE IN. PERHAPS THIS IS MY WAY OF CLINGING MANFULLY TO LIFE. I KNOW THAT I FEEL RIGHT IN WHAT I'M EVERY WHAT I'M DOING. I KNOW THAT MY LIFE MUST BE TO UPGRADE HUMAN STANDARDS. I STILL WHEN THAT I AM MERELY THE VEHICLE WHICH THIS LESSON IS TRAVELLING. BUT SURELY HUMANITY MUST LEARN FROM IT. I SAY AS I THINK OF THESE WORLD WOES AND ASK. IF THESE WERE LEARNED FROM? I CAN'T ANSWER THIS, I JUST BELIEVE THAT I MUST LET PEOPLE SEE AND LEARN FROM WHAT I HAVE GOT THROUGH AND BELIEVING THAT LEARNING CAN BE A LONG SLOW PROCESS.

I thought of a precariously balanced sculpture in my studio. Going to look I found it okay but James Lindsay's door was locked. I looked through the spyhole and he was sitting on the edge of the bed naked covered in blood. I could only think that he had tried to commit suicide and shouted through to ask if he was alright. I went to the staff and told them. J.L. was badly shaken. The cuts were pretty bad on the leg, hand, arm and chest. I then realised he had been attacked. I went upstairs to look at Larry. He was alright. Duncy was standing in the toilet area covered in blood. He was talking his head off as he took off his clothes and began to wash them in the sink. I called him all the fucking idiots of the day and was extremely angry. I did everything I could to stop myself punching him. He kept saying that he asked J.L. to call a meeting and he wouldn't but this was lies. He then told me he was insane and came out with lots of irrational statements. All the while he looked away from me.

I went back downstairs and caught hold of Ken coming on duty and put him in the picture. I then told Wattie. Everyone worked on helping J.L., getting him fixed up. A doctor was sent for. Everyone was shattered.

At this point most people didn't know who had done it. All eyes were fixed on Larry. I made it clear that it wasn't Larry.

Ken called a Community meeting. Duncy sat there calm and composed. It was a remarkable performance. Ken asked the person who had done it to speak up. The Governor was told and he responded by telling Ken and Wattie to lock everyone up and search them. I could see all the old traditional methods being introduced. I refused to be locked up as did Larry.

The staff went through a very loose motion of searching me. Mostly they congregated in my cell to talk. Larry started vomiting with tension and I felt sorry for him. He was afraid that he might be blamed. Duncy's cell was searched and bloodstained clothing was found. They also found a knife. He then started asking staff if he had cut Lindsay's prick. Ken went in and spoke to Duncy and he broke down crying, telling him he had done it.

I sat in my cell thinking. I was shattered as I feel this is the sort of incident that could do us terrible damage. Staff and the Governor sat around my cell chatting. There were many questions as to why. Although there was a lot of understanding towards Duncy it was felt that he had done something inexcusable. There was wild speculation trying to guess the motive but no one was any wiser. Everyone wants to protect the Unit.

The police were called and they interviewed us one at a time. The 'code' came in. J.L. was in a position where he would have to say something and he wanted to do what was best for the Unit but was caught in the 'code' conflict. It was a terrible position to be in. To inform on Duncy would result in him getting more time and nothing would be done for the guy. Also, what would happen if he was transferred to another prison? He saw the police and told them it was Duncy. I saw the cops and told them my part.

There is no doubt that the police were impressed with the co-operation they received. Duncy was charged and taken through to the main prison hospital where he would be kept.

11th MARCH '76 (7.45pm)

The morning after the night before...

Duncy is lying in a bare cell under constant observation. J.L. is below me licking his wounds. This whole incident had raised many questions within me. Yesterday the emphasis was on finding out who did it and this didn't take long with Duncy being caught with the goods. The focus then went on getting J.L. to identify him as the assailant. The Unit was used as the lever to get him to make this identification and it was successful. He was told that to come clean would help as it was a tricky situation and this mess could close the place. He was put in a terrible position.

The one question I have is, what is the purpose of hounding Duncy? What good will it do? It doesn't seem likely that he will get any treatment as he will simply be sent

97

back to Peterhead. I know this will only make the guy worse. The prisoners are being asked to show how good the Unit is by sending Duncy away.

When he was being taken through to the main prison by Ken he was like a docile little kid. The strange thing is that this is possibly the period when we could do Duncy the most good but the legal machinery has moved in and taken its course.

Wattie was saying the Department have been asking if a 'cover up' is going to take place and he proudly says it isn't. They are delighted. Talk is that the Unit has broken the usual prison culture that reigns supreme. I believe this is so but there is no sense breaking it if the answer is just to slap the guy back into jail.

14th MARCH '76
Ken and I have been talking about the possibility of bringing Duncy back. I feel that if he has to go to prison then it should be back here. If he is recommended for hospital treatment then there is nothing we can do. If we can absorb Duncy then we are giving a lesson to society as a whole. They seem to throw people into prisons and forget them. We would be doing the same thing. There is the problem of how J.L. will react. There is the problem of his mother who visits him.

Ken is worried about Duncy in the main prison and feels he is about to blow up.

25th MARCH '76
I spoke to Larry for a spell tonight and he is okay. We discussed freedom and I was saying how there is no substitute for it. Larry remarked that if he was offered the choice between a girl for the night and a gramme of heroin, he would take the heroin. I said that my problem was in coping with the walls and how they restrict me.

The Prisons Department was given an historical document by us to distribute in the Prison Officers' College and throughout the penal service, and elsewhere for that matter. The document gives a rough idea of the development of the Unit since its inception. The beginning of the document states it is for information only.

At the meeting yesterday the Governor pointed out that Mr Meikle in the Department wasn't too happy about the part relating to Communications that states the prisoners can use the phone. The big fear of this is that the press could phone in. He contradicted this by saying Meikle says this doesn't happen in other prisons and that they — the Department — didn't know that the phone was being used by prisoners.

9th APRIL '76

Tom McGrath came in and spoke to the Governor about putting his play on here. It was accepted. Tom and I discussed the play that we are writing and I gave him the material I had done. He is very enthusiastic about it and feels I should write the whole play and he will put it together. I don't want to. I need his expertise and knowledge at the moment and told him so. I would like to do other things at a later stage by myself. We went through everything and he stayed for lunch.

14th APRIL '76

Meikle caught hold of me to ask about the latest work I am doing. He asked how things were with the prisoners and I told him all was well but the Duncy thing had been a blow to us all. We talked about this for a period and he said he had played it down as much as he could, that they were treating it as an incident like in any other prison. I told him how proud we were of the Unit so took it as a personal blow. He said he realised this but it was bound to happen at some time. I then asked him what he would feel about Duncy returning to the Unit. This was unexpected and he said off-hand he could see that there would be wider issues to take into account and that the matter would have to be viewed with the greatest of care. He said he doesn't want to prejudge anything but one would have to consider what would happen if it occurred again...

Ken and Meikle had a session on the Whitley Council

Minutes. Meikle tried to spin it off that these were before he came (In Oliver's time). He said that Ken may be over-reacting to them and Ken replied he hoped he was but time would tell. Ken told him that Department behaviour recently had caused lots of fragmentation in the Unit amongst staff. He told Ken that the Unit is under no pressure to change and that it is still experimental and that the experiment will continue.

16th APRIL '76
This morning I did my exercises then got ready for Tom McGrath coming. While waiting I did some more writing for the play. Tom brought in his wife but she had to leave soon after. He has already spoken to some actors about it and they are very eager to take part. He will type out the first part this week. He is saying that it could be off the ground for September...

17th APRIL '76
When I got locked up at 5pm I was feeling great having just come from a new piece of sculpture.

I wrote up my diary then read up on my OU course but eventually the mood began to change with my mind wandering into the future and wondering what is there.

I thought of the beautiful cool evening, how I long to be walking in it outside this cell. All of this took place while I sat in the semi-dark reading a book. The thoughts on free-dom were only momentary but so powerful that they seem to tear my soul apart. There is something about being alone in a cell, about the inability to rise from a chair, open the door and speak to someone. I would like to get up this minute and discuss this subject with someone. I would like to put these feelings into a piece of sculpture and although sitting typing out the feelings is important there is a tremendous amount of strain and frustration attached to it. During these periods I find it hard to read a book or watch TV, which I hardly do anyway. The only solution at such times is to tackle the mood and try to do something with it.

100

Others lie in neighbouring cells either in drugged hazes or dreamy sleep. Each in his cell bound in himself as I am. Walls separate us from each other.

26th APRIL '76
As I type this the TV is showing Frank McElhone (Gorbals MP) and the Under-Secretary, opening a new security wing at St Marys List 'D' School. He said his heart ached opening this new wing as he hoped that fewer such places would open as he doubted their need. I was very impressed with this.

My children visited me with my niece and her boy-friend... I made a point of getting the children on their own so we could speak. We sat in the sun in the prison yard. Patricia was curious:

'When are you leaving this place' she asked.

'I don't know but I hope it isn't too long,' I replied. 'This place is worse than Colditz,' said James looking round the walls and to the TV monitor focussing on us.

'How long have you been here?' asked Patricia.

'Nine years'

'I thought it was six,' she said.

'I was only a wee baby, wasn't I?' asked James.

'Yes, and Patricia was just born,' I informed them.

'Why can't you come home now?' asked Patricia.

'Hmm, eh, it's just that I can't,' I stumbled. 'Because the court gave him a set time and he has to do that,' said James with protective exasperation.

'Were you in a court and found guilty?' asked Patricia.

'Yes, I was in court and found guilty,' I admitted.

'I've seen that in Crown Court on tele,' she said smiling.

I fumbled and shuffled around trying to hide the inner confusion the dialogue presented me with. I was feeling terribly protective towards them.

27th APRIL '76
The Great Escape – Larry
He holds his palm out to take the multi-coloured bar-biturates, lets them sit there on the surface while he counts

to check the numbers are correct; four reds, four yellows and three pale blues. He counts again then looks, savouring the sight. Quickly he scoops them into his mouth then swallows washing them down knowing the hot coffee will melt the capsules and rush on the tingle. Having taken no meal he knows the effect will be heavy on an empty stomach. Shortly afterwards his hands spring open and shut convulsively with the fingers and thumbs rubbing against each other like antennae searching for the first sign of the on-coming buzz.

An hour passes and the facial expression begins to change, his movements become stilted. His spirits rise and he becomes 'high' though in a moderate manner. He speaks with confidence as though he is master of himself. His company is excellent.

Before very long his mouth begins to hang open, his eyes start to close and his speech becomes slurred. The movement of his limbs becomes totally un-coordinated and the figure pathetic. The drug controls. He has to walk thirty yards to his bed and each step is that of a baby child learning to walk, only this is a grown man. His manner is peaceful. There are times on this short journey when he falls against things and those around him pretend that they don't see this sight — the degradation of man.

He is now at the top of his escape ladder, reality no longer exists for him. Life is a gold coloured haze that blots out the feeling of doom that smothers him in the cold light of day. Deep within he recognises his own weakness — no amount of drugs will blot it out. He can't see a future for himself. There is none because he will not recognise it. The will to fight has left him.

Tomorrow he will waken with signs of the night-before haze still evident as the movements are stilted, the eyes glassy. He looks to the nights ahead and wonders how to fill the time in-between.

The techniques have been acquired so that effort is minimal. He sits and sits, and talks and talks, and talks. The hours are few but long to the waiting man. The cycle of self-destruction has been perfected. He regurgitates the past and throws it in the face of those around him but cannot look at the future, except to the night ahead when the magic rainbow is placed in his palm. Is there a tomorrow?

29th APRIL '76

While speaking to the Scottish Arts Council Committee and telling them that he would like to involve a few artists in his project and named Jimmy Boyle as one, a prominent member of that Committee told the applying community artist that this wouldn't be a good idea. He went on to say Jimmy Boyle had been getting too much attention as an artist and anyway the publicity would hurt the feelings of other prisoners who aren't getting any attention. During this speech the Committee member stated that I had been exploited by Richard Demarco. Personally, I do not and never have asked the Arts Council for any assistance.

The Prison Department have been approached by a number of responsible journalists from the media to gain permission to interview me about my sculpture in order to show how change can take place in a person. They were told that this would not be permitted as they don't want to turn Jimmy Boyle into a star or cult figure. They say that there are lots of other prisoners and one can't pick out individuals.

The sort of problem facing an individual like me in trying to improve the situation is in handling the statements above. Both these groups must have some idea how younger kids in some of the poorer areas of Glasgow look up to me already for my violence and see me as a tough guy. To most of them I am already a cult figure only in a negative context as they want to see the violent part of me. If no information is being presented on the area of change then the authorities are actively suppressing an important issue. I really detest the way they put their argument in humane clothing — that other prisoners will be hurt by all the attention being put on Jimmy Boyle. Shit, pure and un-adulterated. These people are hypocrites who will use any means to prevent change as they have built ivory towers and don't want to be toppled from them by allowing more freedom of expression or they will cease to exist. They feel so strongly about using other prisoners as an excuse that they don't for one minute give any further thought to the conditions that these men are being kept in this very minute. They are aware of the situation concerning other prisoners and know that to allow me to be successful in a real sense, either artistically, academically or socially, is to allow me a platform to put a case for the other prisoners.

Somewhere along the line the original good intentions of these official bodies has been corrupted by individuals who have bent and distorted their responsibility in order to have a sense of power. Now their main purpose is to retain the status quo.

28th APRIL '76
This morning I did my exercises then took my radio to the studio where I worked on a small piece of sculpture. Ken Wolverton (community artist) was coming in as he wanted me to show him the casting technique. It was a relief-type piece so by the time he arrived it was almost complete. We worked on it together with me showing him the short cuts etc. He was delighted with the simplicity.

30th APRIL '76
Today I had a discussion with a psychiatrist on delinquency. He told me that in most cases when he asks kids what they want to be when they are thirty they stare at him then eventually tell him they haven't a clue. As he told me this my thoughts flashed back to when I was a kid — my response would have been similar. I was puzzled that he should find this appalling, the fact that their lives are so empty. I then asked him what answer he would give if the same question had been put to him at that young age. He replied that he wanted to be a doctor. Now I find this truly amazing and alien to anything I have known. I would have found it impossible to predict such a thing at that age, it would have been beyond me. When I say that I mean that I knew my place. No one ever told me but somehow I felt my

place was labouring at something or other and no more. There was a feeling of inferiority that permeated all our lives. I could hardly speak, and was conscious of this, never mind being something like a doctor. The fact is, that by the age of twelve the education system has one 'placed'. Once slotted into this place it is very difficult to break out of. Out of all the guys I was brought up with I don't know one who has a professional position in any field. Being a tradesman is the nearest to being anything in the world. The thought of anyone becoming a doctor is a dream.

26th JUNE '76
I am a human being. You must understand that imprisoned terrorists are also human beings. There is no sense doing away with what you call the barbaric capital punishment if you are going to replace it with a slower form of death. At this very moment I am in a state of total isolation, caught in a trap that is imprisoning my soul. I hate every one of you pretentious bastards who purr up against the leg of the system while telling those trapped within that you are for reform.

Blood is pumping through my whole body. It's passing though my heart to the sole of my feet. I live. I hate; oh God, how I hate... What keeps me from ending it, why have I put off the inevitable for so long? Perhaps its those that I see as the enemy — the cops and the screws of the past who keep me alive. It's hard to believe but it's true... It's hard as I have found more enemies when making a positive contribution than when acting irresponsibly.

You who sit out there, what the fuck do you know? How can I expect you to understand what it means to be in the control of people who look on me as an animal?

I've had a bellyful of pussyfooting with you stinking shits and your cowardly ways. I want to destroy your system. I want to live. I want to walk for a spell without having some great fucking wall stopping me taking another step. I just want to be free. I want to see the stars without seeing bars. I want to be caught in a busy shopping crowd. I want to see children playing nonsense games. I want to see a dog pissing against a lamp post. I want to take my girl-friend for a walk. I want to sleep a whole night beside her. I want to see all of you suffer less. I want away from in-stitutions.

23rd JUNE '76
At the meeting today Ken said that he would like it recorded that Rab is leaving and during his spell here has made tremendous progress in every possible way... Rab was out at the Citizens Theatre working (for that last day). The Governor said he had a letter from the Department refusing Duncy coming to the Unit.

28th JUNE '76
This morning I did my exercises then walked up and down the yard speaking to Ken... all was ready for my going to hospital.

At 9.45 while standing in the yard speaking to Ken, two cops came in — detectives. The Governor obviously knew them. Malky (one of my staff escorts) said there was no need for them as I'd been out before... The cop in charge said he hoped I'd changed as he knew me in the Gorbals.

I was SICK. So absolutely and totally sick. I was told the cops would be with me at all times, even sitting with me in the ward. I just felt bloody angry. I went into the small room and lost the grip on myself. I broke (cried). All these past three years gone for nothing. Here I was, in prison terms 'B' category and with lots of cops. Ken held onto me. My insides were falling apart. This is the essence of power and its corruption, the whole twist of torture through the decision making process. The Governor came in saying I must forget the politics of it and think of myself. He kept saying that it had nothing to do with him or the Depart-ment. He said the decision has been made and the cops were there to protect the Public. This is pure crap. On dis-cussing it in detail he said that if I don't go it will prove that I had something on for escape. I couldn't/didn't argue with this as it is so stupid it's unbelievable. I told him I don't need to prove anything.

106

On reaching the hospital the cops were very pushy and energetic — ultra cautious. On speaking to me one said that he personally sees no need for their presence but that their boss put the high-powered show on when hearing it was me. He told his superior that it would only be for a day or so as I would be crippled after the operation but they were told they would remain throughout. Two of the cops mentioned to Malky that they were embarrassed.

The nurses and sister were upset at all the cops. They remarked that there wasn't any of this last time. Malky and the other staff member see no need for their own presence as the cops have taken over. The whole scene is pathetic but more than anything it has torn lumps out of me. I really broke this morning. I know I did. I am not a hard-man anymore.

29th JUNE '76

I managed to pull myself out of this state of anger and with-drawal to try to find out more about this. I didn't sleep at all during the night as my mind was active... Gerry (staff member) told me his partner is lapping up the cops with their guns etc...

The cops sitting next to me are wearing shoulder holsters and revolvers. They sit staring at me all the time. One of them seems to be friendly but the other sits leaning on an empty bed staring straight at me. I wonder how long he can keep this up. I cannot sleep, in fact I find it difficult to do anything but opt for pretending to read or sleep. Gerry says that even he feels under scrutiny.

I was taken to the pre-operative room where I was greeted by the anaesthetist who asked me how I was. The young guy taking me there enquired who the two following me were. They identified themselves as police, though one was a staff member. The guy then turned to me saying, 'I feel sorry for you'. The two following were being put into green gowns and the cop asked if he needed to take off his cardigan. The nurse replied no. He remarked that it was just as well as it may cause panic; obviously referring to his gun. It hit me then that they were loving this.

Coming out of the anaesthetic certainly amazes me, to think someone has been working on me when dead to the world. I lay there looking around me. Two cops, a man and woman came in to relieve the two already there. She took one cop's gun and put it into her handbag — without the shoulder holster. She sat a few feet from the bed putting her handbag on the floor. After a few moments she got up from her chair, went over to the window to look out, leaving her bag near me. Groggy as I was, I beckoned Malky across to tell him there was a gun in the bag which was near me. I told him to stay close.

Mr White, the specialist, came in to inspect my leg, asking me to lift it. I take it he wants me out of here as soon as possible. The four cops and two Unit staff were present as he did this.

Later the two staff came across to tell me that when I was unconscious the cops had got hold of one of them to say that someone had seen me go into my locker, take something out and go under the blankets with it. They wanted to search me and my locker. Both the staff told them I was unconscious, that they were satisfied and to leave it at that. It was then that Bob (staff member) referred to them (the police) wanting to handcuff me to the bed when I entered hospital.

I feel as though I stick out like a sore thumb in here. Terribly self-conscious. I must get away from here. I am trapped and no good can come of this venture. I must extricate myself from this situation causing as few bad feelings as possible. I must conduct the withdrawal using the highest level of diplomacy. The point is that these cops are brutes. In the past I was very much at home with this sort of thing but my reaction now lets me measure how far I've developed as a person. These guys are actually trained to distrust everyone and everything. They would be the first to deny this but their whole training is geared towards suspicion and hostility. There is no sense me projecting everything onto them as they are only the tools of those above issuing the orders.

The pain of my leg has become secondary. The hard part

is seeing into the faces of everyone around me — nurses, police, staff and patients — that I am not wanted. I feel an alien. I see the patients pointing me out to their visitors. When speaking to everyone as individuals they all state the scenario is unnecessary but none of them do anything about it. Everyone looks to the police before they smile, talk or make any gesture towards me. Meanwhile I am regulating my trips to the toilet so as not to be constantly followed by a gang of watchers.

30th JUNE '76

This morning at 4.30am Gerry told me that a story has appeared in the *Glasgow Herald* saying that I am in hospital. This comes as no surprise the way the cops handled it. David Scott and Scott Devlin (BBC) came in to see me. I have been given crutches and allowed to sit up. This is the fastest anyone's been allowed up. David passed the head of the CID who had just been in. Apparently the cops showed David a photo of Ben Conroy saying that he was the guy coming to do me. I told them this was utter nonsense. A cop was sitting next to us with his shoulder holster and we could all see it.

A matron came across and I explained to her that this was embarrassing for me and I'd like to get out without hurting anyone's feelings. She said she understood and went for the consultant. She brought him down while Scott and David were present and he told me he would have to have four clear post-operation days before letting me out. This was to keep himself in the clear. I agreed with him. David told me that the Nurses' Union and the SPOA were having meetings this afternoon. The latter with the Department in Edinburgh. The issue is over guns being carried in an open ward. There certainly is a lot of activity.

My brother Harry and his friend came in. The cops came in and pulled his friend out and went to pull Harry. He refused. The cop said he was CID. Harry pushed his hands off telling him he doesn't care who he is that he is here to see me. I shouted to the cop that Harry is my brother. Jim (unit staff member) said so too. I was so mad at any scene being

109

made and felt really bad. The whole thing was sickening. All the other patients and visitors were looking at us.

After the visit one of the nurses came across saying to me, 'You are in a bit of a cage here, aren't you?' The tension was tightening in my head and she gave me headache pills. She remarked that the whole action of the police pulling Harry was unnecessary; she had watched it all.

On BBC television David Scott gave the matter good coverage. The piece was pretty long and went into detail about there being no communication between the police and the prison authorities. The police boss said they had a tip-off someone was going to harm me — shoot me. A young cop came in tonight saying this was a load of crap and that the escort came from the top. The press have been on to the ward but have been referred to the hospital super-intendant.

1st JULY '76

Wakened at 4.30am and had to get headache tablets.

Gerry told me that the front page of the *Daily Record* has a full story about me. With the head of CID making it clear that this is a security operation because of my past; that I am a dangerous prisoner and a high risk one, that the police make the decisions where security is involved.

Visitors have been turned away all day. My son James came up to visit me this afternoon and got in okay. He didn't say much but we sat together eating strawberries. He said he had brought his two pals but left them at the main gate saying he was going to visit his aunt. James is a very quiet but very deep boy. I feel he is very close to me.

Bob (staff member) came up to Malky to ask the Governor's home number. Malky asked why. Bob said it was for secret reasons. Malky reminded him that he was on escort with him. One of the cops was present. Bob reminded Malky that he was in charge, that he was the senior officer. Malky replied he doesn't mind him thinking he is in charge but in reality he isn't. They got involved in an argument. I spoke to Bob reminding him that we are living under strenuous circumstances and he should bear this in mind. I told him that solidarity would bring us through this. He turned to me saying that only two people will be able to visit me during visiting hours. I asked him who said this. He replied that CID Chief MacKenzie and Medical Superintendent Anderson had told him. I asked one of the policemen sitting nearby about this. He said it was the first he had heard of it. At this Bob returned, his face almost purple saying he had made a mistake. He said he is under tremendous pressure and feeling it.

2nd JULY '76

This morning I wakened at 6am after having my best sleep since entering hospital. I went to the toilet myself. The two armed cops on duty I haven't seen before but they were tall. Gerry was sleeping in the lecture room, the other staff member John, was elsewhere. Later he told me he had been under the passages of the hospital. I had particularly asked the staff not to leave me alone with the cops but they don't seem to take it seriously.

There was nothing in the press today but I sent a letter to *The Scotsman* on the hospital/police issue.

Mr White came in and found my pulse and temperature were alright. I sat around reading and speaking to Malky and one of the cops. The cop said if ever he was involved with policy making he will make sure I get an even break. He thought what was happening was a liberty, that it was unnecessary. He remarked that the week with me was an experience for him. He shook my hand... Some of the patients came down to say goodbye. I went to see the others, bidding them all goodbye. Malky, Bob and I bought the nurses a box of chocolates. I wrote a small note to them all apologising for any trouble my presence may have caused, thanking them for their support.

I felt the tension ease from me as I left the hospital, felt so tired. It was very confusing for me. I wasn't feeling glad to be leaving the hospital for prison — the Unit. I felt sad at the fact the I wanted to leave hospital but in a way I was numb at going back to prison. Back in the Unit I went to see the Governor. I told him I would like a Petition and that I was writing to my M.P. He asked what I was intending to do. I gave him small but loose pieces of information telling him the rest is for my M.P. He remarked that if I wanted a future I should move to England. He said this showed that the police were out to get me. I told him the solution to this wouldn't be running away from it.

3rd JULY '76
This morning I got up and went into the yard. I sat in the sun with the staff, leaving my crutches in the cell as I don't like them. Last night I didn't sleep. I was weary but had an active mind, also my leg was giving me pain. It seems that a detective sergeant phoned the local branch of the SPOA to ask if it was true that a string of prostitutes were coming from Edinburgh to visit me. Ken got the local branch to take this to their Governor. When he spoke to the Department they said that police have been reporting seeing me in pubs and all other such nonsense. The Governor of the main prison said that whenever he is invited to speak to the Police College they always go on about the Special Unit but particularly about Jimmy Boyle and their hostility towards me.

The Governor spoke to me saying that someone from *The Scotsman* called saying they had a letter from me, asking if it really was from me. The journalist read it out. The Governor said it sounded very much like my feelings and unofficially confirmed it. He said he wasn't to be quoted then asked him to give the Unit a break and leave us for a spell. He told the guy to go to the SIO as he wasn't supposed to speak to him. I told him that I did send the letter... He was in a nervous state saying he will get a call from the Department.

4th JULY '76
The Governor took Malky and Gerry into his office and asked what they were going to say about the letter I had sent to the press. They said there is nothing they can say as it will all fall back on me. The Governor told them this wasn't good enough as they were in charge of the escort.

Malky told him this wasn't the case, the police were in charge of the escort — they took over. The Governor said the press had taken up the letter.

I went into the Governors office. I asked him how he was. He said okay then went right into the article in the *Sunday Mail* which says, 'A row broke out over a letter from a convicted killer'. He said it looks as though the Department and SIO have been brought in. I told him we discussed this yesterday and I admitted doing it. He then got very angry and replied that the press report today was making him angry. I reminded him that all this week I had been lying in hospital being subjected to all sorts of humiliating and degrading treatment and that he wasn't interested in this, that this letter seemed to upset him more than anything else. He then went on about the prison regulations being breached. I told him yes that was right, just as they had by the police, the Prisons Department and everyone else but it's only when a prisoner does so that punishment is called for. I was shouting at him by this time saying that he is only interested in building his own empire and making sure he isn't hurt. I left the office.

The Governor kept saying the whole thing is political now, that it has been taken out of our hands. He shouted at me saying there are more people in the Unit than me. I told him he's fucking right there are more people in the Unit than me, that's what's worrying me as precedents are being set that will affect others.

5th JULY '76
There is no doubt about it, these bastards are trying to destroy me mentally. Blows come in psychological form, ripping through my defences, tearing me apart internally. In the face of this new, but very effective game of destruction I cry like a child. Shattered! No injuries are apparent. What is going on, why?

Retaliation is called for. This violent typewriter shouts bloody anger. Punching holes in the fucking enemy with each tap of the key. Fingers filled with fire and vengeance as they press each lettered key — hatehatehatehatehate.

Fuckers causing mental anguish, I HATE YOU.

They would like to see it. Oh God, they would like to see it. If I were to strike out and hit one of them. 'See!' they would shout. 'Look, the bastard is an animal'. All would turn to me and point. 'Animal, Animal.' they would cry.

What the fucking hell am I doing sitting here suppressing all this natural anger and keeping it under the surface? Does this make me any more civilised? I'm supposed to sit here like some vegetable with a mandarin smile accepting it all.

6th JULY '76

At the meeting today Bill Allan brought up that Davy's mother was sick after making a long journey here. He asked the Community to let Davy go home on occasional visits to see her whenever she can't come here. There was lots of discussion on this and it was agreed it should be left for a week or so.

The Governor brought up the letter from Department on staff follow-up when a Unit prisoner had been transferred. It said the Governors in other prisons are against this and the Department concur with their views. Malky brought up that my mail should be censored for a month as I had broken the Unit rules, that I was accountable to the Community. I answered this by pointing out that I had been taken outside the Community into a situation where they could not protect me therefore I had to protect myself. A discussion followed with Bill Allan wanting to know the reason why I was being punished. He said he had no fears of me doing this again, that he didn't condone what I did but couldn't agree to punish me in this way. The Governor stated if they didn't do something then it would seem that there are two sets of values in the Unit, one for Davy and another for me. Staff pointed out to the Governor that Davy had breached the mail issue a number of times before his mail was censored. It was put to a vote. The Governor and Malky voted for, the rest against.

8th JULY '76
Tomorrow John, a new prisoner, comes to the Unit from Perth Prison. He is serving an eighteen year prison sentence for bank robbery. Nicknamed 'The Bat' because of his bad eyesight and thick glasses, he is an ex-Gorbals guy and we get on very well.

9th JULY '76
John and I had a long talk with him telling me things are much the same if not worse than when I left. He is very bitter about the Parole Board, saying he wouldn't take it if they offered it to him. He is also extremely bitter about his experiences in Perth and Edinburgh prisons. I didn't want to overload him with this place so gave him a small bit and on the whole just listened to him pour out his experiences.

10th JULY '76
This morning I wakened, did my exercises then asked Davy to give me a hand to unpack the sculptures from their cases as they had returned from the York Festival exhibition.

Beth (Americal artist) came in this afternoon bringing a note from Tom McGrath. Tom is always apologising for not coming to the Unit. He is going through a confusing time because of the Unit, or maybe himself. He had a chat with Maurice (lawyer) about me and is afraid the Unit is getting to him. This happens to people when they come here. It makes them look more closely at themselves. Beth said she was sitting with a girl the other day when Tom came in remarking 'The Jimmy Boyle fan club'. Beth feels she has to keep arguing with people that there are more people in the Unit than Jimmy Boyle. I am going to write to Tom.

21st JULY '76
Tom McGrath came up today saying the reason he has been keeping away is that while attending a weekend conference at the Prison Officers Training College, three of the Governor grade caught hold of him during the evening social events and had a go at him about me. They said I was

an evil manipulator, that I had certain people under my control and he is one. Tom said they went on at length tearing me for shit paper. There is no doubt that he got a fright. He said if these allegations are going to be levelled at him then he is going to stay away. He said it was very nasty.

Tom went on to tell me that Lord Balfour of the Scottish .Arts Council phoned him a few weeks ago to say the Arts Minister would be meeting him and Sandy Dunbar, also of the Arts Council, in an hour's time in The Third Eye Centre. He asked Tom to put something simple on show as the Minister would like to be shown round the Centre after the meeting. The reason he said put something simple was, when taking office, the Minister had thrown an abstract painting out saying they are a waste of money. The Minister in question is Under-Secretary of State for Scotland (Education) Frank McElhone M.P. (Gorbals).

After the meeting McElhone went down to the gallery with Balfour and Dunbar. Tom said on approaching him McElhone said, 'This is the man giving me all the problems'. Tom, Balfour and Dunbar looked at each other puzzled. McElhone went on to say 'He gives a man called Boyle exhibitions and glamorises him'. He went on to tell them what I was really like and came out with a stream of filth that shocked all three. He not only verbally assassinated me but stamped me into the ground. He made references that he knew of 'six people I had murdered'. He said kids in the Gorbals are all looking up to the sculpture that I was doing before the sort I was doing now. He went on for ten minutes about me without interruption.

Afterwards Tom said he pointed out that he had my work on show for three weeks and never had he heard any man in the street say anything bad about it and he was shocked that a Minister could talk like that. Tom stated that a relative of someone I had fought at one time remarked that he liked the sculpture and was glad to see how I was doing. McElhone wouldn't listen. Both Balfour and Dunbar were trying to get cash out of McElhone for the Arts, so were cringing at the ferocity of his attack. It ended with Tom arguing the case for more cash and on the way out McElhone turned to Tom telling him to stop being radical, come into the centre away from the left and you'll get the help you need. These were his parting words.

I have never met McElhone but the ironic thing is that I've always been glad to see him get in during an election. His attack seems very personal and the strange thing is I've just had Department permission to write to my M.P. to complain about the police treatment while in hospital. I must get him up here and confront him but I am in a situation where I don't want to fuck things up for Tom. If he is saying this to Tom he is obviously saying it elsewhere so I won't name the source as his mind will do the rest. I want to nail this fucker on this 'six murders' rubbish as this must be the shit being put round about me. They are bastards with their innuendo and psychological warfare. These bastards really know how to kick someone in the balls. It's no wonder Tom had been giving me a body swerve recently. The poor bastard must have been in a turmoil; still, he should know the game these people play but should he? I never expected shit like this. At this point I feel tiny and helpless as the State machinery prepares to crush me.

22nd JULY '76

> *Dear Mr McElhone,*
>
> *I have a very pressing and important issue that I wanted to raise with you but while gaining the necessary permission from the Prisons Dept. I was informed that you had expressed some very hostile opinions of me, and this has put me in a dilemma.*
>
> *It is understandable that people will have very emotional opinions about me and my past. No one is more aware of this than me as I have to live with my past. I am now in prison nine years, and the past three and a half years the Special Unit have given me an opportunity to make a genuine effort to change. All of this with the intention of contributing something back into society. In making this change I've had tremendous support from my family, relatives and*

friends, who are ordinary decent people living in our district. There have been others but the locals have been particularly encouraging.

I realise that there are younger kids in the district who may want to emulate my 'violent ways', just as I wanted to emulate Dan Cronin or Paddy Slowey's 'violent ways', and this is a factor that weighs heavily upon me. My son and daughter are still staying in the Gorbals and like any other parent I am frightened of what's going to become of them, that they could possibly get caught in a situation resembling mine and this I would dread. But for the first time someone with my violent experience is realising that crime and all that it entails is completely wrong and futile. My attitudes have changed from those of a negative outlook to a positive outlook. I want to try and improve the situation in whatever way I can.

The problem is that in making these efforts to change I have received hostility, not so much from the ordinary people, but from the Teddy Taylors and Nicholas Fairbairns of this world. Each rejection of my efforts is a blow to me. By refusing to accept that a person like me can change it leaves the situation rather bleak for 'the man from the Gorbals' people now in prison serving sentences.

I fully appreciate the heavy schedule that you now must have as Minister and understand the Parliamentary situation at the moment but I would like to ask if you could possibly come and see me here in order to discuss the important issue I have and the contents of this letter?

Yours Most Sincerely

26th JULY '76
Ken caught hold of me to say Davy has written a letter to his mother upsetting her to an extent where the doctor took all the tablets out of her house in case she took them. Ken feels his mother is every bit to blame as he is.

Another meeting was called. We were told Davy had gone into the Governor's room where Wattie, Gerry and Mike sat. He pulled out a long, sharp needle and put it at Wattie throat saying he will take his eyes out and flush them down the toilet pan and cut Ken's throat if restrictions are placed on his mail or use of the telephone. Everyone froze and he put the needle away. They tried to get it off him but he refused to give it till he got to phone his mother. Ken said he could and he gave him the needle. Mike stayed while he used the phone. Davy sat in the meeting very tense saying everyone is interfering in his life. It was pointed out to him that his mother had got onto Ken and Wattie and they had to heed her fears. The argument became heated and Davy threatened violence. He refused to see anyone's point of view saying we must get him out of the Unit. He threatened to do a Duncy. He left the meeting but returned to say he is locking himself up and going on a hunger strike till he is moved from here. We decided that things had reached a serious stage and that Davy needed some sort of treatment. Peter Whatmore was present and said this was a matter for the Community. He was asked if Davy needed hospital treatment and replied there is no place he could be put as he isn't ill. Davy's behaviour is more than odd. I think he should be put in an open hospital for help. Peter said this couldn't be so. Everyone agreed if he is going to use violence then he will have to go.

27th JULY '76

Davy is gone. The Governor called a meeting and informed us that he had phoned the Department to put them in the picture about Davy's latest incident. Tom Melville told him they had just received a Petition from Davy saying if he isn't moved from the Unit he will do a Duncy. With the information given by the Governor, the Director of Prisons authorised Davy's transfer. There was a part in me hating this. I said nothing. I couldn't.

The womb that consumed
The penis inserted
Made it possible
for me to be
Here.

28th July '76
This morning I wakened with Davy on my mind. He is on
solitary and anywhere he goes two staff go with him —
exercise and slopping out etc. I did my exercises then went
outside. I did some sculpting with the sandstone and felt
really great. I thoroughly enjoy being back at work again. I
had a letter from Duncy's wife. He goes to court for his
pleading diet on 6th August and the 16th August for trial.
He has been charged with serious assault causing per-
manent disfigurement. There is a Welsh nut who labels
himself criminologist who is making a scene about the
hospital. It seems the Chairman of the Police Federation in
commenting on my letter to *The Scotsman* said that I was
illiterate and the letter had been written by an educated
hand and not by me. This Welshman wrote saying he wants
heads to roll. The Governor brought it to me himself long
after the mail had been distributed so he is a bit panicky. I
thought it very funny.

1st AUGUST '76
Frank McElhone, J.P.M.P.
House of Commons
London SW1A 0AA

Dear Mr. Boyle,
With regard to your letter of 22nd July, I find the
contents most surprising. Could I point out to you
that I am delighted that you are attempting to make
the effort to change, as it is something I have tried to
encourage in all people, who end up in prison.
I should also point out however that many people
have complained to me. Prisoners, the families of
prisoners and people in my constituency area that

120

there are many people, who are serving very long sen-
tences, who don't get the use of the Special Unit, or
the encouragement to pursue an interest in
Sculpture. I am not against these things, but feel that
you have been a victim of too much publicity, regard-
ing your Sculpture, and this has brought more
criticism than it has praise.

Unfortunately, I have been off from Parliament
for several weeks, with a slipped disc and therefore a
lot of engagements had to be postponed and will have
to be fitted in to an overburdened diary, in the next
few months, therefore, it will be impossible for me to
fit in a visit to you, in the near future.

I would suggest therefore, that you should write to
me, on the important issue you wish to raise with me
and I will deal with it as sympathetically as possible.
Yours sincerely

11th AUGUST '76

I was up till 4.20am working on the letter to Frank
McElhone and trying to get things off the ground on this
whole matter. My mind was alive and there was no way I
could go to sleep. I managed two hours then got up to do
my exercises:

Dear Mr. McElhone,
I am encouraged that you are delighted that I am
making the effort to change and was heartened to
hear that many prisoners and families of prisoners
within the constituency area have complained to you
that they don't get the use of the Special Unit or the
encouragement to pursue Sculpture. Like you, I feel
that they should be given the chance and it is great to
see that so many people feel so strongly about it as it
does show a desire to change their ways. It is high
time that what is happening here in the Special Unit
should be expanded and I hope that you as Minister
will add your weight to this. Certainly there is a
financial crisis but the specific areas I am talking

about cost nothing financially and it would be a feather in the cap of Scotland to be showing this remarkable progress at a time when the crime rate is increasing and the financial situation is very bad.

I am rather puzzled by your statement that I am a victim of too much publicity regarding my sculpture and that it brought more criticism than praise. I have heard this statement before from the civil servants at the Prisons Dept., but I can assure you that it is a total contradiction to the reality of the situation. I have piles *of documentation here to prove this and you can see it anytime. I know that there are certain people in 'responsible positions' who are saying that I am being turned into star material etc. etc., but I feel that I should give you a breakdown of the situation. I started sculpting in 1974 and was encouraged in this by the Prisons Dept. It was they who first introduced the media to the Special Unit and in the press handouts declared my remarkable talent as a sculptor. I was encouraged to have exhibitions like any other artist and initially there was a great deal of publicity about it but afterwards both press and the galleries where my work was being shown throughout Britain handled it in a very mature way. In fact I was delighted that the press handled it so maturely while my work was shown in Glasgow. I was very apprehensive beforehand about the man in the street's opinion but let me tell you the response was something that delighted me. You see, what is worrying me is that certain people are too quick off the mark to quote in public when the fact is that it just isn't the case. Let me tell you that last year while in hospital Teddy Taylor was making media statements due to the public having supposedly complained about me being in an open ward with them. It was the very same public who were incensed by this lie that answered him by making a collective statement to the media refuting this. I am very much aware of this tactic and that is why I now keep all the*

documentation to substantiate what I am saying. I must say that I am bitterly disappointed that there is no way you can manage to see me in the near future concerning this very important issue. It is a very complex matter and will be very difficult for me to put on paper but I suppose I must if I am to get it seen to. I was very sorry to hear about your slipped disc and hope that it is much better.
Sincerely

20th AUGUST '76

The Governor... went straight to the court to watch the proceeedings... Duncy was given six years consecutive to his present sentence. The Judge told him had he not received the letters from me, James L., Larry, and the letter he wrote to his wife then he would have been given ten years. The Judge said there were no mitigating circumstances as he had gone into J.L.'s cell and attacked a fellow prisoner while he lay in bed. The radio said Duncy went berserk because his wife was suing him for divorce. The TV had similar reports. Duncy now has an extra six years to serve and what does this prove? What happens to the guy now?

21st AUGUST '76

The press had reports about Duncy's trial and the *Scottish Daily Express* was vile to say the least. The headline screamed BARLINNIE KNIFE ROW and quoted Teddy Taylor as coming up to see what we were doing, that he doesn't agree with the Unit philosophy. It is a complete distortion of what went on in court. The rest of the press, *The Glasgow Herald, The Scotsman* and *Daily Record* are fair...

Ken phoned to say he is getting Hugh Brown M.P. to ask him to fix it to get Teddy Taylor to come in. Ken was very angry at this bastard Taylor jumping on the bandwagon.

31st AUGUST '76

Teddy Taylor M.P. came in... He is a small, balding man who was quite apprehensive though trying not to show it.

He offered us all a cigarette and then I took him round.

His main theme was vandalism and how this problem could be solved. I showed him the kitchen and he could see the knives lying in the cutlery box but made no comment... I showed him inside every cell and we had a brief chat with J.L. as we entered his cell. He asked him about vandalism. He asked what I would do when I got out and I told him I'd probably have to get a job. He said that I am now pretty well established as a sculptor and asked pointedly if I would become a celebrity when I got out. I told him as far as I was concerned I'd try to help the situation in the Gorbals and other districts.

We all sat in the meeting room and had a long debate on the Unit and he was all for what we were doing but should do it without publicity. We discussed this and he was so full of contradictions that it was difficult to accept. He mentioned all his mates and friends who have just come out of prison, some of whom are working for him in the Conservative Party — locally. Then he would say prison nowadays is a soft option and on the other hand state that it must be terrible to be locked up with no privacy. During our discussion he had a phonecall from the BBC and came back and told us the press were waiting on him. He came on very heavy against the Department saying they are a bunch of intellectual civil servants then came in heavy against social workers, psychiatrists, and sociologists. He stayed for three hours then left but first asked if he could come back...

Teddy Taylor held an impromptu Press Conference at the prison gate. We understand he said that it is too soon to say whether it (Unit) is a success or not. He thinks the experiment is going very well and thinks it should continue. This will be on radio tomorrow morning. We understand Harry Ewing is quoted as saying he is glad to see Teddy T. has come into the Unit after three and a half years.

18th SEPTEMBER '76
Today was really good for me as I worked hard and thoroughly enjoyed it. This carving really has a hold on me

at the moment. I like the pieces I am turning out as they are very strong and much to do with what is going on in me personally. Prison ceases to exist and more to the point I become a whole person. I reasoned that what I was doing during this, what we are all seeking, is to become a whole person. All the petty niggles that the mind uses to occupy itself in the fragmented person disappear. I get the most fantastic feeling of being alive. This experience is exactly what I need and want. It seems to put everything into proper perspective and has left me typing this feeling both exhilarated and thoroughly exhausted.

30th SEPTEMBER '76
Roy Rogers had a big influence on me when I was a child, so too did Jesse James and his gang. It depended what mood I was in but they were both good at shooting and getting what they wanted. It was amazing how I would gallop through the dirty backcourts, skirting muddy puddles as though they were deep, dangerous chasms in the Rocky Mountains, letting my clever horse Trigger, guide me safely home. Then I would be Jesse, with the neck of my pullover hiding the lower part of my face as I went to rob the stage or the train. No matter who I was, there was constant vigilance in case those dirty Indians ambushed me, but to be fair there were times when I would be one of them too. I loved Geronimo and always believed I was a true Apache.

Then there was Rocky Marciano; he was the number one hero of the district. Boy, he could really put them away. One punch and they lost their senses. I can remember when he fought Don Cockell, we all sat around the wireless listening, men, women and children. I went to the window that dark night and looked out to the wet street that was empty, hearing all the wirelesses going. The fight game had us all captivated that night. One of the local legends was Benny Lynch who came from our district in the Gorbals so we were brought up on a diet of tales about him. I remember how I used to shadow box on a sunny day or have 'dummy fights' with my pals and we would roll over the streets as though being pounded by the opponent but always I managed to make the last minute recovery to put him away and leave him sprawled on the street.

Tarzan was also important to me as he would come swinging down from the trees and fight off a million darkies who were about to boil Jane in a pot. But then who could beat Flash Gordon who would be trapped in a room with the walls closing in... with me suddenly finding myself thrown into the street to await the next chapter the following week. I would run out of the movies either swinging on an imaginary vine as Tarzan, or driving a spaceship into Mars as Flash. My pal's father, who was big and strong, used to really impress me and others by clenching his fist and letting the muscles on his biceps juggle about while we stared wide-eyed in awe. After a session of this we would all be lying on the ground doing press-ups. One of the real favourites was that man at the Barrows who would let himself be tied with chains and put in a straightjacket only to escape. I would then get my pals to tie me up tight with a rope and squirm about for ten minutes to get out, and would end up cursing them for tying me up too tight as I couldn't get out.

The real favourite though was the gang-fighter in our district as he could really fight. His gang was so tough that no-one in the district would challenge them. Whenever we heard they were going to fight we would run to the meeting place and watch the enemy disperse with a flash of blade. Who could beat them? Afterwards we would pretend to be them and have dummy fights among ourselves.

I tried very hard to be as good as Roy and as bad as Jesse, a winner like Rocky and a loser like Don but very much a fighter like Benny, to have the guts of Tarzan and the speed of Flash with muscles of my pal's father and be as tricky as the escapologist in the Barrows. I then used them all to become the leader of a gang. I was now all my heroes wrapped up in one.

2nd OCTOBER '76
Wattie came round asking if anything had come up during

126

his day off and I told him no. We discussed Larry going into hospital to get his tattoos removed and Wattie felt it may make Larry think about his future. He went on to say Larry and him had a long talk recently, the first in a while. I know that Larry has reduced his barbiturates by one. There is no doubt that he is responding to the hospital outing and I firmly believe if the penal system were to give guys more hope then this response would be common.

John has been in bed a good part of the day. I had to waken him at 4.50 to get up and go for his food before the 5pm lock-up. He was dead to the world. Prior to coming here, John was very much into drugs officially, and any illegal drugs that came into prison you could be sure he was into them. It's not that he likes them but more that he sees them as an escape from the reality of the time he is doing. There is no doubt that the Unit is getting through to him. He is going through a particularly bad period and I will have to make a point of spending more time with him. When he is not sleeping, he is deep in thought and brooding. It's the same with Larry, and the thought has just struck me that he knows more about drugs and the drug scene than most guys on the outside yet when he was outside he didn't know what drugs were. Someone remarked to me that Larry must have been heavily into drugs before coming to prison but the truth was that he wasn't. All the newly acquired friends he has who are part of the drug scene are from prison.

12th OCTOBER '76
Larry came back with heavy bandaging round his leg and hand because of skin grafts etc. The trip went well and there were no police in sight at all. One of the staff who escorted Larry was saying there was bad hostility from some of the hospital staff who were saying that lots of people with serious defects are being turned away because of the waiting list (which Larry had been on for ten years) and yet here is Larry getting this done. After a spell they softened somewhat but this is the sort of attitude we have to break down. The fact that Larry comes from prison

makes his treatment seem less deserving to them and this is wrong. They said that if Larry wanted this he should have paid for it. Instead of playing one off against the other they should be saying that the facilities should be expanded to cater for everyone. Anyway, Larry seems well enough.

26th OCTOBER '76

Joyce Laing said she had bad news for me. She explained that the press had been on to her, two journalists from the *Sunday People*, one from the Manchester office and the other from Scotland. Joyce had been working in hospitals all over the north of Scotland and apparently they had been following her but kept missing her. After four days searching they finally caught up with her in her house. They asked if it was true that she was pregnant to me. Joyce was taken aback by this and went on to ask why they were doing this. The guy said it was a very big story and was hinting at large sums of money if she would substantiate it. They also told her she would be helped with her art work, publicity etc. Joyce tried to find out where they were getting their information. They refused to disclose their sources saying it didn't come from a prisoner or staff in the Unit but hinted at the police. They strongly emphasised Joyce's name being linked with mine in pubs throughout Glasgow. Joyce tried to tell them what the Unit was about but all they were interested in was the story. She was badly shaken and asked what sort of money is being spent on this sort of thing when a newspaper can send a man up from Manchester for four days and two of them can travel all over Scotland on expenses — all in the name of sensationalism. We talked it over and I told Joyce that this rumour has been going around for some time and pops up continuously in different forms, though this is the first time her name has been linked with it. She said she has spoken to Peter Whatmore about it and asked what I thought. I told her I'd speak to Peter also but it should be left to die a natural death. When I did speak to Peter he agreed with this but told me he had advised Joyce to have an off-the-cuff talk with Meikle at the Department. He thought I should mention it to the Governor some time and I agreed to do this.

10th DECEMBER '76
This morning I wakened and thought of my Ma. She is dead five years to the day. I rang my bell to get the door opened then went into the yard to do my run. Snow had fallen overnight. I ran round the yard though taking it easy. The hard crispy snow crunched under my feet as I ran. After my exercises I knelt before the bed and said a Decade of the rosary for my Ma. It's strange, I'm not in the least religious but Ma was so I feel this is the best way to remember her. Only I could possibly know what she gave me throughout my life. I knelt thinking of her and how beautiful she was in standing by me. Also how much she did for my brothers. Doing this is very important for me as I feel as though I'm giving her something in return.

21st DECEMBER '76
A delegation consisting of members of my family and friends approached Frank McElhone. They visited him in his surgery in Gorbals Street and had a long session with him about me and my future. It was put to him that he had been saying derogatory things about me. McElhone denied this saying he knew me well. My brother Harry replied angrily that he didn't know me. They put his back to the wall and extracted a promise from him to come and see me. He said he would visit before the end of the year.

30th DECEMBER '76
At 2.15pm Ken came across with Frank McElhone. He told him his wife and daughter were in the car so Ken said he would collect them. I came upstairs with Frank and we sat down with coffee. He talked about the good work he is doing in List 'D' Schools and in football hooliganism. He went to great pains to describe how he is all for reform in prison and that being an abolitionist of capital punishment he must believe in redemption. He went on to say he had words with Lord Balfour and others about their making

me into a star through my sculpture after having seen the catalogue for the Third Eye exhibition. He then said the more they put me to the fore the harder it will be for me to get ultimate freedom.

I explained to him that over the past four years I had worked constructively but that some months ago I was hit with a very damaging problem in that he as Under-Secretary of State had made public statements to the effect that I had — that he personally knew of — murdered six people. This knocked him quite a bit as it was the last thing he was expecting. I went on to say this is a very cruel statement as it has no foundation and if I had the money I would sue to clear my name publicly. He was in a bit of a state at this as I was unemotional, rational and low key. He didn't even deny it. Instead he rambled on about the good work he does. He was waffling. I pointed out to him the damage this could do me and my future, reminding him that if anyone said to me that a person convicted of one murder had murdered six others I would tend to believe it, particularly if the person telling me was an Under-Secretary of State. People like to think that a person in such a position is responsible. He then went on to say he had never made a public statement about this as it wasn't his Department, therefore he couldn't. I told him that by public statement I mean in an informal social context. He said he appreciated the damage this could do me... I expressed concern as to what was on my file as a result. He promised he would look into this and that he would speak to Harry Ewing about it and tell me in writing that this was not in my file.

He went on to talk about my future and asked what I thought of it and the situation. I pointed out that I was realistic and that I made up my own long-term programme but must have an external programme as an integral part of my development as it's the only logical direction for my future. He wholeheartedly agreed saying that Harry Ewing was being told that I am manipulating everything to get out immediately. I told him I knew where this was coming from... He said he has told Harry Ewing that anything he sends to him he intends sending me a copy whether its good

130

or bad as he doesn't want me to think he is doing the dirty on me...

There is no doubt that he was impressed, but what came home to me is that this guy is extremely limited. I think that he is doing some pretty good work but I am appalled at the calibre of people in these jobs; it must be a contributory factor to the present state of things. Despite the damage McElhone has done to me there is something lively about him but I don't think this balances out the deficiencies.

The only reason he came here was due to heavy pressure. He mentioned his alarm at my brother Harry coming on so heavy and that this will only do me harm. He said the rest of my family were very good. He is gone now and we will have to wait to see what develops from here.

8th JANUARY '77 12.21am

There is a real anger in me. Oh my God, it's almost as though everyone is abandoning their brains. The position is so delicate, so absolutely fragile yet, within this I am holding on by a very thin thread. Larry seems set on a course of self-destruction. If a person is set on this course then there are times when very little can be done about it and I reluctantly admit this. Even so he cannot be allowed to continue on his course as it not only destroys him but all of us.

On the other side of the coin there are others quite prepared to sit and not take part in any of this. Martin Ritt, the McCarthyite blacklisted film-maker said of that era: 'You know my mother said to me at that time, "Marty, what have you done? This is a fair country." That's what the pressure was like. Millions of ordinary people couldn't contemplate what was happening.'

I am so burnt up that I want to sleep yet can't. There are times when I feel it is all too much for me, that it is all about to fall in but from the depths comes this tenacity that refuses to let go. I was speaking to Dr Curran of the Local Review Committee the other day. He started to tell me I'm an exception, that there is no one here like me. I pointed out to him that this was the wrong way to look at it and

131

went on to say the others are improving and showing progress in different ways. Inwardly I was saddened. The Unit can't afford this to be the case. I certainly don't want it to be. I want my ideal to be correct, that every prisoner given the chance can respond in the way I have, can make the most of the opportunities given them. I feel so frustrated tonight, so locked in, so alone, so tired and weary with life.

Tonight I stare at the veins as they protrude from the skin on my arms and hands. Frequently I put my hand to my hair and run it through. Then backwards to feel my neck and round towards the throat, all the while touching skin. Touching, trying to share the feel of myself with myself.

14th JANUARY '77
The Problem Escalates
I am very worried about Larry's involvement with heavy drugs. He is hitting heroin and cocaine at the moment and is looking wasted. I have discussed this with one of the staff at an unofficial level and feel that it should be handled quietly. The reason for this decision is that if revealed that heavy drugs are being used in the Unit the Governor and some staff would panic and it would almost certainly result in the problem being handled in a traditional way. Larry had been getting drugs smuggled in when he was in the main prison system and it was never brought to the surface. The good thing about here is that some of us are discussing and trying to tackle the problem. To be honest, I have seen heavy drugs used frequently in the main system and simply shrugged my shoulders, often wishing the guys the best of luck as anything that beats the system was great to me, but now that my attitudes have changed, I cannot condone this at any level. I also think that to take this to Peter Whatmore would be more than useless as Larry would say nothing and neither would he to anyone connected to the establishment.

Ken told a group of us that last night he was in the Officers Social Club with two others. He went to buy a drink for them. A member of staff from the main prison was sitting cursing and swearing. Ken told him to watch his language as there were women sitting at the next table. The staff member turned on Ken calling him a Special Unit bastard and getting up he kicked Ken on the thigh. Ken said he was livid and grabbed the man but refrained from hitting him.

A discussion took place on this particular member of staff covering a whole range of offences from initiating a group of staff going in to beat up a prisoner (causing one member of staff to leave and join the Unit) to pulling a knife out in the local pub and getting banned. This is the sort of person in charge of us and as my diary has indicated thoughout he is by no means an exception.

24th JANUARY '77
. . . Ken gave me his letter to Harry Ewing, asking if I would type it for him. It is very good as he is telling him that he is going to put a resolution at the Scottish Labour Party Conference in March asking them to back a penal policy on the lines of the Unit. I feel it will frighten Ewing.

25th FEBRUARY '77
Tom McGrath came up and we had a good discussion. It was nice to see him again. He told me he's had comeback to the McElhone saga. Seemingly Sandy Dunbar of the Scottish Arts Council had phoned him a week or so after he had received a copy of all the material from me. Dunbar phoned at the unearthly hour of 9am (Tom's words) asking what he had told me as McElhone has been raising holy hell saying that I have been sending him threatening letters. Tom didn't know what to say as he had to be diplomatic — these are the people who give funding to the Third Eye Centre. He stumbled through by saying I already had knowledge of what McElhone was saying and so he discussed this when I mentioned it. Dunbar went on to say that McElhone had made it clear that he was going to veto a decision that was pending for another administrator of the Arts Council. It seems McElhone does have the power

133

of veto. Tom said he brought this up at a meeting of his Board, one of whom was in the Labour Party. The guy's face fell. It seems Tom had to get Sir William Grey to write to McElhone and smooth it out. They have heard nothing about it since. The meeting to veto the Arts Council administrator was to have taken place the day all the M.P.s coming from the Commons got stranded in a train due to bad weather. Tom said that had he not been in possession of a copy of the documentation I sent him then he would have been wondering about the threatening letter part.

I went into the matter saying I would not have left him open to this sort of thing. At no time did I mention his or anyone's name but relied on McElhone's guilty mind to do it all — it did. Tom said he wasn't concerned if I had mentioned his name as he knows what was said.

We discussed the play that we have been working on and though I thought he had been too busy to start on it, he has. We went over what has been done and it's shaping up well. It will be ready for showing in *The Traverse* on May of this year. Peter Kelly will play the part of me. Peter Lichtenfels will direct it. We will have a long working session on it. We went over the whole thing and he wants to get our lawyers to write up a contract on a 50/50 split so that everything is official. I brought him up to date on my book and the Trust Fund I intend setting up.

3rd MARCH '77
This morning was spent waiting on the Parkhurst Prison people coming. Bob (staff member) went to pick them up at the Central Hotel. Dr Cooper is the psychiatrist and Mr Bryant is the Governor. I took them round and the Governor followed all the way — it was annoying. I was trying to spell every point out to them, concentrating on the areas I thought important. I gave them all the information I could. On seeing the oxy-acetylene equipment the Governor (Bryant) said that red lights are ringing in his ears. I showed him the hacksaw and other materials I use for working. I spelled out to them that these things were built up through 'trust' and through staff working with

prisoners to built up relationships. I showed them the weight room which was a former punishment cell and how we no longer use it to lock people up. I went into detail on the process of this. In the joiners room they turned to me and said I was unique and a special sort of person as I had talent, and was articulate. I came in very strong here saying this wasn't the case and if other guys were given the same opportunities they would be equally successful. After this they went for lunch. While they were away I told the others we were going to have a difficult job with these two as they reminded me of myself when I entered the Unit. The Governor was very tense and extremely 'closed'. The doctor was less so but still closed.

Dr Cooper introduced what they were doing in Parkhurst and the kind of guys they had. He gave examples: one guy an arsonist who has to light fires in order to masturbate and how they have got him over this; the Kray twins both of whom have their personal problems. The discussion opened and it was clear they were here to justify rather than find out. I personally felt they were giving a whitewash of what they were doing.

They said their unit in 'C' wing had effectively cut violence in the penal system. I said we only have to look at the media to see this isn't true. There was silence on this. Denis (Jewish prisoner) told Cooper that with his attitude there is little wonder there is so much trouble in the system. The meeting was very heated at times with Governor Bryant saying little. Everything we told them we were doing they replied saying similar things and it ended up with me wondering why they were here if this was so. The doctor said this place is unreal and that we should be sent back to the main system to be tested. We came in strong on this and pointed out that the one priority of the Unit is not to make them fit for prison but to return to society. They were confused at this and felt we had adopted a technique to handle such questions. They were so full of prison culture and felt that by repeating prison priorities to them we were somehow cheating. Nearer the end Larry got up and left.

I wound the meeting up by saying it was nice having them but I felt we were working in different ways, the one thing that makes or breaks a situation is the staff/prisoner relationship. The doctor said we had exchanged views and they are leaving with some ideas from here in their heads. The Governor, Bryant, who was sitting quiet throughout, was asked by Meikle if he had anything to say. He said he was here to observe and take in what was happening.

I will be surprised if they implement any of our ideas.

4th MARCH '77

This morning I had Neil Cameron and Paul Nolan across from the Craigmillar Festival Society. We discussed the children's play sculpture, Gulliver, that I am designing for them. We discussed the technical side and other areas such as safety and construction. I will do a small scale model of Gulliver for them to submit to their Executive Committee. The project will need £500 for the actual piece of sculpture — it is hoped that kids can run through the body and head. They will get a team of workers from Jobs Creation and they will be local people. They will get finance to go to London to get some experience of concrete techniques.

18th MARCH '77

There is a part of me that dreads wakening to face the wall again. I get out of bed and run round the yard, sit in my cell, talk to the same faces, get screwed up by the same people, stimulated by the same people. Always its the sameness that is killing me. I need external stimulation. I need to live, I need to expand and broaden.

Having entered at a disadvantage and got myself into the rut of the disadvantaged I wonder if it is possible to extract myself from it. I only have one life but am living in a society that wants me to pay with that life for things that are also their responsibility. I didn't set the standards for having to live this way. I am not trying to exonerate myself, all I am saying is that much of it was inevitable.

25th MARCH '77

I went upstairs to read the proofs of my book, *A Sense of Freedom*, and after an hour or so I went back downstairs as I felt something was in the air...

I met Ken and we sat chatting... The Governor came in and dropped a bombshell by saying he has word about a job on the management side of the oil industry. He got word today that he has it. He said he is wondering how to drop it to the lads. He is also wondering how he will drop it to Meikle as he starts on 12th April. He feels that the job has been getting on him as it is a dead-end job for anyone interested in trying out new ideas. He said no matter how bright a person is he cannot get on as promotion is based on seniority. This means that any young man with potential has to suppress his personality and initiative as he is always under a boss who assesses and reports on him. This means the status quo remains as they are, resistant to new ideas.

13th APRIL '77

Hugh Brown and Harry Ewing came in today (an unofficial visit). We talked in generalities, mainly in a light-hearted way about various things. The Governor and staff were present. I get more and more impressed with Hugh Brown every time I see him. We talked about the penal system and I stated that any fundamental change in the system must come from the politicians. Harry Ewing agreed. He said its the inflexibility of the system that gets to him. He gave an example. Jim Sillars M.P. phoned him on a Sunday night about a constituent/prisoner serving twelve months for a driving offence. His father was dying and he wanted to know if Harry could get the guy out to spend the last few hours with his father. Harry said he got onto the Prisons Division and a day or so later they said they had checked it out and phoned him saying there was no truth in the father being in a serious condition and that it was all a ruse. Harry had to inform them that the guy's father had died that morning. He was furious but it was a moving example of what the Department are doing.

Hugh went to speak to Denis (new prisoner). He then popped his head in the door and asked me to explain about my book. In full hearing of everyone I reminded Harry that my family had written to him about its publication. He said he had a letter from my sister-in-law and had heard about the book from many other people. He hadn't read it but certainly would like to. I then explained to him that I felt it would be important for it to be published and gave reasons why. I asked if he knew about the Trust Fund and he did. I outlined it to him for the benefit of those present. Harry Ewing then said he would read it, not to censor it but to see if it should be approved. If it is along the lines he has heard, then he will authorise its being published.

I then took Harry round the Unit. We stood in the hall area talking. He told me he is as hated as I am by the division (Department) as he has a go at them continuously... He told me he knows I won't get into trouble again as I have a future for myself. I said I was aware of this just as I was aware that a section of society demanded I remained in prison till the price had been paid... He went back to the book and said he won't be reading it as a censor but as to its merits on it being published.

24th APRIL '77
Last night I did a very unusual thing by going to bed at 7.40pm and sleeping till 8am this morning. I wakened feeling I had wasted a lot of hours and felt guilty about sleeping all this time. Later while sitting in my cell Malky (staff member) came in dressed in civilian clothes. He had been at the Training College for the past three days on the Assistant Governor's interview course. Meikle and some of the Governors were there. He felt he skated through it and did very well but the last ten minutes let him see the way it was going:

An outside assessor — an old army man — took him into a room saying, 'between us and the four walls the consensus of opinion is that you are your own worst enemy.' Malky asked what he meant and was told that from his reports he is down as anti-authority and seems always to be looking for the bad points in his superiors. He told Malky his reports say that he is wanting to change society and that his antagonistic attitude isn't doing his career any good. He told him to remember what Tennyson said about looking for the good points in our superiors.

It makes me wonder if we are ever going to make any progress.

28th APRIL '77
Had better make a note of the letter from Joe Black of the Police Federation whom we invited in:

> *'Jimmy,*
>
> *Just a note on behalf of Tom and myself to say thank you for taking the time to show us round the 'Special Unit'. We found it very interesting and enjoyed the dialogue with the boys. We are aware that this is a new dimension in the penal system and we thought that it had merit. At least it provides for a frank exchange of views which is necessary if we are ever to understand each other's difficulties and problems.*
>
> *We would esteem it a favour if you could pass on our sincere thanks*
>
> Yours sincerely
Joe Black
General Secretary.

I will read this out tomorrow at the meeting. I think it is an indication of the new and important ground we are breaking here.

30th APRIL '77

> *'Dear M/s Murray,*
>
> *Thank you for the draft copy of the book written by Jimmy Boyle and also for the further page you sent to me on Monday morning (25th April).*
>
> *I will certainly read the book with great interest and from an earlier reading of it, I must admit that I am inclined at this stage to give my blessing in publication. I have no objection to Jimmy Boyle's*

139

reference to me in the book but if you feel at this stage you should now remove it, I will be most content with that as well.

I will write to you again when I have considered the matter fully and assure you that in this respect I will not keep you waiting too long.

My grateful thanks for all your kindness and all my good wishes.

Yours Sincerely
Harry Ewing M.P.

I must admit this was a great relief to me as it overcomes a lot of the fears I previously had in terms of the Unit copping the backlash.

5th MAY '77
Tom McGrath phoned to say he would like to speak to me and asked if he could come up. He did and we had a short talk as he had a taxi waiting outside. Tom said that it is out that I am co-author of the play. A photographer called Liddell and a journalist from the *Sunday Times*, George Rosie, had come to see him. They asked him about my part in the play but Tom said he was extremely heavy with them saying he doesn't want to know the press as they are too irresponsible, even the so-called responsible Sunday ones. They talked and Rosie said he understood what Tom was saying but that he would be most responsible in anything he did. Tom asked me to think it over and if I felt they should come in then he will make the arrangements. I told Tom if I did they would have to slant their articles along the lines that they hadn't been in...

I spoke to Wattie this afternoon telling him the book looks as though it will be out very soon as Harry Ewing is about to give his consent. He said this may have something to do with the fact that the Department put it to their libel lawyers some time ago...

16th MAY '77
This morning I did my run in the beauty of the sun. After

my exercises and cleaning work had been completed I sat outside. Ken brought in the newspapers and there was a piece about me in the *Daily Record*. It was about my book saying it would be published... that the proceeds are going to a Trust Fund.

All the tickets for the first night of our play *The Hardman* have been sold.

23rd MAY '77
The Living Dead - Larry
'The buzz was supreme. On Saturday night I had four diconal (a morphine substitute) which left me with a major decision. Two can give a pleasant glow, but four can take me to the heights. Should I have two nice evenings or one beauty? I decided on the latter. Taking the four, I lay on my bed smoking some hash and felt myself disappearing into the mattress. Occasionally, I had to shake myself as I felt I would disappear into death, yet there was this reckless part of me that said so what? But the other part kept saying Hey man, it's death we're talking about. And the other would pop up and say so what? Life and death. My heart had slowed. It felt so good! The sexual muscle twitched with pleasure — a sure sign of life.'

We talked. Going into great detail, he explained the fantasy as he lay there. A tunnel, worm-like but magnified, was directly ahead. It was a black tunnel with a great death-like attraction that enticed the wanton suicide to dance on its lip. He was aware of the danger yet sought it out.

The other day, his friend had been in to see him. Crippled, he rolled in on a wheelchair. A healthy being who, because of mainlining with a dirty needle, got an abcess which resulted in him losing the use of his lower limbs. A lesson for any man? No. Carrying the cripple up the stairs, they settled into the nest where they broke out the stash and punctured their veins. Music heightened the tone as they disappeared into their own individual worlds. The cripple told the story of his doctor who is a drug pension but who has suddenly taken fright and signed him onto the local Clinic where he can get his drugs regularly.

141

They laughed at the doctor's impotence. They emerged, each on his own cloud, the wheelchair and its occupant symbolising their present and future.

Tonight as we talked he had seconal in him. He talks of Saturday night with deep nostalgia. People tend to complicate his life therefore he isolates himself with drugs. Certainly there is an element of danger and death but these are a part of everyday life. He much prefers to choose his own way of life and death. Recently, he had a massive swelling on his foot, the result of a dirty needle shooting drugs into his vein. Though it was a source of great pain he remarked, 'It was worth it'.

The real pleasure of his life is the Dream Maker. He has eagerly jumped from the lip into the abyss. Dancing through the tunnel of torment on a suffocating cloud, his sexual muscle lies limp as the body shell twitches in pain. Death and beyond. The reincarnation, the new rut: the bowler hat, the pinstriped suit and the brolly. Ahh, the new tomorrow. The Great Dream is out there. Over the hill, somewhere else, but never NEVER here and now.

25th MAY '77

I am going through a very bad period of internal conflict. On the surface, I am very plausible to people and am doing my everyday things but underneath there are faint stirrings that have a frightening insight to NOTHING.

I am feeling the pain of confinement acutely at the moment. Whenever people come to mind I feel a wave of desire to be out. Ken mentioned going to Stornoway for his holidays this year and I am longing to be out of here and into the countryside. Although I try not to look too far ahead I seem to be doing so frequently. I can't see myself getting out of here. I know I have reached the optimum period for release. I can see real difficulties ahead.

On the whole I live day to day with a vague sort of long term ideal of my own future. It would be too painful for me to sit down and consciously plan my every step for the next two or three years. The way to get through this sentence is to keep to the foreseeable future. In spite of this there are

142

times when I get glimpses ahead and still see myself sitting here. They are momentary flashes into the future and somehow they obliterate everything else. They are so painful that I wilt. It could be because of the good weather; the sun is shining and I deeply yearn to walk in the countryside. I want to do the simple things of life but can't.

Being confronted with this brutal reality, the timelessness of which shakes me to the core, I feel utter despair. How do I handle it? These inner defence mechanisms come into action and bury the momentary flashes, but although buried I am constantly aware of their presence. In having a better understanding of my inner machinations, the burial of this painful reality becomes more difficult as I am able to penetrate it, to seek it out and become consciously aware of it. The dichotomy of wanting to know and wanting to hide.

For instance, this very date and time next year, I will be sitting in this exact same spot doing the same thing. Intellectually I am growing and the only way I can live with this expansion and development is in a world large enough to accommodate it. I am growing beyond the Unit and this is dangerous as the restrictions containing me are now becoming effective weapons. I fear that it is all building up to something that could eventually destroy me. With the inner growth there must be a balanced physical growth and in this I mean getting released.

In many ways all of this is very much in my private thoughts but the time is coming when I will have to discuss it with someone who is very close to me. Occasionally I will meet it head on for a fleeting glimpse then run. As time goes on, the encounters with myself get more and more frequent but not lengthier. I sense it all building up to something. These past couple of years there has been a strong sense of freedom in me that is slowly vanishing. As time goes by, any talk of freedom seems to recede into the distance. I am afraid of the past and the nothingness of that existence. I could never dream of living in that world of nothingness again. I thought over a passage from Jung that I read today:

'Understanding is a fearful binding power. At times it

can be a veritable murder of the soul as soon as it flattens out vitally important differences. The core of the individual is a mystery of life which is 'snuffed out' when it is grasped. That is why symbols want to remain mysterious. They are not merely because what is at the bottom cannot be clearly apprehended... All understanding, in general, which is a conformity with general points of view, has the diabolical element in it that kills. It is a wrenching of another life out of its own course, forcing it into a strange one which it does not understand, yet lives and works... We should bless our blindness to the mysteries of others, for it shields us from the devilish deeds of violence...'

This seems to express some of what I feel and somehow gives me great consolation. Meanwhile I get tired and weary, and with each day get more tired and wearier. It is almost as though I've reached the roof and yet I continue to grow but the roof remains strongly in position.

27th MAY '77
I had a visit from Ben and we sat in the sun. He was delighted by *The Hardman* and went into detail about it. I enjoyed hearing it from him as he has experienced most of it.

Ben then went on to tell me how he is coping outside. He said there are times when he lies in his bed for three days at a time, sometimes even a week. He said he isn't depressed or anything but just enjoys being a recluse. He said that his mother is in the house but doesn't come near him, he said he could be lying there dead for all she would ever know. When he does come out she tells him he will sleep his head off. He said that of late he has been getting strong suicidal thoughts. He is questioning his whole way of life and feels he cannot get on the same wavelength with other people on the outside. I was very interested to hear what Ben had to say as I could identify with a lot of it. He feels that his prison experiences have torn something out of him as he has been out three years now and still trying to adjust to life outside. I could see his tension easing as we spoke. He is obviously needing to speak to someone who understands.

144

We reached a very deep level that surprised even me as he talked frankly about his thoughts on suicide and frustrations, but the heartening thing to me was that he seemed to have a better understanding of what makes him tick. He talks well and with a good deal of knowledge about his violent feelings and aggression. He said that he locks himself up in his room like a prisoner and feels quite happy as he lies reading books and watching TV. It's almost as though he has created his own prison outside.

28th MAY '77

Looking around me as I sit locked in my cell with the natural light pouring in through the window, I think of how last week I thought of this week and how it would be the same. It is. Now I look and think and see the barbarity of it. The lock shut tight, alone in the early evening — it's not as though I would be a lonely person by choice. I am a private person who likes to retain his own identity but this is an imposed solitude. I think of the image of the past and how it is no longer me, yet it hangs around me, clinging. I look at the barbed wire that hangs outside my window and want to throw myself at it, not to climb over but as a gesture of defiance. It wouldn't be meant as a gesture of self-destruction though that would be the obvious consequence. It would be more a cry to humanity, to the people of the world as to what they are doing. It's all about these very strong passionate and very tender feelings deep within that have been buried for so long, that have been expressed in snide ways. I always knew they existed but didn't know what they were or what they meant. Having gained this knowledge and having learned a lot about my life and society, I feel my earlier life has been stolen from me. I look to Ben and think of how he has been stolen from, of how he is lying in torment — a free man?

It's time to talk openly about returning to the soil.

29th MAY '77

Last night I went to bed at 8.35pm as I couldn't face looking at the cell walls, doors and windows. I felt exhausted and was soon sound asleep. This morning I wakened and went outside to do my running exercises. While doing so I thought, in the freshness of the morning, of my thoughts of the night before. I thought of the soil and my returning to it. It's inevitable at some point, and the daily struggle in here has reached a level where I am facing each day in a condition of rawness, where exposure to the actual surroundings is excruciatingly painful. Strangely enough the one moment of respite I got this morning was when I lifted a 400 lb weight. I don't know why but somehow the heavy weight matched what I felt. I showered, shaved and dressed. While doing so I looked at myself in the mirror. I looked very healthy and thought of how the external belies the internal.

John has just come in to tell me that he has been with Wattie trying to sort out an outside programme for himself. He was in a state of confusion about it. John's problem is that he has been too long in prison and doesn't have the basic skills to negotiate this for himself; or for that matter, the ability to sit down and think through what it is that will be beneficial to him and his future.

In every sense I love life and people but I have become caught up in this little world that is suffocating me. The alternative to it is returning to the main penal system and that would be like throwing myself onto the barbed wire. It's now about choice, restricted though it may be, I do have a decision to make. It is all about selecting what is best and in this instance I feel that the only feasible choice I have is to return to the soil simply because I am not prepared to accept any of the others. Out of the others, there is the choice between returning to the nothingness of the past or the very painful continuance of the present and I feel I have reached the limit in this.

If I choose to go a certain way then it will be open to all sorts of interpretations. The strange thing about writing one's thoughts on all of this is that it is so inadequate. Certainly it gives insights but shallow ones as the issues and complexity of them are of a multi-dimensional nature. You see, as much as I want to shout out for everything to STOP!

146

and open my soul for everyone to see to give them a look at what is going on inside, I can't. It's about not wakening up. It's more than last night when I went to bed early and wakened to start facing and thinking about it again, to sit here where I left off the night before. There is no sense in kidding myself, as some superficial event may rear its head in the morning and tide me over till the next day, only to be confronted with it later. It's about myself coming to terms with this situation which is incompatible with my present growth and development. The development has to be at all levels or one finds oneself caught in this painful situation — one part tugging, the other part pulling.

The reality of life is that as I sat here a member of staff came to my door to say 'The local shop have no rum and raisin ice-cream but they do have vanilla, strawberry and tutti frutti.' I tell him to get a mixture of all three. I really feel as though I could curl up in bed and sleep till the earth crumbles.

This afternoon my aunt Peggy and cousin came to visit me bringing my two children, James and Patricia, with them. I put on a 'mask' and sat with them, but it was flat, and yet I felt so terribly close to them. I managed to get my children away on their own and have a chat with them. Here I am in this situation just as in previous nights. Is it this, or am I using the confinement as an excuse to avoid the deeper issues lying inside me? Why do I feel as though all that is inside me is blocked in my throat? I feel the best thing I can do is to remain away from everyone for a day or two till I work this thing through. Thank God for the music that is playing — The Brandenburg Concerto.

There was a time when the things that now hurt me never would have as I would have been too insensitive to them. Therefore, is sensitivity a bad thing in a situation, or, more to the point, in a world such as this? No, the answer must be no.

Where do I go from here? It's all a matter of choice. Do I realise what I am considering? Yes, and it is no big thing. It is closing the eyes and leaving, entering a deep sleep to the darkness; it is leaving behind the daytime and the night-time and all that goes on during it. It is stopping the heart, the breath, the sight and sound. It is entering the unknown. Why am I thinking of doing so? Because I have entered a world that has dyed and cast me, like so many others, where certain parts of myself have not been allowed to express themselves; a world that didn't allow my mother to kiss and cuddle me; a world where natural affection was seldom shown. To the present day I am labelled 'Killer', when in fact parts of me were done to death and only now am I discovering them. I look at my fellow convicts and see it in them. I look at my family, my very own children, and see it in them. Entry into a so-called civilisation that murders the soul of man. There is now very little appreciation of the fact that I am blood, sweat and tears. Being labelled 'Killer' I am now a thing.

I think of Jap and when we were in the Cages together. He was a big strapping boy serving a six months sentence and sent to the Cages because he was too difficult for the crews to handle due to his size and build. My heart hung heavy for him. I was a year or so older than him though my life was finished and here he was with it all ahead of him. All he had experienced was orphanages and institutions. I continuously implored him never to get into a situation similar to mine as that was the direction he seemed to be heading in. It was water off a duck's back as no sooner was he released than he was back in again and returned to the Cages. He told of how, when outside and sitting in a pub with a pal nursing the dregs of a beer, a girl, a whore, came in to tell him there was a woman outside asking for him. On going outside he looked at this elderly woman and was puzzled — she was a stranger. They stared at each other till finally she said, 'William, I'm your mother'. He looked at her and then to his pal beside him and they sniggered. He asked if she had any money and she said she had so he invited her in to buy them drinks. They got drunk at her expense. I stood there listening to him telling me this and felt emotionally choked, expecting him to say that he burst out crying at finding his long lost mother, but no, he laughed heartily saying, 'We drunk the silly old cow's dough.' He felt not one thing for her. He arranged, at her insistence, to meet the following day and they did. He took her bag from her and went into a dark entrance. When he returned he gave her the bag to carry for him as they walked along the road. On reaching a cafe, he took the bag from her, opened it, took out a bottle with a rag jammed in the spout, lit it and threw it into the cafe. Both he and his mother were arrested for throwing a petrol bomb. He told me he pleaded guilty to the charge and got her released but he went to great pains to tell me that it wasn't because she was his mother, simply because it's the done thing if a man and woman are arrested on a charge together.

Could I, as I sit here, take the necessary and return to the soil? Yes I could, but I won't. Not because I am afraid to but because this moment isn't right. There has to be meaning to it. I think of Ben and his visit on Friday: 'Jimmy, the working class are their own worst enemy.' He talked about the recent visit of the Queen to commemorate the Jubilee Year and how the old people in the district cried as they watched her. I seethe with rage and tell him about this old woman, who put me in mind of my own mother, who said on TV that her life had been fulfilled as she had seen the Queen in the flesh and shaken her hand on the walkabout. We both sat in this cell and looked at each other with bitter anger when in fact we wanted to fall into each others' arms and weep. We don't need to read Marx, or anyone else for that matter, to tell us, as we are living it; we see, we feel and smell it. It's not so much what we said to each other as we are both still too inarticulate to express what we mean, but we felt it.

I can remember, in the past, time after time, saying to myself 'Why did I do that?' From stealing a bar of soap to slashing someone. Does the woman crying in the street when meeting the Queen say the same thing when she returns to the reality of her street, her house, when she watches the authorities who have put flowers in the area for the Queen's visit come and remove them after she's gone?

God, to think that I am labelled 'Scotland's Most Violent Man'. Is it right that I should think these thoughts

HAVE I REALLY CHANGED? LOOKING THROUGH THE LOOKING GLASS I SEE THE EYES THAT HAVE SEEN THIS FACE SINCE MY TIME BEGAN. THE FLESH, THE BONES, THEY HAVE IT'S ALL THE SAME. THEY HAVE ALL GROWN OLDER. BUT THE INSIDE MY HEAD IS STILL THE SAME THOUGH NEW DIMENSIONS HAVE BEEN EXPERIENCED OVER THE YEARS. I AM YET I AM NOT THE SAME PERSON OF 13 YEARS AGO. I AM A WELL LIVED IN BODY, A WELL TESTED MIND. I CAN ENDURE THE FLESH AS MY BONES HAS BEEN STRETCHED, THE GUT ON MY EMOTIONS PULLED TAUT. THE FLOW OF MY THOUGHTS STEMMED BUT STILL I GO ON. SITTING HERE TODAY I CAN SEE THE SUN IS PERCHED HIGH IN THE SKY THROWING ITS LIGHT THROUGH THE BARRED WINDOW ON THIS COLD NEW YEARS DAY AND I FEEL ALIVE. I SIT HERE, MY 16TH YEAR IN PRISON COMPLETELY DRAINED OF ANY SELF PITY OR ANGUISH AS TO MY PLIGHT. I TRY TO WATCH EVERYTHING THAT IS GOING ON IN A PLACE LIKE THIS SO THAT I MAY UNDERSTAND IT BETTER. THERE ARE MANY THINGS GOING ON HERE THAT HAVE TO BE TOLD, HAVE TO BE DISCUSSED AND IMPROVED ON. I HAVE CHANGED IN THAT THROUGH MY EXPERIENCES I HAVE COME TO UNDERSTAND MUCH OF WHAT IS RIGHT AND WRONG IN PRISONS AND RATHER THAN DO SOMETHING ABOUT IT NEGATIVELY I NOW SEEK VIABLE ALTERNATIVES WHICH ARE CONSTRUCTIVE. SO, YES, I HAVE CHANGED THOUGH THERE IS NO MAN-MADE TECHNOLOGICAL DEVICE TO MEASURE THIS SORT OF CHANGE. THE PROBLEM WITH CHANGE OF THE KIND THAT I HAVE DEVELOPED IS THAT IT TAKES THE FORM OF ARTICULATING LOGICAL AND CONSTRUCTIVE CHANGE IN THE PRESENT SOCIAL STRUCTURE WHICH DISRUPTS THE STATUS QUO AS FAR AS ESTABLISHMENTALLY INCLUDING PEOPLE WHO ARE CONCERNED. THIS MEANS SO-CALLED RESPONSIBLE PEOPLE TO TURN ON ME USING MY LAST VIOLENCE AND IRRESPONSIBLE BEHAVIOUR TO DEVALUE WHAT I SAY. BUT, THIS IS ALL PART OF THE PROCESS OF CHANGE.

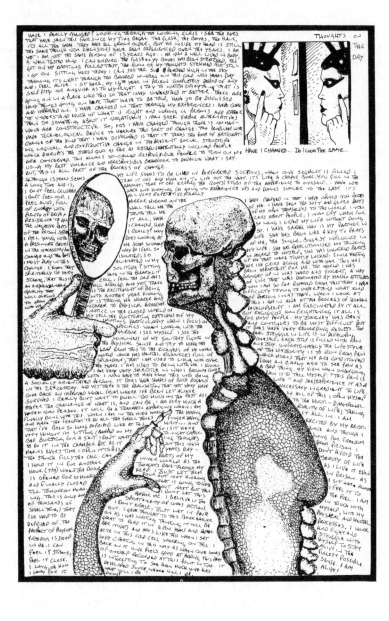

HAVE I CHANGED... Do I look the same...

MY LIFE SEEMS TO BE LIVED IN PERFORATED SECTIONS. WHEN ONE SEGMENT IS FILLED I TEAR IT OFF AND MOVE ON TO LIVE OUT THE NEXT. ITS LIKE A CHEQUE BOOK. YOU FILL IN THE AMOUNT, TEAR IT OFF KEEPING THE (ROOTS) STUBS OF THE EXPERIENCE TO YOURSELF. MOVE ONTO EACH ONE KNOWING I'M GOING TO EXPERIENCE UPS AND DOWNS SIMILAR TO THE LAST. IT'S ALL VERY REPETITIVE REALLY.

MIRROR, MIRROR ON THE WALL TELL ME THE TRUTH TELL ME IT ALL, HAVE I CHANGED, HAVE I REALLY? WHY DOES LOOKING AT ME SEEM SO UNREAL. WHY DO I FEEL SO ISOLATED, SO ALIENATED IN MY SOLITUDE? SITTING HERE IN THE BLEAK, SO COLD AROUND, AND YET, THERE IS THE EXCITEMENT OF BEING NEARER TO PHYSICAL FREEDOM. IT IS TAKING ME NEARER TO ANOTHER YEAR KNOWING IT IS TAKING ME NEARER AND NEARER TO PHYSICAL FREEDOM. JUSTICE IN THE CLOSED WORLD OF MY CELL ITS FLUCTUATING EXTREMES OF MY EMOTIONS PARTICULARLY WHEN I FOCUS ON SPECIFICS. WHEN LOOKING INTO THE MIRROR I SEE MYSELF. I SEE THE LONELINESS OF MY SOLITARY FIGURE IN THE PHYSICAL SENSE AND TRY TO MAKE THE LEAP FROM THIS TO THE RICHNESS OF MY INNER SELF WHICH HAS MENTAL RESOURCES FULL OF SALVATION, THAT I AM USED TO LIVING WITH OVER THE YEARS. I AM USED TO BEING WITH ME. I KNOW I AM VERY VERY SELECTIVE IN WHO I BECOME CLOSE WITH. I NOW HAVE TO THINK FROM THIS INTO BEING A SOCIALLY ORIENTATED PERSON. IT DOES HAVE SHADES OF QUICK ROGERS IN THE 25TH CENTURY. AND YET THERE IS THE REALISATION THAT NOT MANY HAVE COME BACK AN IMPROVED MORE FROM WHERE I'VE BEEN LET ALONE SURVIVED. I REALLY DON'T WANT TO DWELL TOO MUCH ON THE PAST AS I PREFER THE CHALLENGE OF WHAT IS AND CAN BE. AM VERY MUCH A MAN NOW BEING FINALLY DOING MY OWN TIME. WHEN I AM IN THIS WIDE WORLD THE HAVING AND HAVE THE FREEDOM TO DO ALL THE SMALL THINGS. THINGS LIKE THAT I'VE BEEN SO LONG DEPRIVED. LIKE AT THIS VERY MINUTE IN SITTING CALMING ON MY BED BURSTING FOR A SHIT. I DON'T WANT TO DO IT IN THE CHAMBER POT AS IT MEANS EVERYTIME I OR A TO PASS THE STENCH FILLS THE CELL. CAN I HOLD IT IN FOR ANOTHER HOUR (7PM) WHEN THE DOOR IS OPENED FOR 10 MINUTES AND FINALLY CLOSED TILL TOMORROW MORNING. THIS IS ONLY ONE OF THOUSANDS OF SMALL THINGS THAT I'VE HAD TO BE DEPRIVED OF. THE PROSPECT OF PHYSICAL FREEDOM IS DEEP IN ME. I CAN FEEL IT STRONG, FEEL IT CLOSE. I LONG, OH HOW I LONG FOR IT.

I HAVE CHANGED IN THAT I HAVE OPENED MANY PARTS OF ME. I HAVE SEEN THE SOFT AND GENTLE PARTS OF ME OPEN THEMSELVES TO THE WORLD. I NOW CARE ABOUT PEOPLE. I NOW CRY WHEN FOR SO LONG I LIVED MY LIFE WITHOUT DOING SO. I HAVE SARAH WHO IS MY PARTNER IN LIFE. SHE HAS BEEN LIKE A KEY TO PARTS OF ME, THE SINGLE, BIGGEST INFLUENCE IN MY LIFE. SHE HAS REVOLUTIONISED MY THINKING IN REGARD TO MYSELF. SHE HAS UNLOCKED PARTS OF ME THAT WERE TIGHTLY LOCKED. SINCE MEETING HER I'VE CRIED ALONE AND WITH HER. THIS HAS BEEN IMPORTANT FOR ME. THE WORLD I HAS BROUGHT UP IN WAS HARD AND VIOLENT, A WAY BROUGHT UP THAT WAS DOMINATED BY MACHO ATTITUDES OF LIFE THAT WAS REMOVED FROM THE I HAVE SO FAR DIFFICULTY TRYING TO UNDERSTAND WHAT KIND OF PERSON I WAS THEN. WHEN I LOOK AT THIS I AM IN AWE AT THE PROCESS OF HUMAN DEVELOPMENT. I AM FASCINATED BY IT ALL BUT RECOGNISE HOW FRIGHTENING IT ALL IS FOR MOST PEOPLE. MY JOURNEY HAS BEEN AND CONTINUES TO BE MOST DIFFICULT BUT IT DOES HAVE VERY REWARDING RESULTS. THE REAL STRUGGLE IN LIFE IS DEVELOPING ONESELF, EACH STEP IS FILLED WITH PAIN AND JOY. UNFORTUNATELY THE LIFESTYLE OF THE MAJORITY IS TO RUN FROM PAIN WHICH MEANS THAT WE ARE CONDITIONED FROM AN EARLY AGE TO SEE PAIN AS A BAD THING, MY VIEW WAS UNDERGOING PAIN IS TO TELL MYSELF "THIS PAIN IS LIFE" AND SEE/EXPERIENCE IT AS A NECESSARY INGREDIENT TO LIFE. IN ALL OF THIS I OPEN MYSELF TO THE MULTI-DIMENSIONAL REALITY OF LIFE; TAKING IT ALL IN. I AM EXCITED BY MY EXISTENCE AND THOUGH I HAVE BEEN FROM PRISON I DON'T AVOID THE BEAUTY OF LIFE AS I LIVE IT EVEN IN PRISON. AS I SIT HERE AND I FEEL IT TO THE FULL. I AM IN TOUCH WITH MYSELF WITH MY PHYSICAL AND MENTAL PROCESSES. I WORK AND FIGHT AND STRUGGLE WITH MYSELF TO STAY ALIVE IN THE FULLEST POSSIBLE SENSE. I AM ALIVE!

SO I SIT HERE IN THE NIGHT CALM WITH MY THOUGHTS ON THIS NEW YEARS DAY - INNER FACTS OF MY INNER WORLD AS THE THOUGHTS RACE THROUGH MY HEAD. I JUST LET THEM POUR OUT NOT KNOWING WHAT'S GOING TO COME NEXT BUT THIS I DON'T LET THIS BOTHER ME. I BELIEVE IN THE SPONTANEITY OF ONES ACTIONS I DON'T ERASE. JUST LET IT POUR ON AS I AM WRITING THIS BOOK EARLIER I GAVE THOUGHT TO THIS, GREAT TO READ IT IN A FEW YEARS AND AGAIN THINKING IT WILL BE GREAT TO READ IT IN A FEW YEARS AND AGAIN ACTIE IN THIS COLD CELL WORKING ON THIS I HAVE CREATION. BACK IN IT IN THIS WAY AS WHEN ONE LOOKS OF ONESELF RECORDED AT THIS POINT IN TIME. IT IS INTERESTING TO SEE HOW MUCH ONE HAS DEVELOPED SINCE. WHERE WILL I BE WHAT WILL I BE DOING...

or should I do as I have done in the past and fulfil people's expectations of me? Am I doomed to eat raw meat and live in a Cage to satisfy the masses? I come to the present day and watch those very same people who gave me that label say that I am a 'con-man' who is trying to work his ticket out of prison — such versatility I must possess. Could it be that the consequences of someone like me changing would be too much for the establishment to accept? Not so much my changing as my awareness of the games they play and the traps they lay for fodder such as me and those poor souls who cry at seeing the Queen. Ludwig Van Beethoven, your sonatas with Kempff on piano are soothing my savage breast. So much so that I want to rest my weary head and let them lull me to sleep as my whole self is so tired and exhausted. So weary of the struggle and the conflict, of the pain of my past and present life. Tomorrow, I know what you hold. I will speak to the same people, see the same walls and look for the same escape routes — books, writing and sculpture. There is this feeling within me that I have done all that is necessary, that having made my contribution, the continuance is unimportant.

Having spent a good part of the day sitting here in front of the typewriter, I am no further on in bringing the underlying issues to the surface. These thoughts are only fragments of the whole. We can never say how we know it all. We may gain insight to a past but that is about all.

I will return to all of this when I waken, and search for the truth of my soul.

30th MAY '77
Early morning and I find difficulty in sleeping. Getting out of bed, I look out of the window into the blackness beyond. In the far distance, I catch sight of red car-lights as they pass by. TV cameras and searchlights are much nearer but I concentrate on the areas beyond. Ten years, ten long miserable years, and how many more? I hear the sound of a bus as it brakes in the nearby road. I try to imagine the occupants as they pass, sleepy-eyed, drunk and probably returning from parties or visiting friends. How many times

have I passed that way and thought of the prison as a place I had experienced and was going back to?

Later

I waken and do my exercises. While running round the small yard there is a lightness within me but soon afterwards the reality of what I feel hits me. While doing my other exercises I feel weary, not a normal weariness but something much deeper.

I sit in my cell and John comes in telling me that he has clashed with a member of staff. I immediately sense he is drugged and ask him. He admits that he is, saying that he was given two seconal last night as he is having trouble sleeping. I personally wanted to scream at John due to this inner crisis I am in but instead told him that it has nothing to do with the member of staff but comes back to himself and the way he is behaving. John sits there furious and I tell him that I am not going to agree with him just for the sake of peace, as the truth is he is wrong. I reminded him that he has no right taking drugs when he knew he was going out this morning, also that he is sitting here trying to justify the clash he had just had. It was clear that he was upset. Eventually he grabbed me in a jocular manner to break away from the seriousness and the truth of what I was telling him. We laughed and he said he felt much better. I was glad to see the back of him as I was heavy with emotional turmoil within myself, but angered, which differed from the feelings I already had, at someone being so stupid as to give John these pills. I caught hold of Larry and he said he had given them to John from his nightly dose. I didn't go into a bad scene with Larry but let him know that it wasn't a nice thing to do. There was a malicious air about him.

Ken came in later and there was no sense trying to hide the crisis I was in. I explained to him in detail what I felt and he was visibly moved. He came in with what I knew he would, supportive statements. He told me that he was speaking to a politician recently and that he mentioned the fact that I could be released tomorrow and never be in trouble again, but I didn't sparkle as this sort of superficial

152

political talk no longer impresses me. Ken noticed this and we discussed it. He tried to communicate with me but decided that it would be best to leave it. I like Ken tremendously but as I explained to him, the situation that I am in can only be resolved by me. He understood.

It's only when I speak to someone else that I get a proper indication of how deep I am into this 'down'. So far down that were you to shout on me from the surface of your normality then it would echo. Music remains my only companion for the present — Beethoven's Ninth. Somehow the music seems to strike chords that release others deep in the unconscious.

I feel battered and bruised. What has happened to the Spirit? That magical spirit that always lifted me out of the depths of despair in the past. I have gone beyond that, or so it seems. I find myself convoluting in a bottomless pit where there is nothing to grasp onto but my soul.

This inner heaviness that I am experiencing is not unique to me. Others have it from time to time and at varying degrees but the question is why do we hide it from each other? Here I sit alone because I feel others here won't understand, or have enough on their plate, and because I have been conditioned not to share these inner feelings with others. To think that we spend our short living experience on this earth in such a way that stops us sharing experiences that would be invaluable to our existence. My God, it's bloody stupid.

Where do I stand on the fourth day of this encounter? I feel lost. Lost because having gone over everything that I possibly could, I am left with the same helplessness. This is a time when I should be pleased with my achievements as a sculptor, playwright, and author, but no. It comes down to freedom. You can keep a person in the most luxurious hotel and given him what he wants but if you restrict his movements to a room of that hotel then it will become his hell. Ultimately the *need* is for freedom.

31st MAY '77
Still struggling with each moment of the day. Feel lost in

153

the myriad of corridors within myself. The morning sun shines outside my window. It holds no comfort for me. I feel at this moment that I am somewhere beyond. It's almost as though I am in my head. Could it be the hospital?

There is no doubt that it did something to me. It was being confronted by that part of the past that I had erased. Not entirely erased but had somehow left behind. Certainly the memories of the past have always been very much in my conscious but actually to be in amongst it again was crushing. It would be on a par with getting involved in violence again — I see it as unthinkable. My reaction to violence now would be far different to that of the past when I accepted it as part of my life. It was exactly the same as the hospital incident where I was confronted by this situation and instead of reacting to it in a way that would have been typical, I was horrified. I wept. What did this do to me? I don't know and haven't really gone into it. The last time I had this operation the post-surgical pain was bad but this time it was nothing. I think it was because of the brutality of the police presence. The subsequent press coverage was also pretty damaging. Again, the image was that I am Scotland's Most Violent Man and as a result they treated me accordingly. It was almost as though I had no feelings. Again, I couldn't scream with rage as I would then be seen as the animal. What do I do? Fortunately, in that hostile situation the parts of me that have grown so strong emerged and pulled me through, or did they? For if my present state is a direct result of that experience then the damage has been much deeper that I first appreciated.

What about my yearning to be free? I visualise walking in the country, seeing green fields, birds singing, the horizons far in the distance — as far as the eye can see. Oh to walk the streets full of people. To look at my hand and see the clasped hand of my girlfriend, to look at her face and eyes. These are the dreams of the incarcerated. I want so much to taste freedom because for the first time in my life I will be able to appreciate it. I desire the world beyond the walls.

And what about the expressions of my soul? The

hammer and chisel that sculpts the stone from the tenement buildings of my past into a new form for the future. A transformation that is comparative to my own. The ingrained pollution that covers the stone is shorn. I take it in this filth covered condition, devote the time to it and give it another life. When it is complete I leave it with a bright future. The part that I envy in this unfeeling, inanimate object is that its transformation is widely accepted, and not questioned.

And the writing. I need it as a testament to my experience. To reflect, in some small measure, what I feel. To help me see, like the sculpture, the natural development of me — the human being. Threads of life brought to the surface. Painful though it may be there has to be an understanding of what we are doing. For example, many people in this place will notice my absence and presume that I am studying hard when in fact I am going through one of the most painful experiences in my life. I am locked into this crisis where I am questioning my continuance as a human being. What do the days ahead hold for me? Can I pick myself up from the floor, scooping up the millions of scattered pieces, and face the nothingness of tomorrow? The writing can only reflect a surface image of what is going on. This does not devalue its importance. Its very existence may be the key to another person's feelings.

Feelings. Those parts that we all try to hide from each other. The shame, the jealousy, the guilt and insecurity. Our inferiority. Who can put up the most convincing mask to hide the inner turmoil? It's all about chasing illusions that don't really exist. It's like hating some bastard yet when he dies we realise he wasn't so bad after all.

1st JUNE '77
I think of the Unit Community while doing my exercises. The once strong foundation of our Community — the meetings — is crumbling. Crumbling in the sense that it will evaporate into the impotent ways of the whole prison system, be smothered by their stringent restrictions, bound up in bureaucracy. And even if this did happen, people

would still visit the place from outside and say what a fine place it was because it will always be that bit different from the main penal system. They will see it only as it is, unaware of the destruction that has taken place. The bureaucracy is making a perfect job of strangling the life out of us, slowly but surely we are dying. There was a point this morning when I believed that something had lifted, taking the weight off me. It was a moment of optimism simply because I reached a depth last night that had me almost touching the soil. But in spite of this, the weight returned this morning. The *weight*, yes, that's what it feels like. A very heavy weight hanging heavily from a thin thread in my chest, almost as though it's about to snap and plunge into my guts. It's the weight of *life* and the price of being alive.
Later
Having spent the morning reading, thinking and resting, I am feeling that bit brighter. The afternoon of the fifth day and I feel a lightness in my head with much of the pain lifted from my body. What remains is reality. You allow yourself to go through this very painful introspective examination but when you emerge the prison walls are still there. They stand there, high and forboding, a monument to the failure of our way of life, mocking the 'civilisation' of man. I don't know if I can live like this. Only time will tell.

I think of the physically handicapped and what they have to live with. But I compare my situation to the recovered cripple who is forced to remain in the wheelchair.
P.M.
The sun shone down on me. I had entered the world of the living. Sitting on a seat away on my own, I let the heat enter my weary bones. I was absolutely shattered. There was a hesitancy in others as my face was set and I gave out signals to leave me be. There is no doubt that these five secluded days have taken their toll. One cannot experience this sort of thing and emerge unscathed. The fragmentation could be felt and I wondered if it would ever heal. Ken tactfully sat beside me and carried on a low, one-man conversation whilst I soaked up the sun.

I don't know what to make of the past five days but here

I am having gone all the way down. I am shocked at the intensity of the experience and am utterly bewildered by it. The only feeling I have at this moment is that I shouldn't keep this to myself, that people must understand or be aware about this sort of human misery. It is a universal experience but having gone to the depths I feel that something must be done to help others who are likely to make the same trip. Other than that I will have to wait and make sense of it. I really feel brutalised at this moment.

3

He's a man without a colour,
Standing in the rain;
Blankly sees the future now,
With all his hopes in ruin.

Larry Winters

5th JULY '77
After reading my mail I went outside to put some finishing touches to my latest sculpture. While doing so Larry and Denis (prisoner) came across and began discussing it. We had an interesting dialogue on the piece with Denis being quite imaginative. He said it reminds him of a peasant woman who is pregnant. The piece is attractive to me because of its lines. I worked away and finished it.

When staff came on duty after the meal break one of the main prison staff informed them individually (as they entered the gate) that the girl visiting John is a well known prostitute. Ken told me about it. I replied that I knew her and she wasn't. Ken caught hold of John afterwards to ask him about this. John blasted Ken and the other staff. John said he should have been told about this when his visitor was here. I told him no way as it wouldn't be right for his visitor to walk back through the main gate knowing this. John is now along in his cell all bottled up. Ken is reporting this to the main prison Governor in the morning... I brought my new sculpture up to my cell tonight and it sits with two others. I like it and will let it sit there for now. It is a tremendous feeling when completing a new sculpture.

12th JULY '77
I was sitting in the yard when Ken called a Staff Meeting. He had just returned from a meeting with the representative of the local branch of the SPOA. Ken had been given a copy of a letter from the Prisons Dept. to the General Secretary of the SPOA. It contained proposals that all of us consider devastating: 'In our view the time has come to make firm plans for the gradual replacement of staff now on duty in the Unit, which may mean that it will not be possible to rely entirely on volunteers to replace them... Apart from the Chief Nurse Officer, to whom I have already referred we have in mind that we should seek to make the necessary changes over approximately the next twelve months...'

There is no doubt in my mind that they are going to these lengths to 'get' Ken and Malky (prison officer). In doing

this they automatically get me. My strength lies in the relationships I have with staff here and so it vanishes with
them being transferred.

On the prisoner's side, we are in a position where we just
cannot win. With the introduction of staff being detailed to
take duty here the whole concept will be lost. The
Department are frightened by what we are doing here so
they are resorting to this.

14th JULY '77
As I ran round the yard this morning I could hear staff deep
in heated exchanges about the present situation. There
were very strong feelings being expressed and it looks as
though the Department could meet a united staff, which is
very important.

This afternoon I went outside and did some sculpting. I
took a piece of stone and worked, and worked, and worked
getting all the aggression into the piece. It was great as I
made fantastically good progress and sat on a chair
looking at the rough form... The other prisoners are
feeling the effects of the present crisis.

15th JULY '77
The Governor came in and Ken went to speak to him.
Afterwards he came out saying the Governor was shaking
like a leaf. Ken asked him if he had known about this letter.
He admitted he had and that three weeks ago Wattie had
advised him to say nothing about it...

Later this afternoon Ken told me the Department have
also censored the Departmental Working Party Report
which set up the Unit. Ken found he had mislaid his
original copy and asked one of the younger staff for a copy
they get when applying and training for the Unit. Half of
the material has been taken out. The parts omitted are
relevant to what the Unit is doing and the comments made
by the Working Party on the Inverness Cages. They're a
shower of fuckers. I asked the Governor what his views
were on the Department letter. It was bloody pathetic as he
waffled saying that he is making observations of the

situation and intends making his remarks to the Department. Malky asked what his observations were and again he waffled.

The Hull Riot Report was made public today and it is disgraceful as anyone with any experience of the penal system will recognise. It states, 'The staff had shown considerable tolerance in the past towards demonstrations and free and easy relationships between staff and prisoners had tended to obscure perception of what was actually happening...'

27th JULY '77
Neil and John from Craigmillar came in this morning. I had the small-scale model of Gulliver ready for them. They are pleased with it. I'm pleased I redesigned the whole thing. We had a very constructive meeting working out detailed plans.

29th JULY '77
Ben came in today saying he had been to see my play *The Hardman* again last night. He said it was a special showing for Councillors and Judges etc. Afterwards he started chatting to some of them. The general opinion was that I wouldn't get released. Ben made the pertinent point that even the Judge who sentenced me recommended fifteen years so he thought I should get out. They were stumped at this. One of them remarked that I have murdered eight people, and so once again we meet the McElhone myth. Ben replied that he had heard all Councillors are either homosexual or corrupt and they denied this. Ben told them this is the myth going round about them. If they are prepared to believe the myths about me then it must apply to them also. Ben is so funny and brilliant. I thoroughly enjoyed his visit.

Stephanie (my publisher) came up this evening. She said she would like to do a publication of *The Hardman*. I told her I would get in touch with Tom... she heard that Nicky Fairbairn is delighted Pan are doing simultaneous publication of *A Sense of Freedom* as he intends to sue. A big publisher means more money. Stephanie and the Pan people seem slightly worried at this... Stephanie said she received an irate phonecall from a Glasgow schoolteacher saying she thinks it disgusting that she is publishing my book — me, a criminal. She said she had written a book and couldn't get a publisher. It takes all kinds...

30th JULY '77
Kay came in this morning and was saying she is on BBC radio tomorrow morning with Teddy Taylor M.P. It concerns the publication of the book and the Trust Fund I've set up. His opinion is that I am conning everyone to get a parole date. He said that I am not sorry for the things I've done and don't say I'm sorry in the book. He also mentioned Fairbairn remarking that he is going to make a fortune suing the publishers.

6th AUGUST '77
Bruce Millan (Secretary of State for Scotland) states in the morning paper that there will be a review of the internal running of the Unit, and the visits in particular. I can't understand this as Harry Ewing knows everything about the book.

12th AUGUST '77
Ken was called over to the main prison to an Investigating Officer and told he was being charged with a breach of discipline and given all the material relating to it. The charge is that he wrote an 'open' letter to the *Glasgow Herald* relating to material and knowledge gained through his job, and did so without authority. Ken phoned John Renton, General Secretary of the SPOA and he agreed to be a witness for him. He also phoned the *Glasgow Herald* and the assistant editor, Tony Findlay, and he too will be a witness.

17th AUGUST '77
... Stephanie came in and had been to see Tom McGrath to talk about publishing the play. When they came to the

point of joint authorship Tom hesitated, saying he would put a note on the inside saying that I had collaborated. In other words he was taking the whole project over. I feel extremely sad at this and my immediate internal reaction was 'Oh no Tom, not you too'...

21st AUGUST '77
Larry came in tonight and was heavily drugged. He sat down and we talked. He said he is now on six seconal a night. He said he doesn't know how I can work the way I do. I replied that I don't know how he can get drugged the way he does. He shrugged his shoulders and said he would like to work the way I do but can't. We talked about death and I pointed out how we are all dying, everyone, and not just us. I found it very sad as Larry has given up and is accepting his lot. He should fight it every inch of the way. We discussed suicide and Larry said he wouldn't do it as that is what the Department and others want. I sat there looking at him in his drugged state and thinking how this is the way the Department want him.

2nd SEPTEMBER '77
6am and the dark tarmac recedes underfoot with every step I take. The clear blue sky belies the coldness of the air that causes beads of sweat to sit frostily on my forehead and face. Each step, as I run, wakens the still sleepy body as the muscles stretch and contort. Lungs constrict and expand as they take in and expel the cold morning air. The red track suit and brightly coloured shoes are in sharp contrast to the ground level surroundings. Like the mouse in the eternal wheel, I run round the small enclosed yard that is 'L' in shape and has high, thick walls topped with specially designed barbed wire. Out of reach but well within sight, a close-circuit camera focusses on the yard. The anonymous, ever-vigilant eye that accompanies my every step. Windows on the nearby buildings have steel bars and then more steel bars.

I look to the beauty of the morning sky not bothering to look ahead. Each morning, hail, rain or snow, I take this jog knowing its every crease and crack. Letting the silence of the morning enfold me, I look to the one symbol of freedom — the sky. The occasional car can be heard in the distance and like its engine my mind is ticking over. I lose myself in the inner world of thought letting the automatic pilot of familiarity guide my way unseen. I watch a wisp of cloud as it mars the unstained blue. Thin and wispy it moves with the slight breeze and we mark time till the wall changes my direction. Being State property one appreciates the privacy and luxury of thought. I fleetingly focus on my colleagues as they lie in their beds in slumber or listening to the padding of my feet as I pass their windows. Pulling the bedcovers tightly around them they think of my insanity at rising and running at this unearthly hour.

My gaze is distracted by the sight of a beautiful blackbird as it sits decorating the cruel barbed wire. Passing underneath where the bird is perched, I hear its tuneful whistle with a clarity that astounds me. So powerful a symbol of freedom that it nullifies the superstructure of modern technology containing electronic eyes, barbed wire, radar equipment, all surrounded by high walls. I wish myself to be the blackbird as it lifts its beak to throw another loud clear tune. The bird flies off in the direction of freedom. It must have landed nearby as its tuneful whistles floated in from beyond the walls. Visually I look to the sky and audibly to the tune of the blackbird. I am so fortunate.

I think of the sky and the bird, symbols of my future. Tomorrow I will run the same run and breathe the same air. This is the period of torment and discovery. It will finally come to an end but meantime I will roam the abyss. I know it is ahead, the visual impact of what's up there tells me that, the sound of the blackbird that floats in to tell me it all. Ah, the future! Now there's a thought to equal the beauty of the morning and the blackbird. Unlike the past, that dark menacing shadow, I take responsibility for creating the future from this moment onwards. I look at the wispy cloud as it fades in the distance — going in my direction. I want to follow it, to run on air and see the

165

height and breadth of the land, to look as far as the eye can see without walls restricting.

My body functions like a well-oiled machine and I press to keep it that way as my survival depends on it. All of me has to be geared to coping with this purgatorial period that is constantly trying to erode the parts that want to stay alive. The faces of those around me, the feelings that I have about the faces are tiring. We cannot avoid each other. Regardless of what may happen between us, we still have to look at each other all day and every day. I may hate the sight of a person but there is nothing that I can do about it. There are sheer joy moments when one is alone, the techni-coloured world of fantasia where one can create one's wishes and see them all come true. They are never so grand that one cannot believe them in the light of day. I think of myself sculpting in some remote area next to a log cabin with my girlfriend nearby. I imagine myself in a flat with her, having a meal or making love. The simplistic beauty of these dreams moves me to the core. Poignant moments that have a strengthening quality. I roam the countryside with many friends. There is sun, flowers, long swaying grass and a feel of warm intimacy. Hazy moments of love and tenderness that are both dream-like and real. Simple things that I want to do.

Reality, however, is this heaving chest, this sweating body, this well trod path within this small eternal wheel. Reality is here and now. Each step I take is another time and a changing space. I am living in a world of constant change and yet the sameness and repetitiveness of each day eats into me. And so the beginning of another day...

11th SEPTEMBER '77
Larry is dead.
Sitting here with my lunch.
Knock!
Knock!
It was a desperate knock, with Murray Stewart (prison officer) asking me to come with him. Getting out of my chair I went with him trying hard to anticipate what was

ahead. He entered Larry's cell where I could hear slapping — a fight I thought, and so pushing myself forward to pull the standing person off the other, but with an ease that turned it from a fight to something else. 'He is cold and having trouble breathing,' said John. Putting my hands on Larry I started thumping his chest. Rigor mortis had set in. 'He's dead. He's fucking dead!' and they all looked at me. 'Get the doctor for Christ's sake,' and Murray left to do so. The prisoners stood looking at me as I pulled at Larry to make sure. He lay there in a crouched position with the plastic chamber pot still askew under his buttocks. Blood was in the pot, a smattering, some trickles had also co-agulated on his nose, some at his feet. Very little blood in all. His eyes were tightly closed, veins in his neck protruded and the whole pose looked strained as though some massive pain had overtaken him. He was cold.

Internally I was wanting to vomit, was feeling shattered and asked him, the dead body, why? Larry, why, why, why? Next to the blood at his feet lay some pills, sleeping pills. Taking his cover from his bed I placed it over him. Others kept their distance and left it all to me. There was a part of me that recognised the inevitability of it all. Perhaps the responsibility of having to keep things in control held me together as I desperately wanted to run off. To go outside and run for miles, to cry and express all that I wanted to. I sit here shattered but still with a part of me knowing that Larry had played with fire, had seen some of his close friends die over the past years from the effects of drug taking. Knowing all of this it is still hard to take.

Police, the Governor, doctors including Peter Whatmore arrived and all the other legal procedures attached to death were formalised.

And here I was, faced with what I had contemplated doing in recent months. I don't want to end up like this, but the fact is that we all do — none of us can ever escape it. The great leveller of mankind. This man lying there, stiff and cold — useless. I could still feel the coldness and death of him clinging to my skin.

Going into the yard, I let the wind enter my lungs and

cleanse the stench of death from me. Why is it that we all go through the pain of living to end up like that? His lying there brought it all home to me. Why is it that we all fight and squabble together and make life so bloody miserable for the short time that all of us are here? Why do we find it so difficult to let those loving parts of us flow to each other and at least make this short stay something precious?

At the time we found him, a phonecall came through saying his mother was at the gate to visit him. She had travelled a great many miles and was now sitting waiting to see her son, sitting there as contented as I was with my lunch, not knowing that we would be hit by a mighty blow. Throughout the next four and a half hours we wandered around, sometimes in the silence of our own little world and at others speaking with a great emptiness. The police questioned us as to his state of mind and all the while Larry lay where we had found him — dead.

The police photographer took some pictures and a few seconds later spoke to one of the guys asking if he had seen the big football game yesterday and the guy expressed to me the harshness of this. We discussed how these guys are living with this every day and seem to have become hardened to it. Yes, and even society has become hardened to it. John sat in his cell crying his eyes out. Peter made a meal of sausages and eggs. J.L. wandered about with his head in his hands. Denis sat silent. The Governor wanted to know if the prisoners should be searched in order the establish that the formal procedures had been adhered to. One of the staff told him that Larry had always been the weak link and that searching was out of the question. Rape my person while I mourn thought I.

There is no doubt that we all think that it will never happen to us. Stripped of all dignity as the rigor mortis is snapped and you are placed in that coffin, reduced to nothingness. I returned to see him time and again as he lay there throughout the four and half hours. The last time I saw him he seemed slightly more relaxed than when I first set eyes on him, or maybe it was that I got used to it.

There was something about going back to see him lying

there a number of times and it was as though I was trying to understand more about life through looking at this dead friend. Is life as sacred as we would like it to be or is it something we should look on as we do a friend emigrating? The inevitability of death is something that we refuse to look at and it seems to me that by accepting its inevitability we will come to learn more about our own lives. But it is taboo. No-one wants to look at it or accept it. This morning as I ran round the yard, Larry sat on his chamber pot — dead. And all through the morning I did what I did while he sat there dead. Even in this small claustrophobic place he died alone. We are all alone.

And in the midst of the crumbling facades of us all, one of the staff and I tried to focus on the repercussions from this situation. If it is an overdose, where does that leave us? Is this selfish when a guy is lying dead upstairs? No, it is reality and doesn't detract from what we feel for him. We must salvage what we can.

Larry was carried downstairs locked in a green, heavy-laden coffin. I ran to look out the window and see him pass. They carried the coffin out of the gate and it locked behind him. Larry has left us — physically. His cell door is sealed with brown sticky paper.

I have pieced some of it together. Drugs had been brought in. This morning Peter went into Larry's cell at 9.30am and found him sitting on his chamber pot so quickly closed the door thinking he was doing the toilet but he was sitting there frozen in death. Naked and sitting on the pot it looks as though a massive attack locked him into this position. Murray (prison officer) had something to say to him at lunch time and went in to find Larry still sitting there. He went to speak to him but he didn't reply and so he touched him then came to get me. John and Peter were taking Larry's lunch to him and were there for me coming seconds later.

The last time I saw him was last night before lock-up and we were laughing together and I distinctly remember saying to myself that he looked well. Shortly after this he offered Peter some pills but Peter refused them.

After being locked in this cell tonight I looked into the mirror at my image and saw a clear eyed, physically fit human being and compared it to the dead body of Larry. Last night he looked so well, and this morning lifeless. I look at myself and wonder, what will yours be like?

Larry didn't mean to die — consciously — of that I am certain.

The impact of the experience is tremendously thought-provoking. The sight of Larry lying there stiff with rigor mortis made me wonder about life after death. How can there possibly be? There was something very brutal about this shell of man lying there — it is difficult to believe that the spirit of life, as I am experiencing it, would be callous enough to abandon this physical shell as it lay pathetically alone and helpless on the floor. Being so sensitive to life, I didn't want to believe that this is how all of us will end up. It's just like a car engine: switch on, switch off. There was no dignity in the death that I experienced today, it frightened all of us. No-one wanted to accept it. There will never be dignity in death so long as we continue to deny it. Only when we can begin to accept it will we fully understand its meaning. Seeing Larry there today made me petrified of death and only now, locked in this cell very much as he was last night at this time, can I begin to examine my reaction to it.

I sit here feeling slightly afraid. The shadows are cast over the cell as the earphones blast Beethoven's 'Missa Solemnis' into my soul. The depth of the music touches the fear that I feel and soothes it, but the great fear of dying in this cell remains with me.

12th SEPTEMBER '77
The night was very long and uncomfortable and full of symbols of Larry. Two cats meowing outside my window; he had a love of cats. Two singers on the TV singing an old Scottish song: 'Dance, dance, wherever you may be, I am the Lord of the dance said he...' a song that I associate with him. The night was troublesome with little sleep and thoughts racing through my head. I was relieved when the

170

door was opened and I went outside to do my exercises. Running round the yard I felt so tense and full of sorrow but determined to live — not wanting to die under these circumstances. I felt so weary running round but persisted just to prove that I was alive — Larry was dead. It was vitally important for me to do my exercises this morning, nothing but death could have persuaded me otherwise.

From a window looking into the main prison was heard the comment from one prison officer to another, 'The only good thing to come out of the Special Unit was Winters in a box'. No matter how much progress we make this is what we are up against. These are the same people who go around asking other prisoners and staff why we hate them so much.

The Governor called us into the TV room and thanked us for our response to the whole situation and the way we handled it yesterday. Peter Whatmore came in the morning and afternoon. We all sat chatting. He said that Dr. Harland, a pathologist, will be doing the post mortem on Larry.

My day was very busy. It was difficult to concentrate.

Tom McGrath came in. I told him about Larry and we talked about it for a while. Eventually we got on to the problem of the play, the co-author issue. I sorted it out by reminding Tom of the reality. He could do nothing but agree with me. We discussed touring... He has resigned from the Third Eye Centre and intends to take his writing more seriously... It was nice to speak to him and sort things out amicably. I was finding it hard to concentrate on what we were saying as Larry was uppermost in my mind. The news has broken to the press and was on the radio. This afternoon Rab visited us to say the press has been on to him about Larry. We talked about it and he seemed pretty shaken. Tonight he was interviewed by STV and came across pretty bad.

I went along to John Neeson tonight, calling all the others together. I asked John if he was aware of the implications of what had happened. He looked upset and just stared at me. He then said he had done nothing. Peter said that Larry killed Larry. I said I knew that but had heard John had given him the pills. John was looking and feeling as guilty as hell. John said he didn't know where Larry got them. I know John gave them to Larry and told him so. The others remained quiet. He eventually made it clear the drugs came in via the Douglas Inch Clinic and was saying everything except that he gave them to Larry. I tried to tell him that Larry was destined to die this way and that was that. I reminded him that we had to concern ourselves with living and the future of the Unit; the people in it, and its future... I can't help thinking of Larry and how he had to live up to a role that he didn't quite fit. He was just a country boy serving life for manslaughter who ended up in Peterhead Prison and the system there twisted him beyond all recognition. He is the classic case of the guy getting 'used' and criminally educated while in prison...

The big problem has now to be faced by those of us who knew nothing about the drugs Larry had taken. The Department are almost certain to restrict us and there is little we can do about it — they will crush us with it. Larry has left us but his shadow still remains. He got the release he knew he would and I suppose that's about all one can say. In many ways his death has given me a will to live like nothing I've experienced. The fight to remain intact and survive this has put his death in the distance.

13th SEPTEMBER '77
I read my mail and the newspapers which had front page coverage of Larry. The emphasis was on his past violence and his drug taking. On the whole they were pretty sympathetic to him.

I thought over what I was going to do... I called a meeting and outlined to everyone that they were aware of Larry having strange drugs, that there was a lot of suspicion going round about these. I asked the community if anyone knew anything about it. There was silence and after a lengthy time I pointed out that one of us here was responsible for the drugs and I would like him to speak up. Again there was silence. I said that my loyalty was to the

Unit and what it was trying to do. I believed in the community and not any single individual in it. I named John pointing out that I couldn't prove it but knew John was responsible. There was total silence for a long spell; the meeting was very tense. I was feeling very shaky and explained to John that I abhorred doing what I was but for the sake of the Unit and everyone else in it I was doing so. He kept letting out deep, loud sighs. Some others in the group asked him to speak up. John stated that Larry is dead and he has nothing more to say...

Although we all knew that Larry's incarceration in the main prison system and the Unit, along with prison officers, psychiatrists, nursing staff and even Larry himself, were all responsible for his untimely death, the unfortunate fact is that John the prisoner, the most innocent of all these people, was nevertheless the person who got Larry those particular drugs that caused his death a few hours later. This puts us into a dilemma. Should we have joined what is bound to become a cover-up? The meeting ended.

The Governor phoned Mr Meikle at the Department. He said John should remain where he was as they don't want to be seen moving him at this point — before the results of the post mortem. It was only later that Gerry (prison officer) told me he was horrified when listening to the Governor on the phone to the Department. Apparently he told Mr Meikle we had a meeting but nothing of what took place. Gerry said he was shaken by this and seriously doubted the Governor's ability to cope with the Unit. We weren't told any of this by Gerry till later in the evening.

During our ordinary meeting this afternoon Wattie remarked that Peter (Whatmore) has always known that he could be slain for giving Larry as many drugs as he was. His dosage was massive but he felt that he had to do it as Larry was a threat to staff and made this clear. In many ways I agree with him as Larry was so into drugs, in a way they were his life and all he seemed to have. Larry had made it clear that he would use violence if not given his drugs, therefore, the system used Peter Whatmore as the

173

magician. Drugs were what he felt secure with — they were the only alternative for him.

This afternoon John called a meeting. He told us in a very moving way that he had brought the drugs into the Unit — he had collected them from the Douglas Inch Clinic. He said Larry had asked him to take them from a guy who would deliver them to the Clinic and this is what happened... John was on the verge of tears. It must have taken a great deal for him to do this and he was thanked for it. Immediately he stopped talking the Governor told us he would have to rush off and report the matter to the Department. He returned to say that the Department ordered that John be locked up in the Unit till tomorrow morning. Those of us with visits were advised not to say anything.

As I went upstairs the Governor was telling John — in his cell — that the matter will have to be reported to the police. He instructed the staff to take John's shaving gear and other small items in case he tried to do himself damage. John told the Governor he was expecting a visit from his brother-in-law tonight. He replied it would be better if his visitor was told by a staff member that he can't see John as he isn't too well. John replied that this was foolish. The Governor said John could see his visitor for two minutes. By this time John was crying over the Larry thing.

I came upstairs at this point and met the two staff with shaving gear etc. When I asked what they were doing they looked sheepish. I let loose at them saying that they are the staff who are supposed to guide this inexperienced Governor rather than jump to his silly commands.

The Governor came in tonight and had a meeting with staff. Malky (member of staff) came up raging like a bull. He said he was calling a meeting. As we sat there the Governor stated that he realises we aren't happy with the situation and the way it is being handled. Murray (member of staff) said he doesn't want to lock John up as he has been very honest. He said preventing his visitor coming in is senseless. He pointed out that we have never done things this way in the Unit before and we shouldn't start now. Davy (member of staff) said they are being asked to look in

174

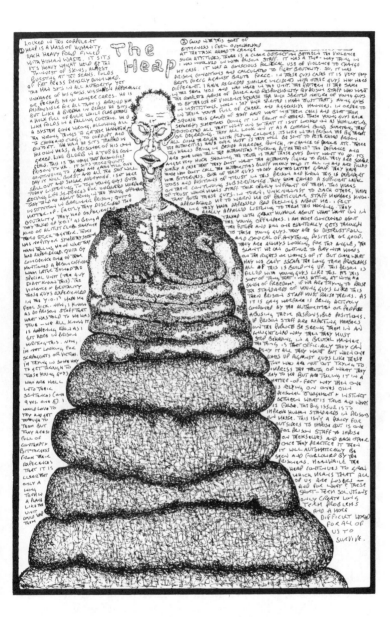

The Heap

① LOCKED IN THIS COMPLETE HEAP IS A MASS OF HUMANITY. EACH HEAVY FOLD FILLED WITH HUMAN WASTE. IT SITS. IT'S HEAVY WEIGHT HELD BY THE THINNEST OF SKINS, ALMOST BURSTING AT THE SEAMS. FOLDS OF FAT PRESS DENSELY DOWNWARD. THIS HEAP SITS IN ALL AUTHORITY YET UNAWARE OF HIS GROSS, WISHING APPEARANCE OR PERHAPS HE NO LONGER CARES. HE IS RESPONSIBLE FOR ALL THAT IS AROUND HIM BUT LIKE A BUDDHA IN REPOSE HE SITS A HULK FULL OF BULK WHILE CLAG GATHERS LIKE FOLDS IN A FALLING CURTAIN. HE IS A SYSTEM GONE WRONG, ALLOWING ALL THE WRONG THINGS TO GATHER WITHIN TO CHOKE AND CLOG TO CORRUPT AND DISTORT. HE MAY BE SITS TRAPPED IN HIS OWN MESS, A PRISONER OF HIS OWN GREED, LIKE BLURB IN A TUBE HE CONGEALS. THIS IS THE IMAGE THAT PASSES MY PRISON TOUR... IT'S INTRIGUING, CONTINUING TO GROW AND GROW, ONE DAY IT WILL BURST AND SMOTHER ALL. I SAT HERE TODAY LISTENING TO TWO YOUNG GUYS SERVING LIFE SENTENCES TO THE YOUNG OFFENDER THEY TOLD ME ABOUT BEING IN THE INSTITUTION IN BARLINNIE PRISON; QUITE MATTER-OF-FACTLY THEY DESCRIBED THE BRUTALITY THEY HAD EXPERIENCED. THEY TALKED OF YO-1 AS BEING A KIND OF ELITIST CLUB. SURELY WE WERE STUCK TOGETHER. THERE WAS NO PITY OR SYMPATHY. IT WAS THEM TELLING ME OF WHAT HAD SURFACED. QUITE A COINCIDENCE ONE OF THEM MENTIONED A PRISON OFFICER WHO LATER JOINED THE SPECIAL UNIT (THE GUY DIDN'T KNOW THIS). THE VIOLENCE & BRUTALITY THESE GUYS EXPERIENCED IN THE Y.O.I. MADE ME FEEL SICK. NOW, I KNOW AS NO PRISON STAFF THAT WHAT WAS TOLD TO ME WAS TRUE — WE ALL KNOW IT IS HAPPENING AND AS I SIT HERE IN PRISON WRITING THIS. NOW, I'M NOT LOOKING FOR SCAPEGOATS OR VICTIMS. I'M TRYING IN SOME WAY TO GET THROUGH TO THESE YOUNG GUYS WHO ARE HELL BENT INTO THEIR SENTENCES (AND 9 YES, ONE 8) I WOULD LOVE TO TRY AND GET THROUGH TO THEM BUT THEY ALSO SO FULL OF CONTEMPT & BITTERNESS FROM THEIR EXPERIENCES THAT IT IS CLEAR THAT ONLY A LONG TERM IN A PLACE LIKE THE UNIT COULD HELP THEM.

② FACED WITH THIS SORT OF BITTERNESS I FEEL OVERWHELMED AT THE TASK AHEAD TO CHANGE SUCH ATTITUDES. THERE IS A CLEAR DISTINCTION BETWEEN THE VIOLENCE I WAS INVOLVED IN WITH PRISON STAFF. IT WAS A TWO-WAY THING IN MY CASE. IT WAS A CONSCIOUS POLITICAL USE OF VIOLENCE TO CHANGE PRISON CONDITIONS AND CALCULATED TO FIGHT BRUTALITY. SO, IT WAS BRUTE FORCE AGAINST BRUTE FORCE. IN THESE GUYS CASES IT IS VERY VERY DIFFERENT. I HAVE RECORDED SIMILAR INCIDENTS WITH OTHER GUYS WHO HAVE IN THE SAME YO1 AND WHO USED IN THE UNIT. THE PATTERN IS THE SAME THE COMPLETE ABUSE OF POWER AND RESPONSIBILITY BY PRISON STAFF WHO WANT TO BY THE USE OF VIOLENCE SQUASH THE HIGH SPIRITED NATURE OF YOUNG GUYS IN INSTITUTIONS. WHEN I SAY HIGH SPIRITED I MEAN JUST THAT; YOUNG GUYS IN THEIR YOUTH FULL OF CHEEK AND AGGRESSIVE MANNERS, IN ORDER TO SQUASH THIS GANGS OF STAFF HAVE WENT WITH THEIR CELLS AND BEAT THEM SEVERELY, SOMETIMES DOING IT IN FRONT OF OTHERS. THESE YOUNG GUYS ARE DISTURBED BY ALL THAT WHAT GOES ON THAT IT ISN'T LOOKED ON AS HUMILIATING OR DEGRADING. THEY ALL LOOK ON IT AS A COMMON BOND. SOMEHOW, THEY ALL COME THROUGH WITH FLYING COLOURS. IT'S LIKE WITH PRISON THE BIG THREAT THE AUTHORITIES HAVE OVER MOST IS THEY WILL BE SENT TO PETERHEAD PRISON. THIS MEANS BEING IN SENIOR HARDCORE BUNCH, IN CHANGE OF AREAS ETC. THERE ARE SOME WHO TELL THE AUTHORITIES FUCKING OFF THE TRUTH THE DEFIANCE AND ANGER VERY MUCH SHOWING. THE TRUTH IS THAT THESE GUYS DON'T WANT TO GO. IT'S SIMPLY A CASE THAT THEY DON'T WANT THE AUTHORITY FIGURE TO FEEL THEY ARE SCARED, THOSE WHO DON'T CALL THE AUTHORITIES BLUFF MERELY END IT ALL AND ARE FILLED WITH BITTERNESS. FOR THESE GUYS TODAY AS IN THIS LATTER GROUP. THEY HAVE JOBS AND POSITIONS OF TRUST IN THE PRISON AND KNOW THIS IS PART OF SUBSERVIENCE, THE ORDERLY UPFRONT OF THEM. THIS YEARS OF MISTRUST WHICH STAFF THEM TURN. UNKNOWINGLY TO EACH OTHER, HAVE THAT BOTH THESE GUYS APPROACHED ME TO WARN ME OF PARTICULAR STAFF MEMBERS KNOWING REALLY APPALLED LISTENING TO. I EXPRESSED BAD FEELINGS ABOUT ME. I FELT TALKED WITH GREAT HUMOUR ABOUT WHAT THAT GUY IN THE YOUNG OFFENDERS. I AM MORE CONCERNED ABOUT THE FUTURE AND HOW ONE EVENTUALLY GETS THROUGH TO THESE YOUNG GUYS. THEY ARE SO DISTRUSTFUL AND CYNICAL OF ANYTHING POSITIVE OR GOOD. THEY ARE ALWAYS LOOKING FOR THE ANGLE. THE SLANT WE CAN CONTINUE TO PLAY WITH WORDS ON THE RIGHTS OR WRONGS OF IT BUT GIVEN WHAT MAY WE CAN'T ESCAPE THE LONG TERM PROBLEMS ALL OF THIS IS BUILDING UP. THIS PRISON IS FILLED WITH YOUNG GUYS LIKE THIS. IT'S THIS SORT OF THING THAT I WAS SITTING WITH WITH A CASE OF FREEDOM. IF WE ARE TRYING TO RAISE THE STANDARDS OF YOUNG GUYS LIKE THIS THEN PRISON STAFF MUST RAISE THEIRS. AS IT IS GANG WARFARE IS BEING ACTIVELY CONDONED BY THE AUTHORITIES OR PEOPLE ABUSING THEIR RESPONSIBLE POSITIONS. IF PRISON STAFF ARE WANTING INMATES WHO PUBLIC TO BE SEEING THEM IN AN ENLIGHTENED WAY THEY MUST STOP BEHAVING IN A BRUTAL MANNER. THE THING IS THAT OFFICIALLY THEY CAN PLAY IT ALL THEY WANT BUT WHEN ONE IS UP AGAINST GUYS LIKE THESE WHO WHO ARE NOT JUST TRYING TO IMPRESS THE TRUTH OF WHAT THEY SAY TO ME BUT ARE TELLING IT IN A MATTER-OF-FACT WAY THEN ONE IS RELYING ON ONES OWN PERSONAL JUDGEMENT & INSTINCT BETWEEN WHAT IS TRUE AND WHAT IS FALSE. THE BIG ISSUE IS TO IMPROVE HUMAN STANDARDS IN PRISONS WHOLESALE. THIS ISN'T A POLICY FOR OUTSIDERS TO IMPOSE BUT IS ONE FOR PRISON STAFF TO IMPOSE ON THEMSELVES AND ON EACH OTHER. ONCE THEY PRACTICE IT THEN IT WILL AUTOMATICALLY BE SEEN AND FOLLOWED BY THE PRISONERS. MEANWHILE THE HEAP CONTINUES TO GROW WHICH MEANS THAT ALL OF US ARE LOSERS — AND FOR WHAT? THESE SHORT-TERM SOLUTIONS ONLY CREATE LONG TERM PROBLEMS AND A MORE DIFFICULT WORLD FOR ALL OF US TO SURVIVE.

on John every fifteen minutes and this is no good. The Governor kept falling back on his statement that he is getting directives from the Department.

Mr Meikle came to the prison tonight. The staff asked that he come to the Unit and see them. Meikle asked to speak to Wattie and it lasted till 10pm so I have no idea how it went.

14th SEPTEMBER '77
This morning Malky opened my door and came in. He said the meeting with Meikle and the staff took place and the Governor sat silent throughout. It seems Meikle said that he understands the staff aren't happy at locking John up and went on to explain that he has to be seen to be doing something. He said he is trying to look at things for the good of the Unit... He asked that visitors be restricted to family and official, those we know but no ex-prisoners or rag-tags, whatever that may mean. He said it's best if John is kept locked up and not seen to be mixing with other prisoners so that accusations of his being pressured cannot be levelled at us. Staff said they can't have this for too long and Meikle agreed saying it wouldn't be allowed to drag on. Meikle said he isn't going to hammer the Unit or be repressive. He has had to answer eighty odd enquiries since Monday, and these were outwith the official ones... Meikle asked the staff how much Larry's being in the shadow of Jimmy Boyle, with the book and other things, brought this on. The staff dispelled this saying it had little bearing on the matter. Meikle asked if Larry could be called a Unit success.

Malky said he got the impression Meikle wanted the whole thing to cool off and that he wasn't interested in repercussions. Malky said he didn't seem to be interested in Larry's death.

14th SEPTEMBER '77 (pm)
The days have become so jumbled it's hard to keep track of the time. The police came in this afternoon and went in to speak to John. He made a very honest statement to them.

They said they weren't sure there would be any charges, saying it would be up to the Procurator Fiscal.

It is my view that the Department are having to be very careful here as they could be accused of making Larry's end inevitable. They offered him no alternative to the drugs. When speaking to Peter (Whatmore) he asked me what could have been done to prevent this happening to Larry. I told him that as far as I was concerned, a lot could have been done. Larry wasn't given any hope and so he took the drugs. It is my view that Larry could have been offered a realistic future but the Department policy towards guys in our position is so horrific that they leave no alternative.

The newspapers had wide coverage of Larry. His family are asking for an Inquiry into how drugs were smuggled into the prison and the press are having a go at us...

15th SEPTEMBER '77

My sleep was restless. I had a dream. I found myself in Peterhead after being transferred from the Unit. I was in the main prison yard surrounded by enemies. Standing nearby but seemingly out of the prison stood Ben. I turned to him saying, 'I'm all alone Ben.'

The door was unlocked and I went into the yard and did my exercises. I felt absolutely drained and bone-weary but forced myself to complete my exercises. Having done so I felt much better. The front page of the *Daily Record* had a story and a big photo of Daphne, a prison visitor, standing in his prison cell. It advertised an exposé on the inner secrets of the Special Unit — Drugs and Sex. All of us felt sick at this. We sat chatting about it and there was doom on the faces of all the staff.

On seeing it the Governor turned a whiter shade of pale. Meikle phoned him to say that he would like a breakdown of all the female visitors we have had and our relationship with them.

The Governor called a meeting when he returned from lunch. He said that Meikle had been on the phone to say that the press in England have been on to him and that it looks as though they are out to do a hatchet job on us.

Jenny (Unit visitor) phoned Harry Ewing and had a re-assuring talk with him about the Unit. It isn't going to close but there will be changes. He said the *Record* had been on to him about the allegations being made by Larry's brother and he told them its up to them whether they print it or not. He said Bruce Millan had been on to him earlier and said he would back him all the way whatever he does. No matter what way it goes things are pretty black but I am going to hang on in there as long as I possibly can. There have been times today when I've felt like screaming — even right now.

Tonight BBC television announced the police know how the drugs got in and have interviewed a prisoner. It says the papers are at the Crown Office for a decision. I went to see John and he is looking very drawn. Jim (ex-Unit staff member) came in tonight and was obviously shocked at Larry's death. He told me that some staff in the main prison hospital wing are rubbing their hands with joy and making snide remarks. Another member of staff said some of the remarks they're making are disgusting.

I had some nice letters from people reading my book.

16th SEPTEMBER '77

This morning I wakened and immediately wanted to pull the covers over my head and blot out what the day ahead was bringing. Despite this I dragged myself out feeling physically exhausted and started doing my exercises. Later I collected a pile of mail but left it aside to go see the morning papers. The *Daily Record* had it all: Larrys mother and sister talking about our being allowed girlfriends, sex, and how I had given Larry a bottle of whisky for his Christmas. They went on and on about how lax the Unit is. I don't know what they are trying to do but it does nothing for their dead son. They state they don't want others to die the same way Larry did but the truth is Larry loved the drugs.

The staff were all jittery and soon after the Governor came in he received a phonecall from Meikle. He called a meeting and announced that he had been given a directive from the Department that no female visitors will be allowed in our cells during visiting time, and that all visits will be supervised from today. This brought another heated debate with all of us arguing that Meikle in taking this action is justifying the allegations.

Malky called a staff meeting and requested that local members of the SPOA be present. Staff want to take legal action against the Winters family and demanded that the Governor get on to Meikle and tell him that by making radical changes in the visiting conditions he is accusing the staff of negligence and prejudicing any legal action they may take. The Governor by this time was shaking and licking a dry mouth. He got on to Meikle in the presence of Malky and Bob and was surprised when Meikle relented and said the visiting should return to what it was but for our own safety we should initiate some supervisory measure and we agreed to this. Malky and Bob will visit the SPOA lawyer. The whole thing has been getting wide coverage on TV, radio and in the press.

The police were in this afternoon and took away most of Larry's correspondence as the Procurator Fiscal has asked for it. I was really sick at this as some of the letters may be incriminating.

Due to the intensity of events during the day all of us seem to have forgotten John. There is also a lot of bitterness against Larry's family as we all feel that they should know better. It is very tense indeed but tonight Denis, Peter, J.L. and I sat speaking and comments such as 'I'm going to ask for Parole on medical grounds' and 'I wish I was a non-smoking, teetotal poof who hated drugs' to 'Do you think we're being victimised?' had us in hysterical laughter — more out of nerves than anything else.

Teddy Taylor has entered the controversy and is calling for an Inquiry. I got masses of mail today containing good responses to the book.

Mosta
Malta

Dear Jimmy Boyle,

I expect you've received quite a few letters from strangers since you wrote your autobiography "A Sense of Freedom"?

When I first saw it displayed in a Valetta bookshop, my thoughts were far from charitable. Like you, I'm from the West of Scotland and I too have a working class background and I was three quarters way through writing my own autobiography.

But I bought your book, albeit grudgingly, and was on the bus going home when I read the dedication. I was moved to tears.

This isn't the first prison book I've read but the others were 'soft shoe shuffles'. Yours was a vigorous highland fling. It isn't the kind of book one enjoys. But I despaired of you, laughed with you, cried for you and finally cared about you. Most of all I am so very very grateful to you for articulating the frustrations and humiliations of prison life. With me, this is a personal gratitude because two boys whom I love dearly are in prison at the moment.

They are my brothers George and James, (Jim), who hailed from a wee place called Hardgate which is near Duncocher which is near Clydebank. (Glasgow boys used to meet me in the dancing and say 'I'd lumber you only I'm frightened I'll miss the last stagecoach!) Our George is serving that most sadistically named sentence 'Her Majesty's Pleasure' in the Butlins of the Bampots known as Carstairs. My other brother, Jim, 'the baby', is serving a life sentence in Peterhead for Murder.

Unlike you we weren't brought up in a slum area. We had an estate (a council estate) to play in. So when George and Jim 'went wrong' local people condemned them, as did judges, as animals etc.

Hadn't they lived in a spotless home and didn't they have a mother who was respected by everyone as a hard working church going woman. Moreover their stepfather had been an N.C.O. during the war and came from a family 'a cut above ours'.

But the inside of our home was a 'socially deprived area'. From the minute we were infiltrated by my stepfather there was no happiness in our home. The boys were aged 11 years and 9 years and they'd come in from school and my stepfather would shout "Get those hands washed on the double". They'd march to the bathroom single file giggling and he (my stepfather) would shout louder.

Eventually as the boys got older – Jim got off the hook a little and George became the prime target. It was "Get those hands out of your pocket when you address my wife" or "How dare you sit on the sink in my home". Then he teased "You know what you are?" and poor George was something different every day. Once my stepfather said "You're a poof". None of us knew what the hell a 'poof' was so we at least got a laugh out of that one. But as you can imagine it wasn't really funny. Getting this mental bullying day in day out wasn't all George got. He was also the only one in our home who got physical punishment because we all ran and he was too proud for that. My mother who, like yours, was naturally kind and gentle, would nevertheless explode every so often and I've seen George's arse bleeding when I finally plucked up the courage to take the belt away from her. He was asked about bruises in school once, and said he fell. He began drinking and staying out all nights as an adolescent and when he returned home one night my stepfather wouldn't let him in and he said "Your mother says you are no longer her son". It wasn't even true but we only found out later.

By then George, who was working as a coal carrier, got fed up walking about covered in dust with nowhere to sleep so he and a mate tried to rob the post office. George went in and asked the assistant for the money but he said "Away home George or I'll tell your mother", so George went out and told his pal (the lookout). Drawing himself up to his full height (4ft.) the pal said "Get back in and demand it". So back he went and she was in the back room. George jumped over the counter intending to grab the money but the girl screamed so he ran out empty handed. He and his pal decided to make their getaway to England – on foot! They'd actually reached Clydebank when they were arrested. Had they been students it would have been looked on as a silly prank but they got Borstal.

Your book is a ray of hope for people like my brothers and a revelation to those who have never been inside. May you go from strength to strength. Actually I could have gone on reading when I reached the end of it. My daughter whose taste in literature is very different to mine, felt the same way. So I feel you have a future as an author.

Kindest Regards.

Mary

Greenford
Middlesex UB 8QJ

Dear Mr Boyle,

I have just finished reading your autobiography "A Sense of Freedom". To say that I am impressed is indeed an understatement. Perhaps the greatest compliment I can pay is the the following request.

I run a small school for adolescents who have been deemed by the Authority to be in need of special education under the heading of maladjustment. You would recognise many of your school mates amongst my students. I would very much like your permission to tape the book for my kids to hear. We would play it over at our morning Assembly. Needless to say it

*would not be used anywhere else and please believe
me not as an "awful warning" – rather the reverse –
to show how someone with spirit and, as you so
generously admit, a little help from his "friends",
can win through in the end.*

   My I wish you every success in the future.

*Yours Sincerely
Headmaster*

*Ballarat, Vic. 3350
Australia.*

Dear Jimmie,

   *I have just read your book 'A Sense of Fredom' and
I have the feeling a word of support from the other
end of the world would be the decent thing to offer,
seeing I got such of lot from it. It occurred to me you
might have suffered a bit from writing your life story.
I hope not. May your effort bring about the desired
reform you have been working for.*

   *There were many things in the book I very much
admired – let me mention a few. First of all it was
beautiful to read of your love for your Mother and the
grand things you had to say about her. She too had
great courage and a deep love for you. As you said she
was a wonderful person and I have joined with you in
offering a little prayer for her.*

   *How correct you are in laying the cause of the
problems of many young people at the feet of the
society in which we live. Too many of us do little to
bring about change, but you cetainly never gave up. I
was touched by your desire to help others and if
possible prevent others from suffering as you did. At
times you didn't think much of yourself but all the
time the goodness deep down in you came to the
surface and it was great to see you were able to
accept the goodness in others – even those you*

183

regarded as your enemies, before we came to the end of the story. I enjoyed your thoughts on Community (p. 252), some day I hope to write more on that theme. Too often we give in when the going gets tough but you always came back, still seeking an alternative way of living and you found enough courage to change heart and accept, even value humanity, when so many had been opposed to you. How many times did you call yourself an animal and deep down there was a humanity so warm and genuine that surged to great heights whenever you were allowed to be human.

Jimmie there is still much for you to do for yourself and others. No man can help others better than the one that has had a taste of all sides. You are not proposing theories but Truths, derived from personal experience. You could not possibly have a more powerful message.

I write primarily to encourage you to KEEP ON, first for yourself and secondly for others. It is possible your life story will return you material satisfaction – good luck to you if it does, but there is a more valuable satisfaction which I feel you are more interested in, the good you wish to others. I hope you will never lose sight of that.

Jimmie we will probably never meet but that doesn't matter. I salute you and congratulate you with all my heart. You probably made many mistakes in your life but you did one mighty deed for all of us when you wrote 'A Sense of Freedom'.

I would like to be allowed to call myself 'an admiring friend'.

Very Sincerely Yours,
Catholic Priest

London SW6

Dear Jimmy,
  I have just read "A Sense of Freedom" and am writing to tell you that I found it extremely moving.
  As a solicitor I have several times acted for prisoners who have been extremely violent while in prison here in England. While I always sympathised with the fact that they suffer an extremely repressive regime I never fully understood their need to fight back. But what they said to me fits in exactly with the feelings that you write about so clearly in your book, that in some situations you have to fight or you have nothing. As a result of reading your book I feel I can understand their situation much better. No doubt this is the same for all who read your book and that is why it is so important that it was written and published.
                          Yours Sincerely
                          Solicitor

Saughtonhall Terrace
Edinburgh

Dear Jimmy,
  I've just read your book, can I just say how much I enjoyed it, it's left me a bit stunned. I'm a bit like yourself, I've been in and out of homes since I was eleven, I'm now 21, the point is, reading your book made me see what I've done to my parents and friends, its no good really, going out to try and make a name for yourself as a hard man, or a great crook, the bit is you do get caught in the end, no matter what! Your book really put the shits up me in parts, and in others made me cry, can you imagine if my mates seen me? When reading the book I sat and thought of the grief you must have caused your wife and family, that's that position I'm in now. I've

185

thought very hard about what you have described in your book, how you feel, what you've lost, can I just say I was out last night, got really pissed, had a great chance to be financially better off, but thought about what you said and declined. The book itself has, and will, make me think twice before I do anything stupid again.

Thanks a lot
Ronald

Geneva

Jimmy Boyle
FOR YOUR NIGHTS
AND DAYS OF FEAR
I SEND LOVE.
Dougal

Dear Jimmy Boyle,
I saw you on the news tonight and I could hardly believe it. You see, I've just read your brilliant book "A Sense of Freedom", and I never imagined you like you are! I thought you'd be really old and horrid! I cried practically the whole way through your book, but as I'm only 15 I can't do anything about penal reform I would if I could. I hope you don't mind me writing to you, but I loved your book so much that I'm going to study it for my 'O' Grades in English. I'm glad you're happier now and can have visitors. I live in Edinburgh and I often pass the Courts in Royal Mile, and its hard to imagine anything 'real' happening there. I think that the Special Unit is a very good idea, but it was probably better before your two friends left. I pray that you'll be free soon to see your children, and I wish you good luck in everything.
I hope you don't mind my writing,
Good luck
P.S. Please write another book soon, I loved the last one. Thank you.

51 Stronend Road
Glasgow

Hello Jimmy
    its been a long time since I last saw you I hope you
are keeping allright Im sorry about how things went
for you at the start as you had it tough well jimmy I
read your book it was some book you came through it
hard I saw you on the TV news it was good to see you I
have seen all the Boys over the South side as I go over
to Tuckers Bar sometimes well jimmy about me I
have been in and out of hospitals about a dozen times
and had shock treatment quite a few times well
jimmy its not much of a life at the moment I am
staying up in possil with my Ma she is 77 years old
and I have to look after her if it wasn't for her I would
be away down in England for a job well jimmy you
must have quite a lot of pals but I thought I would
write to you as I never write much tell everyone I was
asking for them I will close now jimmy hoping you
get out in the near future
                                    from wee Tam

Glenburn,
Paisley

Dear Jimmy
    I'm writing this letter to you after reading your
book A Sense of Freedom it was very interesting to
see how another "Con" lived his life in jail. I'm only
nineteen years old but have already done A/School,
Borstal, Detention and YO's in Bar, Glenochil YO',
Saughton YO's. So your book made me some
interesting reading and put some ideas clear in my
head like it isn't all that glamourours to have a name
or reputation as it only falls back on you as you have
shown. I would very much like to speak to you so as to
see the person you are and come to terms with you in

a frank talk as maybe your book has put others down. I don't really see it as a deterrant to my self as you said in the book you picked your way as I pick mine.

Well Jimmy I hope this letter reaches you if not then maybe I'll meet you some day myself (S/Unit). My Mum worries a lot about me and like youself I love her very much but give her the same patter as you (I'll never get in trouble again Ma) but always seem to do. Why I do I don't know maybe it is born in me like yourself Jimmy. I'm not sure it may take me the same road as yourself before I find out (Jimmy I do not know only God) Some day you'll go free (I hope) Maybe that day I'll start my lifer who knows but I hope not. Many people say your just biding your time soon you'll be a lifer I hope to God not Jimmy as from your book I seem to have the very same attitude (I'm doing life so what have I got to lose 'nothing' only what I have lost "my life"). Well Jimmy I have hard times myself nothing to boast about as I've not done my full stretch yet so hoping you can give me a little assurance against a life sentence then I would be most grateful. I don't know if you have many letters like this but reading from your book and of some things you've done it was a certainty I was destined to follow in your foot steps if I hadn't read your book or if you hadn't got it published so thanking you on a little help and God Bless you for giving me something to think about God Bless Jimmy
Cheers

Yours Sincerely

Ware
Hertfordshire

Dear Mr. Boyle,
I have just finished reading your book "A Sense of Freedom". I thought your book was good and

188

interesting because it made me feel that I never want to go to prison myself.

A member of staff gave me your book to read and another boy has also read it. I am at a Community Home because I used to steal things. In 1974 this home changed from an Approved School to a Community Home. We get on well with the staff generally and call them by their first names. I also went to Latchmere House which is a Remand Home and has high fences around it. At Latchmere House we were locked up for many hours a day. It was not as bad as the places you describe in your book.

I am writing this letter to see if you can give me any advice at all about keeping out of trouble. Are you writing any more books about your life?

I know you have a lot to do, but hope that you can write back to me.

Yours Sincerely

17th SEPTEMBER '77

This morning I lay awake with my mind in a turmoil and asking myself why? Why must I be subjected to this intense psychological pressure? I feel threatened as never before. I realise the gravity of the whole thing. It's not so much the Unit closing, it's more to do with my losing access to the things that are keeping me alive. There is a part of me that knows if I come through this then I'll survive anything. The amount of pressure on is almost crushing.

I sat with Wattie in my cell. He is sick at Larry's family for making these kinds of statements. I was telling him that Peter Whatmore looked worried. Wattie said he knows Peter will be under pressure for having Larry on so many drugs and went on to say that none of them want to bring out the dosage Larry was getting in Perth and Inverness as it was illegal and unethical. Wattie said he mentioned this to Meikle when he was through at the Department. Meikle said he was worried about this but didn't think it would be necessary for people to look back that far. Meikle was the

Governor of Perth at the time. I can remember the drugs Larry was getting in Inverness and it was unbelievable when one saw the amount.

Tom McGrath had a piece in the *Glasgow Herald* about sex and drugs in prison, saying that homosexuality and hard drugs are prevalent and people should understand this. It was a good piece.

I walked up and down the yard this morning and thought of Larry. The finality of death is awesome. I thought of him lying there and wondered if the spiritual side of him continued? I thought of McCaig's *Poem For A Goodbye*.

> The elements which
> Made me from our encounter rich
> Cannot be uncreated; there is no
> Chaos whose informality
> Can cancel, so,
> The ritual of your presence, even gone away.

5th OCTOBER '77

Tom Melville phoned to ask Wattie when our non-censored mail was introduced. He said that Bruce Millan was reading my book and when he came to this part in the book he phoned up to ask the question. Tom was in a panic and suggested to Wattie that Alex Stephen was at that particular meeting. Wattie agreed. This isn't true as the Minutes of the Community meeting show. It's this whole civil service game of throwing it onto someone else instead of fully explaining the truth. I'm sure Bruce Millan would accept it. Tom was saying it has been question after question from the Secretary of State since the whole thing blew up.

Teddy Taylor was on the news a few minutes ago saying he's been sent a letter from an ex-Unit prisoner supporting the fact that drugs, drink and prostitutes go into the place. It is reported to be an anonymous leter.

15th OCTOBER '77

Devil this life of anguish and pain as I sit here locked in this world of forbidden fruits. Each twist and turn, each breath and sigh, each look and laugh — monitored.

Delicately I move on tiptoes — afraid to arouse the emotions of the masses who browse sombrely in the false security of silent containment. Eyes reversed, I look into the matter of their minds searching for signs of consciousness. God, it's frightening, long dark corridors with doors shuttered and bolted to keep out all areas of understanding and sensitivity. Tears, heavy with sorrow, roll from the eyeballs to wash away the dust of time.

Look at them, spread all over the world, self-opinionated bastards they condemn others from a base of ferociously insensitive ignorance. Shallow minds, all but blind, they beat their breasts in self-righteous hypocrisy. Long bony fingers point in my direction 'Him! Him! Him!' they chant accusingly. He bears the mark of Cain, the wrongdoer, the leopard with the branded spots.

Shit, thick and brown with a high fibre content, masses of body waste rubbed into their faces in the hope of fertilizing their brains. Numb, dumb and blunt, they lift one leg and then the other, each limb dim as it stumbles unintelligently on. Blisters on the heel, water on the brain – a mere pinprick could start a flood! Fucking idiots! Pools of pain swim in my soul seeking areas of joy to drown in or that's what it feels like. Leaden lifebelts are thrown my way but sink heavily to the bottom and they call themselves friends, huh! Bastards! Cast off your masks of deception! I scream into the echo-chamber of my soul. Para-fucking-noia is looking over your shoulder and seeing yourself — dogs experience it when they chase their tails. It's like popping air bubbles into your own veins, they soon burst.

17th OCTOBER '77
Tonight the media have announced the date for the Fatal Accident Inquiry into Larry's death. It will be in Glasgow High Court Building on 28 November. The media are already turning it into a circus by stating there will be the tightest security ever mounted. . . it really is shitty.

191

18th OCTOBER '77

The Governor came in. He sent a member of staff to tell us that Meikle and Melville will be visiting the Unit to speak to the staff at 10am. We (the prisoners) were locked up during this meeting. They informed the staff that at 3pm yesterday they had been given authority by the Secretary of State to start in Internal Inquiry. They were seeing ex-staff and ex-prisoners from other prisons. They will return here in three weeks to see the staff and prisoners here. Meikle apparently said that anyone giving evidence would not be liable to disciplinary action if anything is found to be wrong. This is not a witchhunt. He feels that three weeks should cover interviews and two weeks to write up the report to put to Millan. He said the Unit won't close but if the Inquiry reveals areas that should be tightened or restricted then that will happen.

27th OCTOBER '77

I've been sitting here thinking that I seem to spend these days of crises with every part of me alert and expectant, apprehensively anticipating the next move or blow to come our way. I stood in front of the mirror, looking at myself in the shadowy light as I pissed in the chamber pot and thought to myself 'Christ, you can't keep this up much longer'. A weariness overtook me with this silent admission but almost as quickly I reinforced it with a surge of inner strength. I can't afford myself the weakness of relaxation. I seem to spend my days searching faces, listening to phrases and feeling all the underlying tensions as they expand and contract inside each individual. I try to strengthen their vulnerable areas and give them support.

30th OCTOBER '77

Meikle and Melville came in. J.L. was interviewed by them. I was taken in. Meikle informed me that his Inquiry is separate from the public one into the cause of death. He said if during the interview I admit to having a few beers then I won't be put on a disciplinary charge as this is a fact finding survey.

192

He said that allegations have been made by people who know the inner running of the Unit and that part is factual but some of them relate to sex, drugs and drink being in the place. He would like to know the truth of this. He asked about sex and I told him I had never had sex with anyone. I didn't know of anyone else who did either. He asked if it was possible to have it. I told him irregular checks were made by staff during the visits and though it was possible it was unlikely. He asked if I knew of any prostitutes who had come in. I told him I didn't. He moved on to drugs and asked if I'd known of any being smuggled in. I told him we had one incident with Larry in the medical office and John on a visit. I reminded him that drugs, particularly where Larry was concerned were a worry to some of us. He asked me about drink and I told him I had never heard of drink being in the Unit. He pointed out that Rab had admitted this in a recent newspaper interview. I replied that I didn't know of it. . . We left off at lunch with him saying he would like to finish me off on Monday or Tuesday.

I spoke to John when he came out from his interview. He was pretty open with them on the whole incident and told them the Unit had done a lot for him. When asked by Meikle if there should be any changes he replied no and went on to explain that only fools like him will make mistakes like this but this shouldn't detract from the genuine people in the place. John felt his meeting with them went well.

1st NOVEMBER '77

Denis (prisoner) called a meeting this morning. He pointed out that he is concerned at the way this Internal Inquiry is being handled. He said Meikle is asking questions that have nothing to do with the specific allegations being made. He is aware of the way in which past interviews between staff and Prison Department have been distorted and Denis wanted to know if Meikle would come across to the Community meeting at the end of this Inquiry to discuss the Unit problems with us. He said that all of us want an opportunity to talk to him about the place outside of the allegations and we have shown full co-operation with them over this Internal Inquiry and would like them to do the same. This was immediately seconded and everyone supported it. The Governor was asked to speak to Meikle about it.

The reply to Teddy Taylor from Bruce Millan was flashed on the radio news this morning. It stated that no evidence of sex or drink in the Unit had been found but that visits were such that it could have been possible. Staff are now supervising visits. It went on to say that letters would remain unopened but that parcels would be opened and use of the phone has been stopped. The statement refused to mention drugs saying it will be subject to the Public Inquiry. It pointed out that all ex-prisoners would be stopped from visiting the Unit. The Secretary of State said he believes the Unit is a success and the measures taken are simply to safeguard it and people should see it in that context.

That vile little man Teddy Taylor was interviewed and spat his political venom saying he was happy with the result. Millan said it would be foolish to make a final decision on the Unit at this stage as this is only an interim report due to public concern shown.

The Crown Office people came in to interview us. They asked me about sex and I denied sex taking place. They asked me about drink and I denied this. They asked about drugs and I told them about Larry...

The TV news this evening gave wide coverage to Millan's statement. Norman Buchan MP was interviewed. He said he was disturbed that ex-Unit prisoners were barred from going back to visit the Unit. He was worried about the restrictions and searches imposed as they would be harmful to the Unit and the relationship between people there. He was also very concerned about the intention to change the staff.

2nd NOVEMBER '77
The Governor said he would like to speak to me this morning. He said that Meikle wanted my sculpture stored

194

and I looked at him puzzled. I asked what he meant. He was hesitant then said my sculpture work displayed in the hall had to be crated and stored. I really took offence at this and asked what possible reason could he give for this? He said he wasn't sure so I told him that this was not on and is out of order... He told me to cool it and he would try to get more information.

6th NOVEMBER '77
This afternoon John had a visit from his mother. I went in for a spell and she seemed worried. I felt sorry for her as she reminded me of my own mother and the pain I had caused her. She said to John, 'I suppose if you live in hell you get used to it.'

John and I sat speaking. We discussed prison and the humiliation of it. John said he would love to murder a screw as he hates them all. He told me of how when he was in the main prison system he used to follow one round the gallery, watch when no-one was about and have a dummy run as though he was going to do him in. He said he lies and thinks of doing a screw in and said this with lots of anger. I told him I used to do the same thing but now I no longer blame them for my present position. I asked him if we are going to be losers all our lives? I reminded him how we come into prison and think nothing about it. We went on to discuss his getting out and thinking only of returning to villainy. John replied that this is the only alternative to a lousy job.

8th NOVEMBER '77
There was a piece in *The Guardian* about Russ Kerr MP and his group meeting Harry Ewing. It made some scathing remarks at Millan taking the Inquiry out of Harry Ewing's hands. It goes on to say that the group want to know about Larry being on an excessive amount of drugs prior to coming to the Unit, while in Inverness he was getting amounts that were unethical...

At the Community meeting... the Governor said he brought up the sculpture issue with Meikle and said it is really only floor space he is on about and if some of the pieces occupying floor space can be moved that would be fine. He wanted me to know that he isn't discouraging me from sculpting. There was a barrage of questions from different people in the meeting saying the question of arranging furniture is for the Community. The Governor replied that the Controller if he so wishes can over-ride this.

10th NOVEMBER '77
This afternoon I went in to be interviewed by Meikle and Melville...Meikle asked the number of times I had been out to Edinburgh. I told him three... After he had finished with his questions I told him I'd like to mention one or two things. I had been told that he was asking about my role in the Unit, was I too dominating a personality, was I giving them problems? He said the reason he was asking these questions of people he was interviewing was because whenever the Unit was mentioned it was always my name that was there. He said no matter what journalist is writing about the Unit they mention me. He said he wanted people in the Unit's opinion of this, the fact that I get more attention than anyone else, more mail etc. The reply he got from everyone was that I have always been constructive and helpful to people in adjusting to the Unit and have alleviated violence on a number of occasions. He said he is clear on this. I said I cannot separate this from the storage of my sculpture and wondered whether this was a practical way of eliminating that 'dominant personality'. He said he sent a letter here with two points in it referring to me: 1) To ask me to keep a list of all sculptures I have done, where they went to, the price they were sold at and the donated ones. 2) The Governor should discuss with me and Wattie the possibility of finding alternative space for the free standing sculptures on plinths.

24th NOVEMBER '77
...I received a copy of a letter that Willie Hamilton MP had from Harry Ewing on the question of the Unit '...It

196

would be difficult, and inappropriate, to attempt to reproduce all aspects of the Unit throughout the prison system. It has been successful in dealing with prisoners who have proved exceptionally difficult to handle elsewhere in the system, but relatively few prisoners come into this category. More so, its methods are very costly, particularly in terms of staff, as we could not hope to reproduce them on a wide scale. The lessons of the Unit have nevertheless been absorbed and similar concepts — especially the estab- lishment of a close staff/inmate relationship — are applied elsewhere in the Scottish prison system to a considerably greater extent than is sometimes recognised. . .'

What sheer hypocrisy!

29th NOVEMBER '77

I worked till early this morning then went to bed feeling extremely tired. It was 2.20am. I expected to fall asleep but no. My mind was active as I kept thinking about the Public Inquiry. There is something frustrating about tossing and turning in bed within a locked room.

The van arrived and we all went into it; John, Peter and I, along with the staff; some of whom were witnesses. Once out of the prison I tried to look through the frosted windows of the van into the foggy streets. There have been many changes in the east end of the city since I was last there. Most of the houses have been knocked down. Here I was seeing cars, buses, shops and buildings — districts that I have known in the past. It was strange not to feel any emotional tugs. It is as though I have decided never to live here when I get out. It wasn't like other times when I was out or my past thoughts when I would long for the streets that I knew. I felt that I was never going back.

We arrived at the High Court after passing through the Gorbals. A TV camera was outside the court. On going into the building and along the white tiled corridors I felt all the old associations of the place hitting me. I'd have given anything not to be here and yet there was value in being exposed to it. The three of us were locked in a cell for fifteen minutes. The police returned to split us into separate cells. He couldn't understand why and I asked him who issued the order. He said our Governor did. I shook my head with disgust at the silly bastard as all he can think of is negative decisions. I walked up and down then across: six paces one way, three the other. Cold white tiles surrounded me. The steel lined door was covered with prisoner's pasts. There was a small square opening of six inches. I stood looking out of it thinking how familiar it all was. I felt desperately sick and spiritually weakened just standing there. I felt so helpless. I began a long walk around the cell singing 'The House of the Rising Sun'. Before very long I was singing it in a wailing fashion... it was soul singing, it was the pain I was feeling. It was a very powerful experience. How many people have stood here full of fear and all the other feelings that go with a High Court appearance I thought. I wondered how many condemned men had stood on this spot.

In order to get to the court I had to walk up stairs that led into the dock, through this and into the witness box. Once there I looked up to see many of the Unit staff sitting in a row with the Governor sitting alone in the bench in front of them. I wanted to call a meeting and demand why he authorised us being put into separate cells. The Sheriff swore me in. I was asked to give some indication of Larry's state of mind. I said he was in good form the night before. The family lawyer asked if I thought it unlikely that Larry took his own life? 'Absolutely,' I replied. With this I vanished back down the stairs.

The verdict was that Larry died as a result of the ingestion of regurgitated matter while he was subconscious as a result of an overdose of the barbiturate Tuinal. The Tuinal was brought in by John from the Douglas Inch Clinic. He thought that Larry's death might have been avoided by strict searching of prisoners returning from escorted visits. He made no recommendation on this but went on to say that those in charge of the Special Unit should, with a view to preventing further incidents of a like nature in the future, consider how searches of prisoners and visitors are consistent with the aims and methods of the Special Unit. I was left in no doubt that it was one big cover up from start to finish. They really have the system sewn up.

Apart from the publicity, it is all over. There are fears in all of us that Meikle and Co. will institute changes far beyond the ones at present but we will have to wait and see. Meikle, Melville and two other officials were present at the Hearing...

My play went on in London last night...

30th NOVEMBER '77
Press coverage on the Public Inquiry was pretty factual... Russ Kerr MP, challenged Teddy Taylor MP to spend two days in the Unit (Christ, as if we don't have enough on our plates) with him saying he would change his views over that period. Teddy Taylor, is quoted as saying the Unit has become 'a left-wing cause celèbre'...

3rd DECEMBER '77
...This afternoon I had a visit from Sarah Trevelyan. We had lunch together. We discussed many things concerning prisons and her involvement in the Control Unit in English prisons. She works in Inverness at the moment as a doctor in a hospital there. I thoroughly enjoyed speaking with her as we are really into similar things... I showed Sarah round the Unit and soon afterwards she left.

5th DECEMBER '77
...Word came through today saying John is to be moved out of the Unit. It was a phonecall to the Governor from Meikle saying John was to be transferred to the main prison, that he will be put into circulation there even though they don't as yet know if charges will be preferred against him.

12th DECEMBER '77
I am sitting here feeling worn and tired. Late this afternoon I felt like coming up to my bed but instead made some brown bread. Tonight as I watched the TV news I thought

'Christ, the same old blurb and here I am still in this torment of a place'.

Spent tonight buried in deep personal pain trying to deal with this confinement. I am getting many thoughts on the subject, in fact, I seem to be getting pummelled by them. Tonight on Panorama I watched a film on human rights. It concerned political prisoners and had the slogan 'Minds in Prison'. I felt pangs of torment and wanted to shout out what I was feeling. Listening to some of these prisoners, men of high intelligence who are deep-thinking with strong beliefs I thought of how unjust the world is. People in my world aren't brought up to think such things, they are merely the donkeys of our society. Only now, after having travelled a road of misery, am I able to think and believe.

I listened to this man from Amnesty International speak of 'subtle psychological torture' and how difficult it is to detect. I know exactly what he means. I want to sit here into the early hours and try to write what I feel, but how can I? How is it possible to write about this pain, this searing stab that slices through my mind, body and soul? It is not a pain that touches one specific part, it permeates every little fibre in every little way.

22nd DECEMBER '77

Wattie got on to John Renton, General Secretary, SPOA, to ask him about the Internal Inquiry Report. Renton said he hadn't heard anything but can't see much coming out of it. He said if there are any radical changes then they (SPOA) will have to be consulted. He told Wattie that Millan is expected to make a statement about the Internal Inquiry when Parliament re-sits, or during the recess. It will only concern the report and not give details. I had an international telegram from Hollywood:

Feel passionately your story warrants the greater freedom and integrity of film over ephemeral television both for Glasgow relevance and international significance with which Sean Connery concurs. Best Regards, Murray Grigor

I managed to speak to Stephanie. She has been trying to get hold of me to say that two guys want to visit me on Tuesday to discuss a film... She said that Murray Grigor is asking me to stall any decision for as long as I possibly can. The fact is he's had a brief chat with Connery but nothing of any significance so in actual fact the telegram is a piece of bullshit.

29th DECEMBER '77
This morning I completed my exercises then collected my mail. There was a letter from the OU giving results of my exams. I had passed... I was glad to have it done with. James and Patricia came in this morning. We came up to my cell where we made coffee and sat watching TV. It was great being with them. They stayed all the way through to 4pm. Jimmy Mac (staff member) on passing congratulated me on my exam results. James and Patricia asked what this meant so I gave an explanation. Patricia immediately responded, 'Does that mean you get home early?'... Both of them worked hard on my typewriter, writing me small letters...

Harry brought my three visitors in. We had a good chat about the proposed film. Peter MacDougall was very good, a right earthy guy. Frank Roddam and Ted Childs were also good. We discussed the social and political implications of the whole thing and it was very interesting. They feel they could do a TV film almost immediately but that a feature film may be more profitable and worthwhile. They want to come and see me, get to know me before doing the film. They were sensitive to everything and went out of their way to ensure that they weren't putting pressure on me. I liked them as people. I told them I would have to think things over and though the vibes were good tonight we will have to wait and see. Peter is staying up for the New Year and would like to return next week...

2nd JANUARY '78
3.14am. I've been wakened for over an hour, am irritable and restless. The Radio Clyde disc jockey is speaking to

people in their homes via telephone. I get the atmosphere of home parties from it. Pop music is blasting in my ears and I marvel at radio and how it must comfort lonely people. It's almost as though its reassuring me I'm not alone. 3.55 am. One of these days I won't be 'still here'. It's amazing how difficult I find it to think of myself being any-where else. I read some Yevtushenko poetry:

> Consider that city — it is your past,
> wherein you scarcely ever managed to laugh,
> now raging through the streets, now sunk in self,
> between your insurrections and your calms.

> You wanted life and gave it all your strength,
> but, sullenly spurning everything alive,
> this slum of a city suffocated you
> with the dreary weight of its architecture.

12th JANUARY '78

... There was a piece in the new SPOA Magazine on the Minutes of the Whitley Council meeting 16th Aug. '77. On the staffing changes proposed it says: 'The staff side could not accept that lack of volunteers was the cause of the proposed changes and that this was not a manoeuvre on the part of the Department to change the regime of the Unit. It went on to say:
2) The staff side expressed their concern over the impend-ing publication of a book by an inmate of the Special Unit and pressed for an assurance that should an officer be the subject of any defamation in the book he would be given financial assistance by the Secretary of State to pursue a civil action in court.

The Official Side said that it was not aware of any financial authority that would make such assistance but undertook to make enquiries to see whether it was possible.

They then go on to discuss the Inverness Segregation Unit. They are all pressing for it to be put back into action.

18th JANUARY '78

This morning the weather was icy and bitterly cold when I

ran round. I mentally worked on the new sculpture and must admit that I'm getting tremendous satisfaction from working once again.

After my exercises I collected my mail and the papers. There were letters from readers of my book saying how it affected them... they were really nice. I collected my tools and went outside to work on my ideas of early morning. It was cold and icy but I enjoyed working. It's amazing to watch the piece come alive as I work on it. It all began to click and I thought of the process that creates a piece of sculpture like this. First I start out with a rough block of stone and let my hammer and chisel eat into it. I have a vague idea of what I want to do but it's so distant that there's no real form in mind. As I go on it starts to come together, this is what happened this morning. I went into a sort of 'high' and the whole process happened like magic. I fused with the stone. I tasted freedom as I never have before. I thought of how physical freedom is only one part of it. Many, many people on the outside won't have tasted this sort of freedom... David Markham came in this afternoon and we had a good discussion. I was very pleased with his visit. He seems a genuine guy. We had a very open and frank discussion on things. He is the sort of person one can speak to on this level. I am delighted that he is willing to try and get things moving for me as I desperately feel the need for something of this sort to be done. It's strange that as he talked about it I felt guilty of doing something for myself and promoting my case for getting out. I never get into this with visitors who come into the Unit and so talking about it on this very open and subjective level was quite strange and difficult...

19th JANUARY '78
I went outside in the falling snow to work. I lost myself in the piece and felt very close to it. The sculpture has come together so well. It was constantly getting covered in falling snow as I worked and so I had to get a tin of hot water to throw over it so that the snow would melt as it landed. I'm sure people walking into the building must have thought

203

me mad. I can understand this but then if they knew what I was experiencing they would see how sane I am. In this extremely cold winter morning I am glowing, the cold and discomfort didn't matter, it didn't exist. I was spiritually connected to the stone I was working on...

22nd JANUARY '78
All the snow had melted and I could see the ground. It made the yard look naked. I missed the snow. I mentally worked on the piece of stone that stood dressed and ready for sculpting. Peter (prisoner) came out and told me there was something in The *Sunday Post* on the Unit. I thought 'God, don't say all this is going to come up again?' It read SPECIAL UNIT — NEW ROW IS BREWING and went on to say that staff in the main prison are saying procedures haven't been tightened at all and that prisoners there are upset about this. This garbage is such that I suddenly understand why the Scottish people are years behind other countries... I had a walk in the yard with Peter this afternoon. He told me he constantly feels the hammer is going to fall on the place and is always waiting for it. I asked him if this is because of the newspaper report and he said it is. I felt sorry for him. He admitted that he knows he is insecure anyway but he is very nervous about the future of the Unit.

28th JANUARY '78
Getting up I went down to collect my mail and the newspapers. The headline in *The Scotsman* concerned the Unit. It went on to say how an all-party deputation led by Alick Buchanan-Smith and Norman Buchan, MPs, are intending to approach Bruce Millan on the matter to advise him not to make any severe restrictions on the Unit that would damage the atmosphere of the place. In the *Glasgow Herald* there was a headline on the opening of the Inverness Cages with the Department quoted as saying it would be 'humane containment'. The first article pleased me while the second filled me with anger...

There was a letter from Stephanie saying she has sent

204

£2000 (royalties) to the Trust Fund with more to come in April and May...

31st JANUARY '78
Ken came in and we sat chatting till the Governor came in with Lord Longford. We were introduced. I took him around the Unit. He said he had come as a result of reading my book, that he had enjoyed it and thought he'd like to see the Unit as a result... Afterwards we had a meeting with plenty of staff present. We talked about violence and prisoners giving problems in the system and then he asked if we have any questions for him. Denis asked him what he was doing here. Lord Longford explained what he had previously told me and added that he is a peer, that he and MPs can get into places like this... Denis said the present situation is that he has to sit and listen to someone like him when he can't listen to friends or make new friends because of the stupid restrictions imposed on us. Lord L. stated that no one need sit and listen or stay in the meeting if they didn't want to. Denis said that wasn't the point he was trying to make. We explained to Lord L. and asked him to use some muscle to get these restrictions taken off.

The Governor sitting there was beginning to get worried and strained looking, his face beet red, his hands kept going to his face and rubbing it. Throughout the meeting the Governor kept having to leave for phone calls. I went out to make coffee when he came round saying the press are outside in their hoards, hundreds of them and saying he had better get on to the SIO. He was in a bloody panic. On my return Ken was telling Longford that if Millan is restrictive in his final statement the staff will walk out of the Unit as they see this sort of thing being destructive, making conditions intolerable to work in. We discussed the press first telling him the situation was that we were 'hot press' and he was 'hot press' so it would be to the good if he played it cool on leaving.

He told me that he would have recommended my book as Book of the Year to The Times but he did with Wally Probyns as he knew him. I told him I'd prefer it through merit rather than through the 'Pals Act.'

Overall I found him a much harder person than I expected. He was a shrewd, hard politician and for some reason I didn't expect someone this hard. I felt from what I'd heard, read and seen of him on TV, that he was a naive person. But no. He knows what he is doing when he is dealing with the media and this makes it all the worse as he seems impervious to the destructive way the media use him, particularly the way he has given Myra Hindley the 'kiss of death'. This concerned me and is totally different from what I expected. When he left there was only one reporter and photographer.

3rd FEBRUARY '78

The *Glasgow Herald* has a statement from Bruce Millan saying that there were no plans to bring the Cages back into use. He said he wants to make it clear there is no intention of placing prisoners in the Cages at this time. The article and Millan's statement waffles quite a bit... parts stating that the only recent action taken by the Prisons Department has been to identify certain prisoners who would be suitable for transfer should this be judged necessary. No such transfer can be made without Millan's authority and this will be given only if and when it is necessary.

The Scotsman's article about the Cages is pretty detailed and hardhitting. It's obvious that the politicians have been put on the spot with this one — the Department have inadvertantly put them on to it.

I find it ludicrous that the Secretary of State can make this sort of statement when the Inverness staff have been told that Brian Hosie and Sinclair will be transferred from Peterhead to Inverness Cages this Tuesday. They have been told this officially. Millan is saying that he will decide who goes there when in fact the Regulation for the Inverness Segregation Unit recently circulated states quite clearly that Governors will select prisoners for the Cages...

The Regulations for the Segregation Unit, Inverness, state there is a ratio of:

1 prisoner: 1 Senior Officer plus 3 Officers.

More than 1 prisoner: 1 Senior Officer plus 4 Officers.

The rules for the running of the Cages are pretty horrific with no provision for the standard of behaviour of staff in it. Everything is geared towards controlling the prisoner. No mixing with other prisoners in their Cages. It is quite clear that the Department and prison staff have learned nothing from past experiences there.

13th FEBRUARY '78

After being called to the phone to speak to Tom Melville the Governor returned to say that Millan was making his statement to the press (on the outcome of the Internal Inquiry). I asked him if anything had been said and he replied that Radio Clyde phoned to ask for a comment on a Grade 3 Governor being put into the Unit. He said he was surprised. This meant that we all had to sit and wait for news. I thought it appalling that here we were not knowing the contents of the statement and Radio Clyde phoning to tell us.

The staff immediately went off to the SPOA to complain. The local branch tried to get hold of their Executive Committee but they were at the Department. Ken got hold of the Governor to ask him to phone the Department and ask them the content of the statement. He did and Tom Melville is supposed to have said that he doesn't know as it's being released from London. The Governor bolted.

Throughout the early evening, news programmes gave their own versions but they still leave it rather vague as I write this. There is reference to ex-Unit inmates being allowed to visit, that the allegation of drink, sex, and drugs were largely unsubstantiated. Millan was interviewed and I didn't like the way he was coming across about the Unit developing away from what was intended. He said we are now getting it back to what it was meant to be in 1973. He said he no longer sees the Unit as experimental as it has a lot to offer the system. He said it is too early to see it expanded. He said there have been irregularities within the Unit but we don't get what he means on the news reports.

The big thing they seem to be hitting on is the change of

Governor and how a more senior man is being drafted in as soon as possible. They are at great pains to stress that it is no reflection on the present Governor or past governors. I don't know if the present one has the savvy to appreciate that this puts him in a bad light...

14th FEBRUARY '78
Ken caught hold of me saying he went to the Governor telling him that although he didn't particularly admire his performance in here, the way he's been treated in this Report is abominable as he has been made the scapegoat. Ken told him the Department have a lot to answer for as they have put him and other governors into this post without proper training or briefing. He said it was out of order putting this statement out without telling him. The Governor became shaky at this and told Ken he had been told 'in confidence' something about it but nothing about the rest of the statement. Ken was saying that as he spoke to him it was pathetic as he didn't want to criticise the Department. This is what happens to these guys, they become so 'tied' to the Department through blind loyalty that they cannot offer constructive criticism. The Department seems to call for total obedience. Ken said the Governor remarked that it may be in the new Governor's best interests for him to get out as soon as possible.

11th FEBRUARY '78
A letter put by the staff brought the following reply:

> *1. As previously indicated this meeting will be attended by staff only and the request that the inmates should be present is refused.*
> *2. The agenda for this meeting is as follows: 'Confirmation and amplification of the Secretary of State's instructions concerning the future operation of the Unit'.*
> *3. As the meeting is being convened to relay the Secretary of State's instructions for the future operation of the Unit the presence of representatives*

of the local branch of the SPOA or its Executive would not be appropriate. All members of staff should be informed accordingly.

T. Melville.

Ken called a meeting of all the staff about the Department not meeting the measures they had asked for. He got 100% support from the staff saying they shouldn't go into the meeting without SPOA reps.

23rd FEBRUARY '78

I've been asked by Jim Taylor, administrator of the ARC to lend them the Jarrow Heads as they are having a visit from the Duke of Edinburgh on 3rd March. I went down to the new Governor (Grade 3) and asked him about this. He collared me and took me into his office saying he wanted to speak to me.

We sat chatting and at first it was generalities but soon I could see through the facade. He told me that his phone has been ringing all night — his superiors, far above the Prisons Dept. and they were asking him to brief him on the issue of prisoners not having a say in the running of the Unit. He said that his superiors were saying 'this place' is causing too much trouble and would be as well closed down. He said he mentioned this to the staff this morning saying there are people who want it closed. He said if it becomes too troublesome then it could be closed as he knows that Millan was thinking this way at one point, and did I know this? I told him on the contrary I know Millan has always wanted it opened. He said he told his superiors this morning that if they closed the Unit and put the other inmates to other prisons where they would be absorbed, where could they put Jimmy Boyle? He asked me where I could be put. I replied saying I could simply be put into any prison and that's all there was to it. He was playing a game here and I was letting him know that I knew his game.

Tonight John Renton was interviewed on radio and television. He said that when he went into the Working Party meeting this afternoon he was confronted with a document

209

by Department officials and he understands that the document was given to Unit staff on Tuesday. He said the first point in the document meant that the points in it could not be negotiated and this wasn't on. He said that the document, contrary to what the Secretary of State said last week, certainly ended the democratic concept of the Unit. He said it was full of intolerable changes. He said they didn't get past the first post as he walked out of the meeting.

25th MAY '78

Dear Sarah,

Thanks for that lovely card, it touched me deeply.
I must tell you about this dream I had last week.
It was a sunny day here and I met Max in the yard where he was wearing a light grey suit and tie. I felt his attitude towards me was condescending and so I confronted him with this. On doing so he swiftly turned his head to the side as though not wanting to discuss it. I moved to face him saying we must speak. He agreed and we walked towards my cell but at the foot of the stairs I turned to say something to him when this force surging from the pit of my stomach pushed up to the top of my mouth. A gush of blood, thick and powerful, came out of the top gum and covered Max, causing him to throw up his hands and shout 'I'm stained' and then quickly, as though to cover up what he said 'My suit is stained'. I fell to the floor with a feeling of death approaching, and from nowhere you appeared and knelt by my side and held my head trying to stop the flow of blood. You looked with anguish at Max, 'Get an ambulance he's dying'. For some unknown reason I was dragged into a cold cell in the main prison. It was filled with debris and pools of filthy water. You sat with my head on your lap this time imploring a screw, standing at the door clutching a baton, to get me out to hospital. He said he couldn't without orders from his superiors. You kept insisting you were a doctor, but still he wouldn't

210

budge. At points many recognisable faces appeared in front of me and I told you I was going to die. You told me that I wasn't but the eyes said different. I ended up lying on a stretcher in a hospital with people moving around but no one interested in my situation. At this point I wakened...

Yes, it is okay for you to bring Sam... I look forward to meeting him. Till such times as I see you, look after your soul.

17th JUNE '78

This morning I wakened with the sun shining through the bars on the window. 'I'm going out of here,' I thought. Pretended to be numb to it. Getting up I went downstairs, collected my mail and looked at the official paper lying on the Governor's desk.

I went out to the yard. Ken came out and sat beside me. He immediately told me that he sees this being played very close and straight as it is vitally important for the November Parole Review. In many ways it's like starting all over again, building up trust in another area but within me there is a frustration as I look at Ken and part of me resents his 'prison officer' attitude.

My own feelings are a mixture of frustration as I would like to do some simple things like go into a shop and purchase something for each of the prisoners. At the same time I look on this as a new beginning so don't want to screw it up though I hardly see going into a shop as screwing it up. My one desire is to see into the distance, to see for miles without a wall blocking the way. It is 1.15pm and I feel the excitement building up inside me. This morning when lying in the sun I kept getting this vivid image of locking myself into a room in the Arts School and killing myself so that I would never have to return to prison. It's difficult to believe that I will finally walk out of here for good one day. I know that I will. This is just the beginning.

My first impression of sitting between the two doors and watching the one open to let us into the outside world was overwhelming. There is no feeling on earth like this. To suddenly see people, cars and most important of all, wide open spaces is unbelievable. As the car drove down the approach road I felt tears about to come pouring down. I was blitzed by the movement: people, traffic, space, noise, colour and all that one could never imagine unless one had been locked away for all these years. The feelings within me were tremendous. Men stood about while their wives shopped, women stood looking into shop windows, were being served in them, and children were running around. I was being bombarded by a million little things. We met the guy at the Art School which he unlocked and showed us round. I was thrilled at seeing the Rennie MacIntosh building for the first time. I had known it since I was a child but really, was seeing it for the first time. We looked at the various exhibitions in the place; sculpture, paintings and so on. The building itself was the real work of art — quite outstanding! Later I went into a shop and bought some food. It was an Italian food store. The smell of food was fantastic. I bought Pizzas for the guys, some cheese and olive oil for myself.

All too soon we had to return...

29th JUNE '78

> *Dear Sarah,*
>
> *I find myself sitting here thinking of you, not really having anything to say but simply wishing to communicate with you. Basically, I'm interested to see and hear how things go after those rapid-fire lettes with highly inflammable content. It's strange how twists & turns lead to confrontation with areas that one thought oneself immune from.*

26th SEPTEMBER '78

Ken told me he met David and Vladimir Bukovsky last night for half an hour or so. They got on okay. They both came in at 9.30am and we had a chat in my cell. David left Bukovsky and I to talk and we discussed the dissident issue. It was enlightening and what struck me was that they

212

have a much wider base of appeal than comes across in the media. He described the conditions of prisons there, of the social conditions outside Moscow. He made the interesting observation of how the authorities there tried to beat and torture prisoners into submission but found that this made them more violent. And this meant that the society became more violent. The authorities then had to use a more subtle approach. We later joined the rest of the Community and had a lively discussion. . .

5th NOVEMBER '78
This morning I wakened early and on going downstairs found Ken and the other staff reading the *Sunday Mail*. An article by Ruth Wishart on the Cages was using excerpts from Malky's Dissertation. I thought it was an excellent piece of journalism. While doing my run I thought of the impact it would have on the Department. They would be furious. I was also interested to see the Governor's reaction. After my exercises I made some brown bread and spoke to the Governor who had just entered. He mentioned going to Springburn last night to buy a *Sunday Mail* at 11pm. He was first in the queue. He was angry at the piece, calling Ruth a silly bitch. He said he had two roles to play: community member and Governor. He said the former was spitting fucking mad — forgive the French. The second would have to wait the official response: a Disciplinary Code for Malky. I played dumb on this and remarked that Malky would be furious about the Dissertation being published and asked who did give it to Ruth Wishart? I then reminded the Governor that the Department had a copy of it, as did others. He came out defending the Department saying they would never do such a thing. . .
It was interesting to watch the Governor's dilemma here. He kept reassuring me he was against the Cages but thought this article was damaging to the prison staff. He explained that although he had to go along with the democratic decision of his Association he had let his feelings be known that he was against them. He then went on to tell me that it was him who had updated the design of

the Cages; a concrete mound for the prisoners to sit on and a small metal sheet onto the wall as a table. It made me want to vomit...

6th NOVEMBER '78
I'm just this minute back from outside — what a feeling! Wattie and Gordon came in early. I told them about the possible police presence and we agreed to play it low key. We left the prison — everything hit me, again... It was great seeing Gulliver; we stood beside and on him. A sleeping concrete giant; he is well used by the kids who play on him.

10th NOVEMBER '78
This morning I wakened and said a full decade of the rosary to my Ma. When the door opened I went to do my exercises. Afterwards I collected my mail, amongst which was a letter from Craigmillar with some photos of me on Gulliver.

In the morning papers there was news that Millan had okayed the media going in to see the Cages. I think this is a good thing though feel people won't see them as being bad after the portrayal in *The Hardman*. They will try to put them over in a humane way so I have written to Ben and Paddy Meehan asking if they will get in touch with STV and BBC to speak to them when they are shown. A Bruce Millan statement has come through as I write this. He has conceded the issue to the SPOA. The Cages are to be re-opened. What a weak shit of a man, what a tragedy. I feel sick and I know that all the prison staff will be congratulating themselves and feeling all-powerful which means they will be exerting this on the prisoners. It really is sad.

11th NOVEMBER '78
Amongst my mail was a signed copy of *To Build A Castle* by V. Bukovsky... I sat with Wattie who told me that the material was in for my Parole Review...

I am heartsick at Millan giving the okay to the Cages opening. I thought about it deeply for a while. It isn't that I

214

personally want to 'defeat' the authorities on this, it's having had the experience of that situation and knowing that it damages everyone involved. I feel bad when I think of our horrific experience there being pushed aside...

15th NOVEMBER '78
Listened to a report on the Cages issue and Ken being interviewed after his Labour Party meeting last night. He was very strong stating that the use of the Cages was unacceptable, they would cause more trouble for SPOA members and further damage prisoners. He was also widely reported in the press... I'm hoping he hasn't left himself open to breaking the Official Secrets Act...

I had a chat with Wattie and he was telling me that there was a call from the Department yesterday asking for Davy's (ex-Unit prisoner now candidate for the Cages) psychiatric report. It was put into the post by the Governor last night. I am hoping this is as a result of a detailed letter I sent Hugh Brown two weeks ago requesting he do this.

In the papers this morning the Cages feature prominently. Photographs of a Cage (in colour). The *Daily Record* and Gordon Airs (no less) were openly condemning them and the media view seemed to be unanimous on this... at least it's something.

The Governor came in this morning as we sat in the kitchen speaking about them and looking at the photographs. He leaned over and looked then remarked without mentioning the rights or wrongs of the Cages, that the table-shelf and bollard designed by him look nice...

Wattie was telling me that feelings about Ken in the main prison are running pretty high. The staff there are furious. He said there is talk that they may toss him out of the Union for disloyalty...

17th NOVEMBER '78
I sat in my cell typing when a knock came to the door. A voice said the Governor wanted to see me in his office — it was 8.45am, unusually early for him. On going down I found Wattie and Peter (staff member) sitting with him. It

all looked very strange indeed. The Governor was pure white. He opened a file and brought out a letter saying that he was hauled up to the Department yesterday and given this, and asked to account for it. The letter was the one I had sent to Ben, containing the Instructions for the Operation of the Inverness Cages and asking him to go to the BBC and STV studios with them. I also urged Ben to give his views on what like it feels to be kept in a Cage. It was returned with the words 'gone away' scribbled on it. The GPO sent it to the Department. I was now plainly in shit street. Nevertheless I pointed out to him that I would have to take the consequences but in my view I felt so strongly about the Cages that I had to do this. The Governor then said he wanted two senior staff to search my cell. I told him that first I'd like to call a Community meeting and tell the others.

I explained to everyone and there was silence amongst them. I tried to cool the situation by saying I had done wrong but I knew what the Cages are like and desperately want to stop them opening. I also respect the Community but it was a decision I made.

While in the Governors room he asked me if a member of staff had given me a photostat of the Instructions and I told him no. While my cell was being searched he called staff into his office one at a time and asked if they had given me a copy.

Later:

One of the prisoners told me that when my cell was searched he immediately thought I was going to be shanghied (transferred) so he took a knife up to his cell just in case. It is obvious that they are all feeling insecure and so I tried to tell them, tried like hell to put it into their heads that they must keep this place going at all costs and make sure it isn't looked on as a one-man show. It was hard to convince them. They felt if I went it would only be a matter of time till it closed. I felt at an utter loss on seeing this attitude. Rather than support what we were doing they were resigning themselves to its inevitable collapse which is something I don't like.

216

Sarah came in the door this evening and I left her to go to another meeting... Afterwards I returned to spend the rest of the visit time with her. I was glad she was here as it allowed me to speak the matter over with someone outside of it.

22nd NOVEMBER '78
Community meeting: The Governor produced his file of all the material relating to the Inverness Cages document I sent to Ben. He said he found a copy of letters I had from The *Sunday Times* and Ruth Wishart. He was sitting like a shaky judge on a three legged chair. He asked what everyone thought of the situation and demanded that they speak up. They did by telling him they had taken action yesterday (a meeting at which he was not present) by imposing restrictions on my mail. He said he totally agreed with this. Wattie censored my mail this morning and did so with the embarrassment of someone who knows me, and the efficiency of a prison officer. The more I get into it the more this whole process of imprisonment cripples me with humiliation and degradation. Instead of getting used to it I get more and more hurt by it.

25th NOVEMBER '78
Malky came in today and we had a chat. He is looking very well... I agree with Malky when he says that I'll get nothing out of the Department in terms of parole. And from what I gather Ewing is saying it looks like the politicians are accepting what the Department people are saying... I sat with my kids eating sweets and drinking coca cola. During this James came out jibing at Patricia saying two of her pals were debating a film of a prison with one of them saying it's Barlinnie and the other saying it's some other prison. Patricia suddenly burst into tears. James was scornful of this saying she's stupid... I felt this slice deeply into me...

4th DECEMBER '78
The Governor called a Special Meeting. He opened it by saying that we haven't seen much of him for the last two

weeks as he's been having continuous talks with the Department. He intimated that a Department person has been trying to impose the Secretary of State's Rules on him, telling him to get down here and implement them. As a result of this a personal clash has developed between them. He was accused of not 'Governing' the Unit and not obeying an order. He said he sought support from his Association and got it. They said the S.O.S. rules were shelved because of the non-negotiable tag. He went on to talk about the fears going round about another Unit Governor being broken but in this instance it wasn't the case, and more to the point had nothing at all to do with the Unit.

13th DECEMBER '78

Peter came in saying there was an announcement on the radio that the *Daily Express* in Scotland had a piece about me... It was an extremely vicious piece. The front page was covered by an article stating that the Parole Board shouldn't let me out. Inside it used pieces of my sculpture to say how terrible I am — clenched fists etc. The article regurgitates my past and has people like Teddy Taylor and Joe Black, and an un-named prison officer having a go at me. It said things like, the public are dead against me getting out... It was ferocious. It was a piece set on destroying the impartiality of the Parole Board. There is no hiding the fact that this article hurt me deeply but I tried to get beyond this to understand why? I know why, and its to do with people like me trying to gain status as human beings. It's because I've come to symbolise change, and in fact it shows the hysteria of some people in certain positions who are afraid of the implications of my changing and the apparent success of the Unit.

15th DECEMBER '78

The *Express* had a follow up article quoting from Joe Black saying that he agreed with the *Express* article and that if my behaviour is exemplary after fifteen years I should be let out. The editorial said I should be kept in to the last second of the last day of my fifteen years...

21st DECEMBER '78

The headlines in the paper blazed that Davy is to be sent to Inverness. I felt sick and terribly sad. There are clear inconsistencies. On the one hand we are being told a Committee will be set up to decide who goes into the Cages, and today it states Millan has decided. Davy will go to the Cages for a short, sharp lesson and then be put to a long term prison to complete his sentence. What appalls me about all this is the amount of ignorance from Millan down. They have no idea what they are doing and it's all to do with short term revenge.

26th JANUARY '79

This morning after my exercises I read in the morning paper that a staff member in Inverness, a Mr Darling, was sentenced to Life Imprisonment. He had eleven years service and went to Inverness as a volunteer for duty in the Cages.

The Court of Inquiry into the dead patient in Barlinnie prison hospital has been postponed for a month, what is going on?

I was given a copy of a reply from Harry Ewing on the Cages issue:

'The Secretary of State has decided that the Inverness unit should remain an integral part of the Scottish prison system but that no prisoner will be transferred there without his personal approval. There are no 'cages' in the Unit, which comprises a number of extra large cells each divided internally by a grille which provides a measure of protection to the Unit staff. However on the instruction of the Secretary of State trials will be made to find an alternative method of providing for staff safety.'

17th FEBRUARY '79

I sussed Wattie wasn't looking too well and asked him what was wrong. He then pushed aside the papers he was working on to tell me that last Thursday when the Governor had left, a 'Staff in Confidence' envelope came in. Wattie opened it. He said he began to tick off some of the papers and came to the last one which was his own annual report. It was pretty devastating and said he did anything to avoid crisis because he is into his last year. Wattie said he couldn't believe it as it was the Governor's report to the Department about him. Wattie said on the back of the report was an official question stating, 'If the report is critical of the officer, have you informed him? If not why not?' This was left blank and the Governor hadn't mentioned it to Wattie. He said that later that afternoon he and the Governor worked on the Duty Roster but he couldn't bring himself to mention it. He said he just felt terrible and couldn't mention it to anyone. He said he did so to his wife and she immediately reacted by telling him to go to the Governor as the truth is that the Governors have constantly run from crisis.

20th FEBRUARY '79

This morning after my exercises I sat with Wattie. He seemed nervous about confronting the Governor but determined to do so.

Wattie confronted him with the report and he was at a loss. He mentioned to Wattie that he sent up a supplementary report (something unknown until now) giving an explanation as to what he meant in the report Wattie had seen. Wattie asked him what crisis he had ever dodged in here. The Governor seemingly bumbled and mumbled and stumbled his way through saying he didn't actually mean that. What he meant was that someone of Wattie's rank and service should not be in a crisis situation. Wattie reminded him this isn't what he said. The Governor replied that he would ask the Department for a copy of the supplementary report to show him. Wattie said he wants to see it but this isn't the end of it.

27th FEBRUARY '79

I had a telegram saying that Jeremy Issacs and Peter MacDougall want to visit me on Friday to discuss the film of *A Sense of Freedom*...

28th FEBRUARY '79

Darling Sarah,

It was lovely to spend that evening with you in celebration of your birth. It is a night I shall cherish for it captured all that is beautiful in life, and the fact that two people coming together can create such feelings in a setting such as this says much for the human spirit.

However, life is an ever-changing role in a series of dramas – and I feel my life has had more than its share. It would be too easy for life to be monotonous and dull. Mine is full of 'aliveness'. In saying this I don't mean that it's full of what is good in life. It means I am open to the pains of existence, and my position is unique in that I seem to be the source of so many people's fantasies. I sit here wondering if you have any idea what I am up against, of what you've put yourself in for in connecting yourself with me...

2nd MARCH '79

I made lunch for Jeremy Issacs and Peter MacDougal. Peter is now working on the script of SOF. He is now filming in his home town of Greenock. We had a long talk about the Unit, with Jeremy asking pointed questions. He is a Glasgow man. We discussed the book and Jeremy said he has talked with the people at STV... He said he had a handshake on the deal and is now going to sign up the contract. He will bring up John McKenzie, who will direct the film. He also wants to bring a quality camera man. We discussed the appalling state of Scottish television with Peter saying neither of the companies here will touch his work.

Peter and I arranged to meet on Monday to sit down and talk about the material. We all discussed the sort of pressures that would be put on us getting it off the ground. Jeremy said there will be plenty but has told the STV people that he must be given a free hand to get this thing going. He said he wants to do it his way and will handle any pressure or controversy.

4th MARCH '79

Wakened from the misery of last night into the misery of this morning — shit! It's this gut-sapping part of the situation that gets to me...feel like screaming but decide against it. I turn some lively music on and let my body shake the tiredness out of it while I put on my track suit. This works wonders for as I hit the yard I get into the rhythm of running...bastards, bastards, bastards...just let it all pour out and begin to feel distinctly better...

Quite spontaneously I made breakfast as a sort of celebration. Afterwards I walked into Larry's old cell where a pigeon now stays. I was intending to put it out. Behind the door lies Collie (new prisoner) — sudden flashback to Larry lying there. He's depressed to fuck. I sit talking to him about the pigeon and we laugh. All the while I want to tell him, 'Make it on your own kid — don't reach out'. At the end of the day it is down to him. I won't help to create illusions for him. Instead I'll help in practical ways. Perhaps I'll move a mountain for him.

1st MARCH '79

Teddy Taylor (shadow Secretary of State for Scotland) was interviewed by Ruth Wishart in the *Sunday Mail*. He admits that conditions in Peterhead are terrible but goes on to say that he wouldn't change them as people there are convicted criminals. He said he wouldn't close the Special Unit down but would see that there was not publicity about it. He would concentrate on deterrence...

9th APRIL '79

Malky, Gerry, Ken and I had a good dialogue going this morning. This afternoon the Governor phoned the Department to tell us that John Maxton, the prospective Labour candidate (opposing Taylor in Cathcart) was coming in later. The Department man said it was okay but would contact the political office to clear it with them. He did and was told that Maxton should contact Bruce Millan or Harry Ewing. He did, getting hold of Bruce Millan who told him the Unit is a very sensitive area and that he should leave it alone but if Taylor mentioned the Unit once then he has complete authority to walk straight in here. We saw this as a cop out by Millan. By coincidence Ken met an Assistant Governor from Barlinnie who told Ken he was also going to canvass for Maxton in the Cathcart district. He mentioned to Ken that the prospective Tory candidate was being shown round the main prison at this moment. Ken was pretty angry at this and is going to try to get hold of Millan at the Prime Minister's talk in Glasgow tonight.

3rd MAY '79
This morning I lay awake listening to the results of the General Election. I was delighted to see Teddy Taylor being thrown out but bitterly disappointed to see Margaret Thatcher getting in. It all makes for terrible times ahead for the poor and needy. I stayed up all night and listened, feeling moments of elation to terrible disappointment. . .

Ken came in this morning and he looked tired. We agreed that Teddy Taylor was merely a consolation prize as the general picture is bad. . . A member of staff pulled me into the surgery to ask if I'd heard anything about my parole, had the Governor spoken to me about it? I told him no. He then went on to tell me that Jack Crossley of the Sunday *Observer* had called him to say that he had it from a number of good sources that my Parole Application had been refused. It stated I would be considered again next year. He is doing an article on it this Sunday . . . My personal reaction to this is one of numbness as the way in which I've been told doesn't make it seem real. I don't know if this is delayed action. . . we'll see. One thing I do say, it is abominable that I should be told third or fourth hand.

4th MAY '79
George Younger has been appointed Secretary of State for Scotland. According to many people he seems to be an okay guy. Let's hope so.

11th MAY '79
There was a piece in the *Daily Record* on conditions in

Peterhead. Prisoners there sneaked out a letter stating that conditions in the prison are worse than the Cages and Renton of the SPOA agreed. It pointed out that prisoners are kept on solitary for a year at a time and have to eat their food off the floor.

At 11am Mr Allan came in with the Governor. He is a small man with black greying hair and a moustache. He has strong looking hands. On taking him round he listened intently. We all assembled in the TV room. He was asked by the Governor to give his views. He said he is just new to the job and to the penal system. He went on to say how he wanted to know more about the place. He emphasised to us that the previous Secretary of State had made it clear that when breaking new ground in the Unit he should take personal responsibility for it. He said the judgement as to what should be passed on to the Minister lies in the hands of the Department. He said that being civil servants they have political masters to follow and went on to say they have no idea how the new Administration is going to look on the Unit, that they are waiting to see. He was using some hardline phraseology when saying 'Your very congenial surroundings' and 'It's an airy fairy world' . . . on confronting him with this he said he is being devil's advocate or just a bureaucratic mind at work. He agreed to give us reasons for refusing anything we ask for and went on to say the communications between us and the Department would improve. He would be down on a regular basis. He made it clear his hands are tied as far as decision making is concerned.

5th JUNE '79
I spoke to Dr John Basson and he was telling me he is on the new Advisory Board for 'difficult prisoners'. This group will recommend what prisoners should go to the Cages in Inverness. He was asked to go on it along with Mr Allan. Peter Whatmore was asked and refused. I didn't get a chance to pursue this as other visitors came in to see me.

7th JUNE '79
The morning papers had articles on the STV press con-

ference stating that they are filming *A Sense of Freedom*. The *Record* continues its attempt to seem fair and grudgingly has to concede certain points about me, but very grudgingly and makes its usual negative noises. It's this whole issue of how these papers feed off crime and yet are quick to moralise. In many respects I no longer see all of this as about me, it's about people in general and the future. I am merely the vehicle in which this lesson is travelling...

8th JUNE '79
This morning I was up early and said some prayers for my Ma before the door was unlocked. I had a restless night and dreamt about rats in the Unit biting me on the chest. It was a troubled night and my brother's marriage splitting didn't help.

After my exercises I collected my mail and read the papers. A piece in the *Daily Express* quotes Joe Black, the Police Federation man appealing to the public to boycott my play... Basically, all of this reinforces that it isn't simply about me. It's the struggle between civilisation and barbarism. Guys like him in these influential positions are certainly not trying to understand the social ills that surround us. They want to state that anyone having problems is either inadequate or criminal...

Petition: James Boyle: 5/73
            Life
Please inform the prisoner in reply to his petition of 7 May that the copy letter from the then Governor of Inverness Prison dated 9 February to the Governor of the Special Unit at that time which was sent to him and various members of the staff at the Special Unit, was submitted to the Serious Crime Squad of Strathclyde in an attempt to establish how this letter came to be sent to them.

Exhaustive enquiries were carried out by the police in Glasgow, Edinburgh and Inverness in an effort to establish the identity of the person(s) who sent the letter. They were unable however on the evidence available to them to establish who sent the letters and their investigations proved inconclusive. The Department is most concerned that a letter from one Governor to another Governor should have found its way into the hands of an unauthorised person, who was able to send copies to James Boyle and to members of the Unit staff; this is clearly in breach of the rules and regulations governing official correspondence and every effort will be made to ensure that there is not a repetition of this breach.

With regard to the rumours which he has heard about the alleged attitude of some members of the Department towards his work, these are completely without foundation and like all rumours should be ignored. His undoubted talent as a sculptor is recognised by the Department and any publicity which has been attributed to him in this respect will in no way harm the concept of the Special Unit.

16th JUNE '79
... This afternoon I had a visit from Peter MacDougall who has just completed the first draft of the script. He described it to me in detail saying he will send a copy when it is typed. We then went on to discuss what direction it will take... We talked about many things related to it and Peter opened to talk about himself. It was a really good talk and I thoroughly enjoyed it. We find ourselves very much on the same level.

17th JUNE '79
The morning was beautiful and so we sat in the sun.

As we sat there the Governor came in the door with Ken. They both looked glum and the Governor veered off into the Unit as Ken approached us. He told us that he was being transferred to Lowmoss Prison. He said that he met the Governor in the car park by chance and he invited Ken to his office in the main prison. Ken said that the Governor then told him about the transfer. He stated to Ken that it is his (the Governor's) doing as they just don't get on. He said he has had this in mind for some months now. He accused Ken of not being loyal to him, saying that he isn't committed to the Unit and that he is here only for his own personal gain. Ken accused the Governor of wanting a staff of arselickers. The Governor told Ken he wants him out as soon as possible.

We are all shocked at this but immediately set about looking for ways to overcome it...

This afternoon was shadowed by the news of Ken.

18th JUNE '79
This morning I was up early and out doing my exercises. Ken came in after 8am and we had a talk. He was in to sort out material as he was defending three staff colleagues in the main prison who were on Disciplinary charges. He is very controlled and thinks the whole thing is a set-up. Most of us suspect the same. Wattie came in quite shaky but settled. He informed us that he has known since Tuesday but couldn't tell anyone.

SPECIAL MEETING:
MONDAY 18.6.79
Staff Member: Said that there was news yesterday of Ken being transferred from the Unit. He said that he wants to express his fears about someone being posted out of here, and asks what the reasons behind the posting are. He says that he sees Ken as a figurehead in the Unit and finds it strange that while we still have not resolved our problems with the (new) Working Party, and our future, Ken is being moved out. He said that the other thing that bothers him is where he is left if Ken can be treated like this. He asked if it means that if he confronts or questions the Governor he might be moved. He said that if that is the case then there are serious implications for everyone in the Unit.
Staff Member: Said that he feels exactly the same way.
New Prisoner Said that he would like to ask where this leaves him. He said that Walter is due to go soon (retire), Jimmy Boyle may go soon

too and Ken is to be transferred. He said that we will be having new staff and new prisoners and there will be no experienced people.

New Prisoner: Said that he was going to ask the same question.

Staff Member: Said that the reasons for the transfer are not what worry him. He said that staff in the Unit are all volunteers and should therefore be allowed to continue working here as long as they want to...

Staff Member Said that he has made the point before now that there is no way that he will go back to working in the traditional system so he is out of a job if he is posted like Ken. He said that people like Ken have given a lot to the place and it is wrong to cast them aside.

Staff Member: Asked if it's a case that staff are subject to being posted...

Wattie: Said that although there is nothing in the original Working Party Report to cover this it has been the unwritten rule that whilst staff still operate under general staff rules they were allowed to stay in the Unit unless they asked to leave. He said that if it's the case that Ken's activities upset people they should be saying so, both to Ken and the Community so that it can be discussed.

Staff Member: Said that although he is leaving the Unit he believes in it. He said that since Larry died we had had a set of rules, a Working Party on the Unit whose sole function is to ensure the implication of these rules, a visit from 2 of the 7 Working Party members (a farce) and now the transfer of Ken. He said that he sees a disturbing pattern in all this and he is afraid for the future of the Unit. He said that if he had not already asked to leave the Unit he would have if the rules had been implemented. He said this place will never work if these rules are implemented. . .

Prisoner: Said that he can see the whole concept of the Unit being destroyed if this goes through.

Governor: Said he will not talk about the transfer itself as Ken has the right to appeal and will no doubt exercise that right. He said that the reasons for the transfer are his and his alone. He said that he had made the decision, not the Department, although they had granted his request to transfer Ken. He said that he gets a lot of satisfaction from the fact that the fears expressed today are the same fears he has to take into consideration when he makes such a decision. He said that having gone through them all he still decided that Ken should be transferred. He said that P.C. (prisoner) used the word manipulation and that quite often managerial decisions are seen as manipulative. He said that as far as he was concerned this decision is not a manipulative one. He said that in the Unit's situation such manipulation would be destructive. He said that as far as a personality clash is concerned that any decision based on that would be a bad one. He said that if anything, he and Ken could be considered of similar personality in that they are both single minded. He said that the fear that Ken's transfer is part of a bigger game involving the implementation of the rules is groundless. He said the rules played no part in the decision he took. He said that his commitment is to the Unit document of standards, not the rules. He said that he had already expressed his fears about the possible implementation of the rules. He said that as far as staff fears about being posted if they fall out with the Governor are concerned, he has the same problem with his bosses. He said that this would not be a reason for him to recommend staff transfers. He said that everyone is aware that the Governor's role in the Unit is a split one with responsibility to both the Community and the Department.

Staff Member: Said that (the Governor) has not really answered the questions he opened the meeting with and is obviously not going to discuss the transfer although one of the fundamental principles of the Unit is that the Community discussed what affects people in it. He said that he thinks there has been some type of managerial decision which could be taken on any member of staff in the Unit, or indeed on any prisoner.

29th JUNE '79

Ken met with the man from the Department. He told Ken it was in his own interests to go back to the mainstream nursing and this the reason for his transfer. He went on to point out that Ken's annual reports were of the highest calibre and were held in the highest respect. Ken said he really opened up on him saying that Malcolm Rifkind (new Tory Minister) is alleged to have said that Ken is being transferred because he is a 'discipline problem...'

There seems to be a spate of problems in other prisons throughout Scotland. Davy (out of the Cages) is charged with two stabbings in Peterhead. Another prisoner there is charged with two stabbings and breaking a prison officer's nose, and two staff in Polmont Borstal have been suspended and one charged with theft.

7th JULY '79

In *The Scotsman* there was an article and photograph showing some Lords being installed into the Knights of the Thistle Order. It showed Lord Cameron, Lord Douglas-Home and some others who are part of the Scottish Establishment. Although Cameron sentenced me this had little to do with it. My anger is about what they represent. On another page was an article on Len Murray, General Secretary of the T.U.C. receiving an Honorary Degree at St Andrews University. I felt the same about this. All these forms of patronage make me sick as I think of all the wonderful ordinary people I know living in Glasgow, people housed in ghettoes who are doing more than any of these people. There was a photograph of the Queen and some lovely children walking in this procession and I thought of all the kids in places like Easterhouse, the Gorbals and other areas who would look just as lovely but never get the opportunities these privileged kids get. Our kids grow up to fill our penal institutions...

12th JULY '79

This morning I had trouble getting to sleep... the strain on me was considerable. I kept waiting for someone to come and tell me that my day out was off... John and I went onto a bus which took us to Duke Street. We walked to the nearest stone merchant in Gallowgate. Sarah was waiting there and it was fantastic to see her. Being with Sarah was beautiful... We walked hand in hand along Sauchiehall Street and it was fantastic...

14th JULY '79

This morning I got up quite early with Ken on my mind. Going downstairs I sat with him and the other staff. We talked about various things concerning the Unit. The newspapers came in and on the front page of *The Scotsman* was a headline about Ken: 'Barlinnie special Unit leader fights transfer'. I hope to hell it does some good.

The Governor came in and Ken sat in his office with him. The Governor wanted to see me. He read out a letter approving my 'C' category and approving my sculpture exhibition at Stirling. He also stated that I could go to the exhibition but not to the official opening. Now, I find this interesting as I didn't ask to be allowed out. It strikes me that what is happening here is that the authorities are giving me this sort of thing but at the same time putting the knife into Ken. They don't want to be seen sabotaging the Unit... On speaking to Ken he showed me a letter from the Department which stated he has to get his apeal in if he is going to but meanwhile the Governor is to continue making arrangements for his transfer and it's to be no later than 23rd July. They are going all out to railroad Ken...

Ken is really shattered as this virtually means that come what may he has only a week left in the Unit... it is brutal.

18th JULY '79
Tonight the prisoners had all their visitors in for a social evening. I had my aunt Peggy, her son Freddy and Sarah in. The Governor gave a speech assuring the visitors of the continuance of the Unit and how glad he is they are here. On finishing Sarah said she was sorry that he didn't take the opportunity to mention Ken's situation. Betty and Mrs. L. (two prisoners' mothers) came in and they had a good session with the Governor on this.

A member of the nightshift came to my door tonight. He said the Department are on the phone and want to know if I was in a pub tonight.

19th JULY '79
Ken said he was exhausted as he has been phoned all day and night by the press. He also had to write out his appeal.

In the papers this morning was a statement that I had written to a newspaper about Ken. It was front page news in the *Glasgow Herald*...there was a piece in the *Record* both of which were good...

The Governor came in and said that his phone has been going all last night with newspaper enquiries... He informed me that he had the press onto him about a letter that I had written and there was talk from the Department

232

about desciplining me. He went on to say that he would not take any formal action as emotions were running high at the moment.

Sarah came in tonight and was very shaken. Two *Record* reporters had been to the hospital to see her and had later come to her house. She spoke to them giving her views of the Unit, told them she wouldn't discuss her personal life or relationship with me.

21st JULY '79
This morning I wakened feeling slightly relieved. Lying on the floor I looked up at the ceiling for a spell and felt the weight coming onto me. What would today bring.

Sarah's father — John Trevelyan — was in the papers telling them what a charming chap I was! He seems to have handled them with some skill. Wattie came in this morning and we sat chatting. He was of the opinion that Ken's transfer would not have been reversed unless Jesus Christ himself intervened. . . I told Wattie that Ken had a moving letter from Larry's mother expressing sorrow about his transfer and reminding him of the contribution he had made to Larry's short and tragic life in the Unit.

Ken came in looking taut and worn. He had a briefcase with him to empty his desk. I was at a loss what to do and sat with him as he did this. Both of us were on the verge of tears and felt literally crushed. Agonised thoughts raced through my head — what are they doing to this wonderful man? We talked in a rambling fashion, both of us finding it extremely difficult to say anything to each other. We held an informal Community meeting and most of us were near to tears. Wattie opened the meeting by saying how despicably he thought Ken had been treated and that he personally wanted Ken to know that it had been great for him (Wattie) to have worked with him over the years. Ken talked but the tears were at surface level and his throat choked. He said we must continue to fight and that we mustn't let them frighten us off because of what was happening to him. I eventually spoke telling Ken that our testament to him will be solidarity of the Community, the continuance of the Unit and the satisfaction that the prison authorities will never regain credibility amongst any of us in the Unit. The meeting became too much for Ken and he abruptly left.

His exit left an emptiness, a hollowness and tremendous feeling of loss. This man has been tremendous in his caring for individuals. The establishment have condoned his downfall in their deceitful and calculated way and yet have left no tangible evidence of having done so. Anyone like Ken who tries to do something effective within the system is soon squeezed out and rendered impotent.

And now as I sit here I can let the loss of Ken enter into me. I want to feel his going to the full. I want to soak up every last bit of it so that I never forget what the small-minded, petty men of this world are capable of. It is a pyrrhic victory for them. I am trying to imagine how someone like Ken will survive in this outpost they have sent him to.

23rd JULY '79
Wattie was telling me that the Chief Officer in Barlinnie prison called him over to his office this morning to tell him that his Governor had instructed that under no circumstances is Ken Murray to step over the gate at Barlinnie prison. Also, that they are not providing transport to Ken's new post where he was to start this morning. . .

24th JULY '79
This morning I wakened feeling pretty beat but got up and went down for my exercises. . . I met one of the staff who told me that I am on the front page of the morning paper — saying that I am to be transferred to Dungavel prison. The adrenalin started pumping. There is a feeling of strength and sureness almost as though I'd been expecting them to make some sort of move towards me.

On seeing the article I was quite untouched by it, PRISON MOVE FOR BOYLE and the leader inside was headed GOOD MOVE FOR ALL. The general feeling in the Unit was that a deal had been done and I was being moved. The article stated that their sources had made it clear that the transfer was on and only needed clearance from the Scottish Secretary. It stated 'sooner rather than later'. Immediately I took steps to prepare myself mentally for such an eventuality, giving thought to the sort of pressure I would come under in the main system. I felt calm knowing that I could cope with whatever came my way.

This evening Malcolm Rifkind, Scottish Under Secretary responsible for prisons was interviewed on television by David Scott about the Unit and the continuing allegations. Rifkind was nervous and didn't handle the inverview very well.

This evening Sarah came in and was apprehensive about the impending transfer. She was expecting me to be moved at any time. I replayed the interview and the part where it was stated that I wouldn't be moved. It eased her some.

26th JULY '79

I was shown a copy of last night's *Evening Times* where Harry Ewing is reported as saying the Unit should be moved to Greenock prison, away from Barlinnie. He claimed this would benefit the work of the Unit, curb the threat of a 'personality cult' amongst prisoners, and reduce strains and jealousies affecting prisoners and prison staff in the main prison of Barlinnie. He goes on to state 'It is far too small and one person in an establishment — whom I do not propose to name — can impose his or her personality on that small establishment.' He goes on to say 'If the establishment is bigger that person must learn to live with the establishment.'

3rd AUGUST '79

> *Dear Jimmy,*
>
> *I am suffering from severe 'Unit withdrawal symptoms'. Your note was helpful in my battle to face this unreal situation. I am being treated very badly but I am fighting. It is rather ironic to discover that I have to justify the upgrading of the nursing post here. It is clear that no one considered the*

implications of the move. All the Governors have dis-
appeared and I am left trying to negotiate with an
A/G who doesn't know the time of day... I am sure
that I will eventually win but it is tough going...

30th AUGUST '79
Darling Sarah,
*   The Governor in a confidential exchange with*
Malky told him that I will be going to Edinburgh
prison but prior to going the Governor of that prison
will come through to see me. It seems that my present
Parole Application will be rejected, possibly next
month or October and will begin again the next
month – November. It seems the provisional release
date will by '82...

31st AUGUST '79
I was in the yard when the Secretary of State, George
Younger, came in followed by his minions. Wattie
introduced us and we stood speaking about my sculpture
and his love of music...

23rd SEPTEMBER '79
This morning I went downstairs to be met by the Governor
coming in. I told him that I intended raising a personal
issue with Mr Allan when he came next but thought the
Governor should know about it. I explained that Sarah
and I wanted to get married and would like to do so with
the co-operation of the Prisons Department. He was most
calm and said he was very glad we have come to this
decision, it didn't surprise him and he is delighted to assist
in any way. I told him Sarah's family and my own were
behind us. We then discussed ways in which it could be
done as I told him I'd prefer it without any publicity, if
possible.

18th OCTOBER '79
I had Jeremy and Peter in for lunch to discuss the script.
The meeting lasted three hours, was wide-ranging and very

probing. We discussed specific areas and the fact that STV is doing it and the fears they have — turning me into a star. Jeremy asked questions related to the mythology surrounding me...

24th OCTOBER '79

Darling Sarah,

Well, Mr. Allan was here today as expected. It was very much as my own sources had told me. He said that last year's Parole Application has been rejected and the new one will start almost immediately – 3rd Nov. During this period I will remain here. He stated that my paroles out will be opened up considerably next year and then mentioned the recommended minimum saying they have given a date to a guy before the recommended minimum.

I asked him about our getting married and he gave me the same thing he gave you but went on to say that he is sitting in a meeting tomorrow on this question as two more guys in Edinburgh want to get married. He suggested that I leave it for now and let the case be discussed over these two guys and he'll keep the Governor informed. I asked him what time scale he is thinking of and he said weeks. I told him we'd like to get married without any publicity and as quietly as possible and he was in agreement.

22nd NOVEMBER '79

Amazingly Mr Allan phoned the Governor today to ask him to tell me to put up a formal request to get married... My Parole Dossier came down and has to be returned to the Department by 4th Feb.

29th NOVEMBER '79

Sarah, the sheer poetry of this morning spent with you is something that all people should experience. I cherish my sensitivity as it makes me 'feel' this to the core. I love the way your presence makes me happy and full of love. I get tremendous satisfaction from

*the way we discuss things and although I totally
dislike my present circumstances I have the ability to
see that it is providing an opportunity for us to
connect in this way, despite the obvious difficulties...*

19th DECEMBER '79

The Governor came out into the yard where I was sculpting
and told me I can now go ahead and make arrangements to
marry Sarah as word has now come through, giving permission. He also told me that I will be allowed out once a
week to purchase groceries between the hours of 10am —
3pm. The Department suggested my going out on different
days. I was really bowled over by all this. I immediately
phoned Sarah and she was delighted. I cancelled another
visitor for tonight to make way for her coming in. It really
is good, good news. I am feeling tremendously strong at the
moment...

4th JANUARY '80

Sarah came in this evening shortly before Giles (Director
of Citizen's Theatre). She had been to Balfron (village) to
lodge the marriage papers and it felt good. Giles came in
and we had a good meal and discussion on the Unit, our
marriage and other things. It was a lovely evening.

5th JANUARY '80

Lay in bed feeling a virus bad in me but eventually got up. I
felt shaky and stuffy.

Wattie was in and we wished each other happy new year.
He seemed snappy today and we talked about his retirement being just round the corner. He seemed to be feeling
this. I asked him if he was conscious of it and he replied that
one day he just won't come into work and that will be it. He
seemed pretty pessimistic about the future of the Unit and
said that it would be good if I was moved before he went or
shortly afterwards. He said the place isn't the same.

11th JANUARY '80

Davy and I left the prison just before 10am. The weather

was dank and muggy but in no way detracted from the sheer joy of being out. It was wonderful going into the flat. Sarah and I kissed and hugged excitedly. We went shopping and I bought various articles of food and clothing. It was fantastic, utterly fantastic walking down the streets. On the one hand I felt normal, it all seemed so natural but on the other I was walking on air. I bought some clothing for the wedding day...

14th JANUARY '80
I was hit with my photograph in a front page splash: 'A taste of freedom soon for murderer Boyle'. It went on to describe informed sources as disclosing that I would be going out shopping with an escorting officer. Inevitably, it regurgitated the past. It was so unnecessary but beyond this I wondered where it came from, who released it? I could only think of someone in the main prison or the Department. I started thinking of the wedding day and how it could mean the press getting on to this. The Governor came in and I showed it to him. He was shocked and got on to Allan, at the Department. His immediate response was that it was the police, saying that the wording of the article was similar to a previous letter.

19th JANUARY '80
This afternoon Sarah came in and we spent a really good afternoon together. We discussed the arrangements for to-morrow and our visit to Father Anthony Ross. Afterwards we'll go to Margaret's for lunch (my sister-in-law). We went into the possibility of the press appearing at Balfron the day we're to be married and agreed to be diplomatic. Both of us hope they aren't as it's our day and we would hate them to be there... Sarah is being quite realistic about the day saying that in real terms getting married won't dramatically change our lives due to the physical situation of my being here. However, we will try to make it special whilst at the same time realising it won't be perfect.

20th JANUARY '80

This morning while running round the yard I thought of the day ahead and felt the freedom seep into me. Thoughts flickered through my head like a movie screen, it felt wonderful knowing that in a few hours I would be outside all of this... I thought of when I was in Borstal and one would get out like this though through my adult experience it is different; it is all for real now whereas in those days there was no belief that it was.

The day was pleasant weatherwise. We stopped at a shop down the road and I bought the Sunday papers, an insignificant action that brought me much pleasure. This was the first Sunday I've been out in thirteen years. As I went for the papers the church bells rang and it was beautiful...

We then drove to Sarah's flat... I felt excited running up the stairs. Taking the flat keys from my pocket I opened the door. Sarah walked round, not hearing me and the look of surprise on her face was funny. We warmly embraced and it was great. I scurried all over the flat like a dog looking for a bone... the happiness in both of us could be seen on our faces. We sat having a coffee. Sarah and I called her Dad and he wished us well. We went to Margaret's and had a meal... Sarah, Davy and I went to the Gorbals and into St Francis chapel. It had changed though the basic structure was the same. All the old nostalgic thoughts raced through my head; it was here that we came for candles when our electricity was cut off; and where we came for confession and had our sins cleansed away. The sheer power of the catholic church suddenly weighed on me. It was here that we kissed and embraced, almost a consummation of our marriage. I thought of my Ma, and somehow she was more real in this old building full of memories. I thought of how she would have loved to have known Sarah, of how proud she would have been of all this... We met Father Anthony Ross in his flat. We talked about various things and then the ceremony... He looked tired but there is always a spiritual liveliness about him.

From here we drove to Wilton Street and dropped Sarah off. This is the sad part of the day, the opposite of the beginning. I have to get into the frame of mind that this is only a start and that we are moving in a positive direction. Nevertheless, it is hard, very difficult. This stress is important and should not be cast aside...

I could see Sarah was feeling it and leaving her was the hardest part. It is so natural our being in the flat together, a place that holds a lot of comfort and security for us; there is a feeling of 'home'. I feel so happy with her and know it's where I should be — that day will come, it will come soon.

26th JANUARY '80

I felt sort of tense this morning but couldn't put my finger on the reason why... Sarah came in saying that a journalist, Phil Davies, from the *Sunday Mirror*, called her at midnight last night saying he knew everything about our plans to marry. He said he would do a sympathetic article. Sarah replied she had nothing to say. The journalist then told her he knew about the ceremony taking place on Friday and that Anthony Ross would be doing one privately in the flat afterwards. Obviously this guy knows everything. Sarah asked who his source was but he wouldn't say...Sarah refused to give him anything and put the phone down. Later a free-lance journalist called saying he was a friend of the previous chap and perhaps he could persuade her. She refused. Shortly afterwards they appeared at the door... This morning when she got up and went out they took a picture of her, obviously they'd been sitting there all night. Phil Davies said he isn't blackmailing her but if she doesn't speak to them they'll give her address and telephone number to all the newspapers. Sarah told him this is blackmail... All of this hit me like a ton of bricks...

It has serious implications as it seriously curtails the arrangements we had for that day. I know that it will screw up the flat ceremony and means that it will only be a short Registrar ceremony and back to the prison... Sitting here I am realistic enough to know there is little I can do though I feel terribly hurt at being betrayed in this way. I feel fragile as I've been caught in a vulnerable spot in that an issue of this kind heightens my impotence due to being in here. It leaves Sarah out there on her own having to deal with it all in a practical sense.

27th JANUARY '80
This morning I lay awake, not sleeping a wink. There was a feeling of total impotence and frustration. I wondered what the papers would say and kept my ear to the radio in the hope that something would come across. It came on the news at 8am and was the first item. I was deeply upset and felt that something most private and personal had been raped. Getting up I dressed in my exercise gear and went out to pound the yard. Jesus, it felt much much better than lying here locked in this cell. I thought of Sarah and wondered how she was coping.

Malky went down for the papers. The front page of the *Sunday Mirror* and *Mail* was 'Boyle to Marry', and showed a photo of Sarah. Going through the articles I could see comments attributed to Sarah which indicated the pressure she must be under; and I am in here *protected* from it fucking all! I sat with staff reading them and they had an appreciation of what Sarah must be having to deal with...

28th JANUARY '80
The night was slow in passing. I felt terribly restless, sweat pouring from me as I tossed and turned while waiting for the door to open so I could burst out of my cell... after a laborious wait I threw myself into the yard with the adrenalin surging through my body.

The morning papers splashed headlines covering the story. The *Record* had a photo of Margaret (the woman I already had two children with) wishing us all the best. On the whole the press coverage was sympathetic though I was feeling the effects in a different way being aware that Sarah was out there on her own and having to do duty at the hospital. I knew how difficult it would be for her...

This afternoon I was bound with pent-up anger and frustration so got the gloves on and battered the heavy punchbag...

This evening Sarah came in and she was looking tired. We embraced and she just cried. . . It has all been too much for her and this is the first we've been together since.

29th JANUARY '80
Wattie came in and soon after I had a call from Sarah. She was angry at a vicious article in the *Express*:

THE CHEEK OF KILLER BOYLE
Scots are staggered yet again by the astonishingly successful effrontery of killer James Boyle, the most notorious and most pampered man in Britain's jails.

This week he caps his unprecedented privileges by getting out of Barlinnie's special unit to marry 29-year-old psychiatrist Dr Sarah Trevelyan, but it is not a romance that captivates the nation. Law-abiding people are deeply disturbed that a dangerous felon, serving life with a 15 year minimum and a further 12 years on top of that for creating mayhem in prison, should be allowed so much scope for intimate, personal activities.

NOT ONLY IS BOYLE GIVEN PERMISSION TO BE MARRIED. HE WAS ALLOWED OUT TO BUY HIS WEDDING CLOTHES, AND APPARENTLY HAD LUNCH WITH HIS FIANCEE AT THE SAME TIME. He has been permitted to visit her home on several occasions. And she visits him twice a week in the Special Unit, where the visiting hours are nine to twelve and two to five daily. Yet the Prisons' Department claim that Boyle is being given no special privileges and assure us that his marriage is not a stepping-stone to freedom. To say the least is it not a strange, unexpected, match, between a half-educated thug and killer from the heart of Glasgow's Gorbals and the gently-nurtured, highly-educated daughter of Britain's former film censor.

She does not find it strange. She initiated the court-ship by becoming a Special Unit visitor after reading Boyle's book. One may wonder how the romance may have flourished had Boyle's 'control unit' still been the cages at Porterfield instead of the Special Unit at Barlinnie.

Dr Trevelyan is one of the large group of academics and intellectuals who have been campaigning for Boyle's early release. He has served 13 years of his life sentence.

IT WOULD BE A SOURCE OF SURPRISE, SHOCK AND ANGER TO EVERYONE IN SCOTLAND IF BOYLE WERE TO BE RELEASED BEFORE THE 15 YEARS NOMINALLY DECREED BY LORD CAMERON HAD EXPIRED.

Justice has to be seen to be done — and it has to be seen to be served.

I explained to her how the *Express* was a nothing paper which is desperately trying to get readers in Scotland. Sarah said that someone had been up at the door and torn the nameplate off. I am wound up knowing that Sarah is having to deal with all this.

30th JANUARY '80

This evening Sarah came in and she kept herself very strong though I could see the strain on her face. I am deeply moved at the way she is handling this whole thing. We ate some food and talked. She said Phil Davies of the *Sunday Mirror* made an offer of £10,000 for a series of articles, including photographs. Sarah had the presence of mind to ask him to give it in writing. He said that now our address is known the money may help to buy another flat! We both discussed cheque-book journalism and how it seduces people into selling their souls. Sarah will reply in writing saying she is refusing their offer. We intend to keep all this documentation in order to do something about it in future... In all that is happening at present the media are writing their own indictment... In contrast to this we are both receiving many many greetings from people in letters, cards and telegrams. Some of these from unknown people...

31st JANUARY '80

God, I feel weary this morning but once in my track suit and out running I felt much better. My nerves were jangling in my stomach. The press have been outside the prison since 6am. When we left the prison a cavalcade of cars pursued us. There were hoards of press, radio and television journalists waiting for us at Balfron. On getting out of the car I waited for Sarah and we walked through flashing cameras and questioning reporters. I kept saying 'no comment' as I had been instructed. In the Registrar Office we were ushered into a small room.

The woman Registrar proceeded with the ceremony and had to stop to mention that she was nervous and I appreciated this admission from her as it added warmth to the ceremony. We slid our rings on and took photographs before leaving to push through the mass of journalists.

Once back in the prison we sat in my cell with Heidi and Margaret (our witnesses). No sooner had we settled in than the Governor wanted to speak to us. The media were crowding the main road and they were harassing people. I got the feeling he wanted Sarah to go and speak to them. She was firm and stated that they should be able to do it. At the end of this debate it was agreed that the Governor and Malky would go and tell the journalists that Sarah would appear at a press conference later.

Sarah was near bursting point and I was angry at the Governor for being so insensitive. On returning to my cell Sarah was in tears and being comforted by Margaret and Heidi. I asked them to sort out some food and we sat alone. Sarah burst into deep sobs. I knew what she was feeling... oh I knew. Anthony Ross came in and he sat with us.

Once Sarah had washed and sorted herself out we then sat in a triangle of 'silence' and got into the feel of our being married. This was a strengthening silence which seemed to bind us all together. There was a powerful atmosphere of love. Anthony read out two brief passages on love which were appropriate. He then gave us his blessing and all three of us stood embracing.

Sarah distributed little gifts to the other prisoners as we wanted them to share in it. I was concerned about the press conference and suggested she take Anthony with her. She jumped at this and he graciously accepted.

I sat on edge listening to the news and watching television. It was given prominent coverage on the national news. Sarah gave a fantastic interview and came across as a very warm human being. Some moments she was fragile, the others strong. . . at least we've come through this with dignity and left the others who tried to turn this into a circus looking ridiculous. . . I am now a married man and feel it has been the right decision. Only Sarah and I know the truth of what we share and feel. This is a special moment in our lives.

1st FEBRUARY '80
Lay in bed till 7.30am feeling extremely tired. Getting up I dressed in my track suit and went out for my run. I kept thinking of yesterday and that I am now a married man! I am wondering how Sarah is coping, can't wait to read the newspapers and phone her. The press coverage is massive. . . in all it is pretty fair but on the whole I am aware that this marriage, this happy event has shown the press up as nothing more than vultures who will stoop to anything.

I phoned Sarah and she is full of the joys, and I'm infected by it, am so happy that she is happy. We both know the score, we both understand the fight on our hands but there is now a solid base; we're in it together. We both laugh at our being man and wife knowing that this will take some getting used to but feel good about it. The headlines in a paper is a quote from Sarah: WE'LL MAKE THIS MARRIAGE WORK

I sit with the Governor and Wattie, both of whom are delighted at the way Sarah dealt with the press conference. The Governor tells of many phonecalls he had from people in the Department stating they were delighted and moved by Sarah's courage in dealing with the media. This evening Sarah came in bringing some Italian food and both of us were overjoyed to see each other. We sat eating and she remarked how, spontaneously, she has decided to be known as Dr and Mrs Boyle. I laughed at this and felt good. I think it important that she made this decision on her own and am glad she did so. We both share our bumper mails and it is good to know we are getting support from so many people.

Kelvingrove
Glasgow G.3.

Dear Jimmy,
Just had to write and let you know that I've only now read your book (what a cracker) I mean very good by that. And as we say here in Glasgow, I had an honest to good greet. I came across it by chance one night in my brother's house, but I had to leave it there as he had just started to read it himself. Well anyway I ordered it myself at my local newsagent and got it within a week. By God Jimmy you've come through the mill. I felt an old hurt wound open up while reading it. And I'm only going back 4 years ago, when my favourite brother who is the youngest in the family got sentenced to 5 years. You see Jimmy we were so close then (and still are) It just about broke my heart when he was sent to prison. People used to think me daft the time it took me to get over it. I think I went through every day of his sentence with him I couldn't eat, couldn't sleep, couldn't face my work. The only thing I was good at was getting (blitz) out of my mind with booze. I remember one night, I was so God damned full of the stuff, hailed a taxi to Barlinnie, and stood outside for about 2 hours singing all the Johnny Cash songs I could think of. Don't know how to this day I never got hailed inside. And this is honest Jimmy, on my way back down the road, the eyes a pure mass of mascara wae the greeting and the snotters tripping me, this voices pipes up and says 'Thank Christ for that, RENT-A-MOUTH is going home'. I would love to have shook the guy's hand,

because I had a bloody good laugh to myself the next day thinking about it (Hope it wasn't you Jimmy) Ha Ha.

Well I went to visit Barlinnie to see my wee brother (as I say) he's now 32 and I still call him that he was then moved to Peterhead and I never saw him till he came back down to Barlinnie for the last 6 weeks. There's a lot of things you write in your book that I identify him with you. He was a bit of a rebel at times, but a good hearted bloke well met. The family used to shout and bawl their heads off at him, but my wee mother Nellie and myself were the only two who really understood him he used to always confide in me and to this day he still does. While he was inside his wife divorced him the only sad thing about that is he hasn't seen his wee daughter since, but the good part of it Jimmy, is that since he's come out of prison he hasn't been back. He's got quite a good job on a building site and he's now met a nice girl and they've set up home together. And may I say this Jimmy and I truthfully mean it, I wish you and your lovely wife Sarah all the happiness to come. You deserve it and I'm praying for you that you'll be granted parole before this year ends. Hope you don't mind me writing I'm just one crazy mixed up sister.
God Bless you Jimmy Boyle
from Margaret, a friend

Cramond St.
Glasgow G5

Dear Jimmy,
I only finished reading your book, which was given to me as an Xmas present by one of my sons. My husband and I are pensioners and retired so we read quite a lot to pass the time. We liked your book so well it touched us to the heart, so we felt it right to write to you even as strangers to tell you in our own way how happy we are for you, and to wish you every happiness in your marriage which we saw on telly.
And to say we hope it will not be long until you are home with your lovely wife and be happy.
Good-bye
God Bless

St. John's College
Oxford

Dear Mr Boyle,
I hope this letter gets through to you as I wanted to tell you my relief and happiness when I read in the paper the other day about both your imminent marriage and release from prison. Having read "A Sense of Freedom" I found it very depressing to think that you were still in prison and going to remain there for the foreseeable future. I haven't totally sorted out my attitudes to the penal system but your book among others has led me to reject the principle of punishment. Bertrand Russell compared the penal system to a garage which treats cars that don't go by saying "you are a very wicked car and I won't give you petrol till you go" instead of trying to find out what is wrong. One sees after every violent crime splashed across the headlines "MONSTER" or "SAVAGE" or "ANIMAL". But how often does one

250

see that all important word "WHY?"

The only use I can see for prisons is as a way to keep violent and anti-social people away from Society while reminding Society that it is to blame and not any 'moral guilt' of the individual. The whole penal system has been built up and is still justified on the principle of guilt which I see as a direct link with the idea of original sin. If we could only learn to look from the effect to the cause we might prevent the spread of the illness instead of desperately trying to repress the symptoms when they surface. In that respect it is depressing though not altogether surprising that the Tories have just increased spending on 'Law and Order' while cutting nursery-school building projects in half.

Your book has helped to make me think and for that I thank you. Nobody who reads it can afterwards believe in the 'conventional system' and that can only be good. (I lend it to people here). I see "A Sense of Freedom" as a great and necessary donation of sanity to a controversy which seems sadly short of it.

I would like to end this rather muddled but sincere letter by wishing you all the best for your return to civilised (!) society and your plunge into matrimony.

Yours Sincerely

Weybridge
Surrey

Dear Sarah,

This is to wish you every happiness and success in your marriage. I am writing to you as though you had joined my own family because it feels like that! Two of my friends who have read "A Sense of Freedom" feel the same. We couldn't be more pleased to hear of the engagement to an attractive intelligent girl to one

251

of our own sons. You must both have needed courage and faith to get married before you are able to live together, but that is what so many did in the wars, and at least your hopes and plans are not likely to be upset by enemy action. It is really something to come through a childhood such as your husband had and overcome the bitterness. The direct style of his writing has made me feel I have known him all his life. I would think you have chosen a man of courage capable of deep affection. It must be good to feel he is like a man born again – a man who will not ultimately let the past make him a prisoner. At the marriage of a young friend of mine, her father, who was the priest conducting the service, spread himself in this address on the difficulties to be encountered in the daily lives of married people, and it is true that none of us escape tensions in close relationships. However you have before you an opportunity to make a contribution no other couple could make to the well being of children in the poorer areas, and in the direction of prison reform. No-one can put the whole troubled world to rights, but it is nice to be able to do a little to help people.

Yours Sincerely

Uddingston
Glasgow G7I

Dear Mr. Boyle,

Let me first of all congratulate you on your marriage, and wish your wife and you a happy and successful future.

I would also like to add a few comments about which I feel deeply. You are, more than anyone, aware of the vile resentment and hostility your situation has caused among that (unfortunately large) section of society which feels that criminals

should be boiled in oil, left to rot etc... the
"Hanging's too good for them brigade."

Despite this beknighted viewpoint, there are a
great many people, not just sociologists seeking
material for their next thesis, or middle class ladies
seeking lunch dates with youself in order to thrill the
others at the next coffee morning, but ordinary
people who on a simple moral level believe that, as
Anthony Ross put it, an individual can be "reformed"
or "rehabilitated".

Mr. Boyle, these people have argued on behalf of
you and the Special Unit in bars, cafes, railway
carriages, buses and places of work all over the
country. They are called everything from fools to
'trendy liberals' – but their faith in man's ability to
reform himself is unshakeable. So much of that faith
is invested in you.

Well, I've said it. Maybe I am a crank – I don't
know. I don't expect a reply – I just hope that my
words might come back to you some lonely night
when you might be feeling pretty low, and who knows
– maybe they'll help a wee bit.

Good luck – Stay Strong

6th FEBRUARY '80

As the day progressed the Governor asked to see me. In his
office I was faced with Wattie and two other staff members.
The Governor then told me that my day out tomorrow had
been reduced to two hours instead of the usual five. Also, I
wasn't to meet Sarah. The Governor said that he and his
senior staff were furious at this as George Younger had
previously stated I would get five hours weekly. I asked
him why I was being punished? He replied that he couldn't
answer this. One of the staff said that we didn't want to get
into conflict with these people again and although I can see
the sense in this I am angry.

7th FEBRUARY '80

I lay in bed till 11am. I felt really tired and couldn't face anyone downstairs. One of the staff came up and asked if I was going out for the two hours? I told him yes. I must admit that I had given thought to telling them to stick their two hours. The staff member then told me that a letter had come from the Department, signed by Mr Allan, the Controller of Operations, confirming what he said yesterday. Downstairs the staff member showed me the letter. It stated re our phonecall yesterday and because of the publicity last week there are certain restrictions he wants carried out:

1. I've not to meet Mrs. Boyle
2. I've to state which shops I'm going to and return immediately from there.
3. The outing has to last a maximum of 2 hours.

The staff member and I went out at 2.15pm and drove to Great Western Road. It was beautiful being outside. I thought, if I had been a weaker sort of person how stupid it would be for the Department to exert this sort of pressure as the temptation would be to run off.

The Governor phoned the Unit after we returned. He was at the Department and told Unit staff that Mr Allan told him that the cutting of my outing was an arbitrary decision by the Secretary of State himself till such times as he meets his junior Minister. The Governor said he was happy with this meeting and had an opportunity to make his views known. I had a chat with one of the staff this evening. He said that the position is that his (S.O.S.) decision is making it intolerable for staff as we have it in writing that my hours will be five on outings and that this will be increased after a month or so. He said that he pointed out to the Governor today that if this isn't sorted out there'll be no staff left here.

8th FEBRUARY '80

Two staff members, in the Unit for a week, gave their views to the Community today. The first started by telling us his pre-conceived ideas of the place, pointing out that his colleagues in the prison he worked told him that Jimmy Boyle ran the place and everything revolved round him, and that the Governor was in my pocket. He said that his week here showed him how untrue this was and he was surprised to see how it worked in reality. He said he could work here and would like to. The other staff member gave similar preconceived notions saying the same things and how amazed he was in the changes in people here. He talked of how I had handled the knock-back of my paroles and could never have believed it could have been handled this way. His coming here had shown him the reality though he said that if he did come here he would find it difficult to adjust to this way of working.

11th FEBRUARY '80
The Governor called me in and said my paroles are now back to five hours. He said Younger stated this himself before receiving the Governor's submission. He said that they don't want me meeting Mrs. Boyle. He didn't agree with this and was sharp in his comments. I know they are very sensitive to the press taking a photo of Sarah and I together but explained they had and that we're married now. I said that Sarah and I don't want publicity between now and my parole reply and they must give us credit for being circumspect in this. He agreed with me saying I should speak to Allan when he comes down next week...

14th FEBRUARY '80
There is a piece in *The Scotsman* on those jokers refusing STV access to some council houses for the film. It is quite witty:

'Use of flats for Boyle Film Refused.'

James Boyle, best-known inmate of Barlinnie's Special Unit, was at the centre of a council-house wrangle in Glasgow City Chambers yesterday.
It was not that the recently-wed Boyle had prematurely applied for a council house in his native city

— but because Scottish Television had requested the use of council flats to film scenes for a programme based on Boyle's autobiography *A Sense of Freedom*. However, had Boyle applied for apartments in the City Chambers itself, the reception could not have been cooler.

Not one of the seventeen councillors on the tenure and rehabilitation sub-committee were sympathetic to the request. They were outraged at any connection being made between violent conduct and their city.

There was laughter when a council official reported that STV had said the play was not about Boyle, but his autobiography. But the laughter stopped abruptly when Conservative Councillor Dyer moved to reject the request. He thought vacant property should be used to house Glasgow families... although the city has 3000 untenanted homes.

Councillor N. Stobo, Lab. said he didn't want Drumchapel to get the same image as Easterhouse through adverse publicity.

'It would not be in the interest of the people of Drumchapel to associate Boyle with the area,' he told the meeting. 'I am not anti-Boyle, I am pro-Drumchapel, or any other area in the city this crew want to film.' Councillor Stewart, Conservative, felt it was no part of the council's function to aid the glorification 'of this particular individual'. He added, 'He's had enough glorification. We would only be giving him aid and succour. When one considers the things Boyle has done and how he is held up to public esteem as part of his bid for reinstatement into society, I don't think we should have anything to do with it. He should have been hanged in the first place.'

A spokesman for STV said: 'It appears the emotions running on this issue are unjustified. The idea is to take a book about a criminally-violent man and consider what society can do about him!'

I find the hypocrisy of these politicians, both locally and nationally, difficult to accept; and yet, there is something hysterically funny about them. I should look on all that is going on as one would a continuous stream of clowns which evoke responses ranging from the deadly boring to the absurdly funny. I've got to stop their rantings from hurting me and this is possibly the best way of doing it; in my mind I'll fit them all with bulbous red-noses, outrageous costumes and flappy feet.

26th FEBRUARY '80
This afternoon Mr Allan came in and I opened up the meeting on the subject of my paroles explaining to him the unnatural strains placed on me as a result of not being allowed to see Sarah. He referred to a letter he sent to Sarah saying the publicity is the main problem here and that they haven't shut this off by any means and his general attitude was sympathetic. He said that people like Sproat and Fairbairn MPs, have been writing letters about me saying I am getting more privileges than other prisoners. He said that I am getting similar privileges to other prisoners. I then asked him if I am getting treated differently and he admitted that I am a victim of my own popularity/notoriety and agreed I am getting less than others. I told him that I am asking supporters of mine to keep a low profile and as a result they are having to deal with negative ones from Sproat and Fairbairn. He told me that lots of letters received immediately after the wedding were positive and I pointed out to him the amount of support Sarah and I had received from unknown people.

On the subject of violence there were some strong statements made when we were discussing our violent backgrounds. Allan stated that there were moments when he has been filled with tremendous anger but has never reverted to striking anyone. He said he's now fifty-three years old and has never hit anyone in his life. I explained to him that where we come from violence is a part of ones upbringing. I said that within the Unit one learns new skills and techniques as a substitute for violence; that when one develops these areas of oneself then violence becomes less necessary. One of the prisoners stated that there have been times in here when he's been so angry he desperately wanted to attack someone and stab him but what prevents him is that he knows there is no danger of the other person attacking him; whereas, the thing in the main system is that if conflict arises then 'Get in first' is the name of the game.

Throughout this meeting and this particular topic Mr Allan opened himself and so the Community responded to this. It is a lovely process and one that lets us see the human face of a bureaucrat.

14th MARCH '80

BOYLE SHOPPING TRIPS BANNED
Glasgow Herald

Scottish Office Ministers have placed a ban on controversial prisoner James Boyle's weekly shopping trips to buy supplies for his fellow inmates in Barlinnie's Special Unit. Last week, on one of his shopping expeditions Boyle, a convicted killer, had a 'chance' meeting with his new wife and they were seen in a restaurant together.

This latest episode proved the ultimate embarrassment for Scottish Office Ministers who had been unhappy with the publicity surrounding Boyle on trips about Glasgow under escort of prison staff...

A Scottish Office spokesman confirmed last night that Boyle's outside visits had been suspended 'for the present'.

16th MARCH '80

FURY AT TV FILM ON KILLER *The Observer*

A Television company's attempt to film the life story of rehabilitated Scots murderer Jimmy Boyle in Glasgow's meaner streets is proving almost as bizarre as the man himself. The £350,000, 90-minute blockbuster from Scottish Television's studios is derived from Boyle's autobiography *A Sense of Freedom*. Before filming got

258

underway there were outraged squeals from Glasgow district councillors. They felt that Boyle — described by his trial judge as 'a menace to society' — was being 'lionised and glorified'.

Scottish Television defended their actions: 'The film will portray Boyle as he was, a vicious, ruthless thug. In no way will it show him to be a martyr or a hero.'

And Sarah? In the midst of this whole mess we are both surviving under trying circumstances. Moments that we've had have been stolen, like thieves in the night. She represents that soft underbelly; she is the soft loving part of me. She is my vulnerability. And the tears that I would want to shed at this moment are pouring through my fingers, these fingers type with all the emotion of a man who is crying... In the past few weeks I've raised the inner question 'What have I brought this lovely person by marrying her?' Both of us knew it would be hard but never this hard. The brutal harshness of the political and bureaucratic processes have taken their toll.

Those moments when she has come seeking refuge in my arms, crying wracking sobs, her anguish all pouring out, I give her all that I possibly can, that soft vulnerable part of me flows into her, the strong exterior guards her. 'When will all of this end?' I ask myself. And there are those moments when I have cried...

The conglomeration of boiling emotions within me at this moment have an intensity that is bordering on bursting point. I am a man filled to the brim. So full that I want to close my blazing eyes to prevent the overspill of anger.

I must push my way through this, must emerge healthy and strong. The weight, the burden, the pressure that is on me must somehow be overcome. It must! And in telling myself this, I extend it to my loving woman. We both must survive this; together we must thrust our way forward, letting no-one and nothing stand in our way.

22nd MARCH '80 Evening

I tell you dear paper, sweet confidante in my isolation, that I am this good night dancing in my feelings. I am in touch with my joy. Though the snow is thick on the ground I am warm and happy inside. I am at this moment the personification of love. I feel deeply the breadth and depth of my woman. How do I describe it?

If I close my eyes I feel the intense waves of ecstasy race through my entire body, my heart seems to have quickened just as it would had I taken drugs. But there is no chemical could match this. If I close my eyes I find myself anywhere but here, no-place specific but the sun is shining on me, it smiles, it actually laughs. I am alone as I've been for thirteen years. The happiness within me is so intense that I can almost see it bounce off the walls as it shoots from my body. All I can do is share it with the inanimate objects but most importantly, with myself. I feel 'high'. At this moment if I were outside I would go to her and share it.

27th MARCH '80

Four prison staff from Grendon Underwood prison (England) visited us today. They paid for the trips out of their own pockets and came in their own time. They've been looking at a few places in Scotland so didn't come specifically to see the Unit. It was interesting to listen to their views which were a mixture of good and bad. They complained about not being allowed to get closer to the prisoners in Grendon, and yet were disgruntled at having put prisoners on a disciplinary report only to see him fined a paltry 50 pence! They used this example to indicate the lack of Governor support. Some of the staff were good but from what we gather they are seriously inhibited by professional staff. They have doctors, psychiatrists and psychologists as well as therapists. We explained the Unit concept and how we do the job ourselves. They talked of how staff are put into Grendon and don't want to be there and they tend to cause trouble. One of the guys said he didn't want to be there but had to lump it.

28th APRIL '80
A source told me that the Parole Board are wary of me because of the pressure to release me. Apparently there is no talk about my being transferred to Perth Prison but that Edinburgh is more likely with my being put into an artistic situation so that I could pursue my work.

Ken came in and it was lovely to see him. He told me that rumour has it that although Malcolm Rifkind is sympathetic, he is wanting to abide by the sentencing Judge's fifteen year recommendation. Ken said Rifkind is ambitious and that there is no way he is going to move for me, and that the Labour mob are the same.

Sarah came in and it was nice to have her, Ken and I standing in the Unit again. We then had to sit down for lunch (Wattie's retiral lunch) with many other people. Sarah had to leave soon afterwards. I presented a crystal decanter and glasses to Wattie and made a speech which gave some perspective to his role and contribution right from the start. Wattie shook my hand warmly and then stood up and gave a speech. He was torn right from the beginning. It was a moving scene. He is a lovely man with lots of weaknesses that show him to be a sensitive human being. Wattie, retiring after thirty one years in the Prison Service made no bones about it, the Unit and his years here were the most difficult.

9th JUNE '80
I had a call from Frankie Miller who has seen the film and says it is very good. He thinks David Hayman, acting as me, has done a great job. Frankie said it is strong stuff and he loves it. He is working on the music for the film and will have it completed for Friday. He wanted my permission to title the song *A Sense of Freedom*, and I agreed. He is getting Rory Gallagher to back him musically.

18th JUNE '80

I went out for the shopping and was widely recognised by people... We had lunch in Sauchiehall Street and two girls asked Ron (escort) if I was Jimmy Boyle... I sat next to a guy on the new tube and he asked if I was me. I told him yes and he said he had read my book and loved it.

There was a piece in the evening paper saying I had been nominated for Rector of Glasgow University... The Governor came in saying he's been on the phone to press all night about this.

1st JULY '80

After the Community meeting the Governor caught hold of me to say he's been onto the Department and the Director has said that final word of my parole will come sometime in September. This floored me as I was expecting it much sooner. He said that although it's September that doesn't mean there won't be movement between now and then. It will go to the Board in August and at that meeting he expects two of their members to come and interview me. He said he has to be careful what he is saying but there are no negative noises.

3rd JULY '80

This morning I wakened feeling totally exhausted and drained. Getting up I sat waiting for the door to unlock. I couldn't help but succumb to the negative feelings concerning my parole. By the time the door was opened and I was out doing my run I felt physically drained.

I just can't go on. Despair was so deep in me that I sat for a long spell on the rowing machine in a daze, desiring to have a nervous breakdown or something, anything but having to live with how strong I am. I sat there in that condition, dazed, numbed and near to tears but still telling myself that I've got to do those exercises. This is what I hate about myself at times like this; I keep going and live through this torturous situation.

12th JULY '80

This evening Sarah came in looking much stronger and brought some food with her. Going out to work this morning she found the nameplate torn off the door again. When she went downstairs to the street her car tyres were let down and the paint-work scraped with the words 'Killer Boyle'. Sarah showed a strong front here but I was shaking with anger. She said she was at first but gave some thought to it and tried to understand it. We both thought the likely perpetrator would be the guy who is writing anonymous letters to us. I am afraid for Sarah. She tried to alleviate this by showing a remarkable strength. We both looked on it as some badly damaged guy who has fed on the media pap. When the Mirror journalist tried to blackmail Sarah into giving her a story or he would publish the address of the flat, this is what he was putting her in for... All this bureaucratic nonsense about not being able to see her when out for the groceries doesn't help. I want to comfort her, support her in a practical sense... Internationally recognised as husband and wife we must act like secret lovers...

Secret Lovers

Perhaps I'll be there waiting in the shadow
out of sight; unnoticed by others passing-by.
Try not to be conspicuous when you approach;
I prefer the anonymity and the solitude.
There is something profoundly comforting
about living in the shade; far from the glare.
Should we meet then make it betwixt and between;
if possible in the softness of dusk.
Let your movements be slight and subtle;
a flick of your wrist; a smile on your lips.
It is enough for me to see you; to feel your
presence; to smell your sweet smell.
Make it so the observer sees nothing;
not even the casual brush of our bodies.

We should remain apart yet together in all
but the obvious; our secret shared.
Forgive my discretion it's simply that I hold
precious our love wrapped in intrigue.

14th JULY '80
This afternoon two of the staff returned with the new
prisoner. He immediately went into the Governor's
room and then came into a Community meeting. On
entering one could see he was under extreme pressure
and making nonsensical noises as though he was in
control of the situation. This let me see just how much
pressure there is on people coming into meetings like
this. The Governor opened the meeting by asking if
there was anything anyone had to say. One of the
prisoners wanted to know the position between the new
prisoner and Jimmy Boyle. The new prisoner came in
saying we know the score so there will be no trouble. I
then explained to him that I would be no threat to him in
terms of violence. He said the same. He seemed to relax
after a few minutes. He said he wanted out and that was
why he was here. There was some discussion on the Unit
and then we were left alone.

In many ways I couldn't help feeling sorry for him as
he is under tremendous pressure and so steeped in prison
culture that he was at a gross disadvantage. The contrast
between guys entering the Unit like this and those who
have been here was never more clear than now. We
discussed the past and he tried to justify everything
saying that he hadn't raped guys, hadn't bullied them
and so on. We talked about this and I let him get it off his
chest. He said that he was hated by everyone and that
people kept putting the mix in for him and that he never
did many of the things people accused him of. It was
interesting listening to him justify his position telling me
that he didn't grass me in the High Court trial all those
years ago.

On talking about the Unit he said that he is only
intending to pay lip service to it as there is no way that he

intends grassing anyone. At the same time he won't do anything in here or get involved with anyone. He said it is okay for me as I'm not going out to live in the world I came from whereas he is. He said he is concerned about his son now who is in the nick and so on. At one point he became so emotional I thought he was going to cry. I tried to be as sensitive as possible with him while at the same time making the boundaries of the Community plain. I tried to point out to him that I can appreciate and understand him saying the things he is at the moment but that it isn't as simple as what he is saying. He said he doesn't want to get involved or take on what I have done. It is quite clear that he is intent on paying lip service to the place.

He mentioned that at one point he had considered coming down here to get me and had spoken like this to the Interview Team. But, now all he wants is out. He said that he has to save face now and doesn't want to be seen pulling with me or being too friendly with me. He talked of having lived with hate for me for years and I can understand this.

27th JULY '80

I sat with a member of staff. He asked me how things are going between the new prisoner and myself. I told him there was an uneasiness between us but that this was to be expected as he is loaded with old prison culture. The staff member nodded at this saying the new prisoner is obsessed with me — his hatred that is. We agreed this is to be expected but that he must be encouraged to look to the future. The staff member said he spent most of yesterday afternoon with him and continuously he returned to the subject of me. He asked if he should condone this and let him get it out. I said yes but the consistent message to put to him is that the past is the past and he must get on with the future. I explained that if we were to continue to harp on about past conflicts then all we would be doing is wasting time de-bating the rights and wrongs of that period — which was eight years ago — instead of the present and future.

28th AUGUST '80

While sitting talking to some of the others the papers came in. The front page headline in the *Glasgow Herald* says BOYLE TO LEAVE BARLINNIE SPECIAL UNIT. It stated I would be told today that I was being transferred to Edinburgh or Perth and that I would be given a date for a year's time. There were inaccuracies in the article but nevertheless it gave me a feeling of being from an authoritative source. The article quoted a prison source. I was very angry and immediately thought of Sarah.

I phoned her. . . she asked what the news was? I told her there was no truth in it and expressed my anger saying the article was opening up all my expectations of a parole reply. Sarah said someone from the *Herald* called her at 11.30 last night telling her he got the information from an official source. She refused to comment. This morning a reporter from the evening paper was at the door at 8am. Sarah told her to 'Piss off'. I asked Sarah to go to the editor of the *Herald* and complain about this article as it is tearing us apart emotionally. Sarah, rather shrewdly, advised me to see the Governor first.

The Governor came in and I let him see it. While reading it his only response was, so you're being moved next week. I told him Sarah would like to go to the editor of the paper and complain but we need a denial or confirmation from the prison authorities. He replied that he'll speak to me at 10am. He said he's expecting a call at 9.45, giving a reply to my parole. He expressed anger at the press getting this saying he had to leave the prison yesterday to go home and make calls about me and that only three people knew this information: Mr Allan, Mr Hills (the Governor of Saughton) and himself. At 10am he spoke to me saying my release date is Nov. 1982 and that I'll be transferrd to Saughton Prison, Edinburgh. Next week Mr Allan, Mr Hills and Mr Ogilvie, Assistant Governor from Saughton will come to Barlinnie to discuss with us what my programme will be. I replied to this saying whilst I was pleased to have a release date I was disappointed it was so far away. I was also concerned about the conditions under which I would be transferred to Saughton. Sarah came in and I told her the news. As we sat discussing it the Governor came in and Sarah was forthright in telling him how stupid it was to keep me in this length of time. His response was that he would have it otherwise but those above deemed '82 as the time. We said we would challenge this.

This evening the news came over the BBC. There was a lengthy television piece saying the Prisons Department have broken precedent by issuing a statement about an individual prisoner. It stated I would be getting no preferential treatment.

It's been a momentous day. The one clear thing is that I have a date and from my point of view it's tremendous to have a release date. All of it will take some time to sink in and next week will let us see what Saughton has to offer.

29th AUGUST '80
I spent the morning writing letters seeking support about the distant parole date and transfer. It won't do any harm.

The press coverage was pretty wide and accurate in issuing the statement that Sarah and I gave. There was speculation about my imminent transfer to Edinburgh. The press took relish in describing the contrasting regimes; my leaving the soft-option of the Unit for the harshness of Saughton. When reading all of this I could understand Sarah's trepidation. I am merely blanking it till I know what the decision is come Wednesday. The Department are stating publicly that I am getting no preferential treatment and yet they are coming through here in a high-powered fashion to sit and discuss things with me. This in itself is preferential treatment — I don't see them doing it for other prisoners.

I can see the effects of my transfer seeping in here. There is concern amongst people about my going. The new prisoner is certainly hit by the decision about me. He said he can't help but see it reflecting on himself (a twenty year recommended minimum).

3rd SEPTEMBER '80

Sitting here I couldn't help feeling trapped. I certainly didn't like the position I was in. JL said he wished me well but was fearing the worst. On entering the main prison gate building I found the door to the Boardroom. Malky and I could see Mr Allan with his briefcase standing outside. We entered the room and all the people standing there sat down. Edinburgh team: Mr. Hills, Governor of Saughton, Mr. Ogilvie, Assistant Governor and a Principal Officer. Glasgow team: Our Governor, Peter Whatmore, Malky and me.

Mr Hills wasted no time in opening the proceedings by saying that I was coming to his prison and he would now outline what would happen to me. First, I would be going into his prison like any other prisoner.

1) I would be going into 'B' Hall for 4 weeks.
2) To Forth Hall for 3 months.
3) To Pentland Hall for one month.
4) To 'C' hall for the rest.

I was told nothing about what would happen after this, only that at each of the above stages I would be consulted. I was then asked if I had anything to say or to ask them. I told them that what they were telling me was that I now have to learn to adjust to Saughton prison instead of adjusting to life outside. I asked them to explain the logic of this. Mr Hills replied that this is to be the laid down procedure for any prisoners coming from so-called 'untrainable' prisons. When I challenged them on the points about my conditioning and training here and what they had to offer, they were speechless. I mentioned the things I do here, shopping, art, visits etc. and comparatively speaking, what had they to offer? None of them could answer this. I was told that I would be put into a prison uniform and given three half-hour visits every two months and that my mail would be censored... They were telling me that I wouldn't get any special treatment and yet Ogilvie explained that I would be the focus of attention on visits so could have mine in the overspill room.

On returning to the Unit I immediately called Sarah. I

told her briefly and she knew I was holding it all in. God, this is the hard bit, this is the one bit that kills me. I just don't know what the hell I'm going to do. I called a Special Meeting. On explaining what had happened to everyone they voiced that they were sick and made this known. Peter Whatmore said that he had made his feelings known to the Controller and was disappointed. The Governor said that Ian Stephen forcefully opposed it and he did also. They had a go at Mr Allan but apparently he was carrying the message from someone else. Whatever, it is patently clear that there is no support for the move by any of the professional consultants. They, as well as the Governor, will make their views known in writing. The Community will too.

I was barely holding myself together. The new prisoner made an interesting remark saying that his cousin on TFF (Training for Freedom) in Saughton was given immediate parole and he can only imagine it's because I am going to Saughton.

Tonight Sarah came in and we fell into each others arms. I fell apart and cried deep sobs of pain. Going back there is like a nightmare. That is my past and I feel myself being dragged into that tunnel, far into the muck of that life. Oh, am I never going to get away from it? What, just what am I to do with this heaving knot of emotion inside? I held Sarah with all the pain in my arms. I held onto her for love's sake. Why, why are they doing this? I am naked and vulnerable — that system will creep into me, it will tear my insides apart. I feel deep, deep anger. I feel the full weight of the nightmare on my shoulders. I am caught, trapped and feel that they want to shut me away... feel them wrapping a blanket over me, feel so helpless to do anything about it.

At this writing I am like an open sore... I worry for Sarah, don't know what I'll do without her and yet know that the love we have will bring us through though this rings rather hollow at this moment. My tears are running and this is the man I am now.

4

In solitude and peace
Think deeply
I am you and
You are me
Only space lies
Between us.

Larry Winters

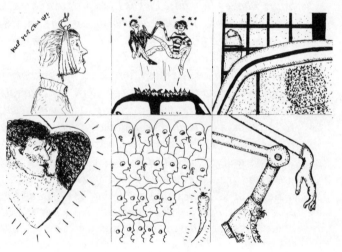

8th SEPTEMBER '80

Darling Sarah,

Well, here I am lodged in my new place of residence. The contrast is sharp and startling between here and the Unit. A simple thing like writing to you on prison notepaper is very strange. I'm trying to gauge my reaction to all the things that pre-Unit were things I took to without thought. At the moment I am pretty bewildered by it all, and felt just like a first offender. I feel anonymous wearing this coarse prison uniform... although only here a few hours I have pin-pointed what I feel will be the major problem for me; the dull and boring routine. Having been used to a high-pitched, dynamic routine where intellectually and physically I was disciplined I now find myself in a situation where little opportunity is given to develop these areas of oneself. For example, in this hall I understand there is no facility or access to the gym. Also running round the yard would be out of the question. I'm aware of the fact that I've got to improve and set myself tasks. I've got to keep myself alive and free in every way that I can.

Being in 'B' Hall is the beginning of the induction process. At this point I have no idea what it's all about. I can see there is an abundance of material to research and look at. I don't have a dictionary, sketchbook or drawing pens yet but hope my Governor's Request will resolve this tomorrow.

I have a large window in my cell which lets in lots of light. It's an ordinary house window with bars. There are two beds so I take it another customer could come in at any time. Already I am becoming conscious that this letter will be censored. I'm wondering what is and isn't permissable; if it isn't then my letters to you will help us. Prior to the Unit I'd have known all of this and anyway being so steeped in it I'd never have put anything in a letter

272

going through official channels. Now the difference is that I'm interested in exploring new areas and taking note of what is really going on. I'm allowed re-creation with other prisoners two nights a week. I'm just too bewildered by it all to comment... The cell light is switched off at 10pm so I'll have to find something to while away the other four and a half hours. I have thrown off the foam mattress and one lovely possession is your photograph...

9th SEPTEMBER '80

Darling Sarah,

I now have my own pens, sketchbook and dictionary but would not like these to be seen as concessions as it's ridiculous that such things should be taken away in the first place.

Today was interesting as I spent the best part of the morning in the mailbag party. It was an incredible experience. But, first things first. I went to the doctor for a cursory check-up and on entry was marched in and told to stand side-on, on a small black board sitting on the carpet. I don't know why. One of the things that concerns me, and came more to the fore as the day progressed, is the rigidity of the regime. All the decision making is taken away from the prisoner and I can now see at first hand how the system makes prisoners dependent on it. As much as I try to detach myself from this, it will be impossible. By being in it one falls prey to it. What I find ironic is that the undoing of all this was very difficult for me in coming to terms with the Unit and latterly in helping other prisoners re-learn social skills... I'm still confused by all of this as it really is severe, much more so than I could have imagined. In a strange sort of way I want this to be with me throughout my stay in this place. I'd prefer the continual pain of culture shock to the acceptance of life in here. I can never erase from my mind the problems I've seen guys have in the Unit as a result of this system. I feel the

273

transfer so much because I know that even though individuals here have the best will in the world to do good they haven't my insight or awareness of what just being here does in terms of personal damage. There are some heartrending stories here. I'll tell you about these when I see you. Basically, I'm feeling severely the loss of my creative outlets. It is difficult to explain to the non-creative person what this means. The procedure in 'B' Hall seems to be that prisoners are given nothing so that when they move on to other halls they will appreciate the petty concessions: the 'carrot' system which in effect works in relation to a smooth running penal system as opposed to gearing prisoners to cope with life outside. The horrifying part is that every single prisoner here will return to society sooner or later. They have to fit into the system which means it does not focus on the needs of the individual.

10th SEPTEMBER '80

The hustle and bustle of early morning ablutions permeate the air. Everyone makes for the sinks which sit in two large archways. While shaving one guy tells another, 'It was on the radio that three cons have escaped from Perth.' The other stops his razor half-way down his cheek, 'Did they get away?' The other replies, 'They rammed a lorry filled with concrete and the cops are looking for three hardened criminals'. Humour does play an important part in people's lives here. I did a few exercises on the floor: press-ups, sit-ups and some yoga...

> *Darling Sarah,*
> *I'm now having to leave for breakfast and won't return to my cell till the evening... I won't be able to write any letters till tomorrow which means I can't send any off to you till the following day...*

11th SEPTEMBER '80

My Dearest Sarah,

I'm so at sea in this place that I'm trying hard not to be drawn into it. The whole process is so insidious that it's like a creeping disease. The 'them' and 'us' is quite strong. I'm listening to everyone but trying to remain detached. I'm now working in the engineering shop which is okay in terms of being left alone to get on with it though I have to contend with the boredom. There is nothing remotely related to life on the outside. Yes, my conditions are spartan to say the least but that isn't a complaint. As I said before I can't enthuse about an extra shower or pair of socks a week as part of the upgrading scheme. Guys in here talk about other halls and the 'perks' there as though they are meaningful. This affects me deeply as it has no relevance to their lives outside... I'm puzzled by your letter as you keep (twice) mentioning that you'll see me tomorrow (14th). The position is that I have to book a visit and the only vacancy was the 28th, so I'm concerned that you may make the journey here for nothing... The visit will be for one hour round a small table under supervision. Alternatively, we could use the $1\frac{1}{2}$ hours at half hour intervals but these would have to be through a glass screen. Let me know your thoughts on this? You won't believe this but every Friday night everyone has to polish their cell floor and a Governor comes round on Saturday morning to inspect it. I needn't tell you that on Friday we got our weekly change of socks, shirt and underpants, all to match the floor I suppose!

27th SEPTEMBER '80

Darling Sarah,

Well, I've just this minute returned from getting my extra pair of socks etc. in this new Hall I'm in. The whole structure of the place is almost identical to the other only this one seems older and more worn. The cell is very much the same only I'm on the bottom flat. Being here again raises the question, what is all this about? I've just been given a sheet outlining the rules of this particular hall. One of them states the four visitors will be allowed on any pass, this includes a babe in arms. What saddens me is the way other prisoners in the previous hall were all hung up about wanting to get to this one. At that point one begins to see the uglier side of it. The Assistant Governor has just come in to do his inspection, and we talked about my being here. He himself appreciated that it was all a waste of time but that I've just got to go through with it. He said he was surprised I was put in here and not on TFF. The one stand-out feature is that no-one here seems to have any control over my present circumstance. I get the distinct impression they are all observers watching the train go by...

Sunday:
Beautiful morning outside and I know you'll be making your way over here for the visit...

You looked great even though I knew you wanted to break down and hold me. I wanted to but what was so important was holding ourselves together. Just to hold and kiss you was wonderful, to look at you and feel you close. Sarah, this they'll never break. This was our first visit and I was truly in need of it though the appalling lack of privacy was most difficult to accept. I'm sure you'll agree with me when I say it had a cattle-market feel to it. At least we can take some comfort from knowing that our experience of it is limited. Some guys I spoke to afterwards were in the first year of a life sentence. It's so depressing. Can you imagine trying to keep a marriage together under such circumstances...

29th SEPTEMBER '80
I went on request and spoke to the Hall Assistant Governor, asking to be put on the Special Escorted Leaves

276

Scheme (SEL). She said there is a big waiting list but wasn't very clear about any of this.

11th OCTOBER '80

> *My Darling Sarah,*
>
> *I was told officially that I can go out on SELs. Prisoners, having done a certain length of time can get four of these outings a year; each four hours in length. However, the problem is in getting a member of staff. It's all done on a voluntary basis. Here is what I have to do: approach a member of staff and if he agrees I get a form from the Hall desk and fill it in. I then have to save up £1 from my weekly wages and put this into my personal property. I can go out two weeks after this. The first SEL has to be in the vicinity of Edinburgh.*

18th OCTOBER '80

I approached another member of staff today and asked him to take me out. He already takes guys out and says it's a lot of pressure on him and the few staff who do. He refused me but said he would ask one or two of the staff on my behalf. It is a crazy system in that it's extremely difficult to get staff to take me out. One guy I know said he has asked thirty odd staff members. Another guy told me he has asked fourteen. He has been trying to get his since April. You can see how frustration builds up in people as a result. The two guys I spoke to are pretty bitter and so as we get into this part of the system one is faced with problems hitherto concealed... For lunch I had a baked potato with a scraping of cheese on top, one small roast potato and a scoop of mashed potato — the sput in all forms! This is my veg. diet!

22nd OCTOBER '80

It's tremendous to see the effect all our outside support is having. Apparently the Department has been swamped with letters condemning my transfer and on top of this the hunger strike and court action by Joseph Beuys and the others has them jumping... I had an interview with the Governor, Mr Allan and a Mr Whyte, education man here. They tell me that negotiations with Edinburgh University have fallen through as they have been pushing to get me on a course when it is into term. The University said they will take me full-time '81 — '82. The problem is that none of this was worked out well in advance. The public pressure has caught them with their pants down. So, it's back to the drawing board. Mr Allan suggested that I do something at Craigmillar or Wester Hailes or at Ricky Demarco's Gallery. They will contact the community groups first as this is my preference... I hope to hear from them very soon. I must admit I'm pleasantly surprised at this turn of events — we're winning! As for the SEL, I took the opportunity to mention this to Mr. Hills. He said he will raise it on Monday. As you can see they are all aware of the situation but no-one is doing anything about it. Yes, the ironic thing is that even with a 'D' category one needs an escort. The crazy system is this — make sense of it if you can — that one guy goes out alone one day a week to college but when he goes on an SEL he has to go with a prison officer...

3rd NOVEMBER '80

My Darling Sarah,

It's amazing how good I feel since seeing you yesterday. The contrast between 'before and after' showed in your mail. One card showed all the cracks of stress and strain, of how you were letting it bite into you and eat you up. The other showing the magic of us together and what we do for each other... I approached officer No. 10 and yes, he's taking me out on an SEL. I wonder if you could make space on Tues. 24th Nov. between the hours of 2 – 6pm? I can tell you, knowing you will feel the same on reading this, that it was pure relief when he said yes. I thought it would be nice to have a meal and we can go and look at the new flat...

7th NOVEMBER '80

My Darling Sarah,

It was great to get your letter today and find out all that you've been doing. I'll go into this later but first let me bring you up to date on events here. The Assistant Governor explained to me that the Wester Hailes management team will be coming to see me on Sunday afternoon to interview me for a job in their community. As you know the Governor and Mr Whyte went to see their activities earlier this week. The management team there have put feelers out to the grassroot groups to get their views on it. There is a possibility that I'll be working on their Art Festival programme. Initially it would mean my going out two days a week with this expanding to full time after January. The Wester Hailes group would want to issue a statement to the media on the Monday, if it is agreed I go there, and this way take the initiative.

9th NOVEMBER '80

Darling Sarah,

The Principal Officer came in to give me a hurried look at the parole conditions for my going out. It stated that I'll be allowed out every Tues. and Thurs. between the hours of 9 and 5pm and that I would be under the guidance of Laurence Demarco; that I won't be allowed alcohol, that I won't meet the press, take part in any commercial or private business, make any pre-arranged meetings with anyone outside the Wester Hailes group; that I have to stay within the Wester Hailes area and if not back in the prison in time I will be arrested.

Shortly afterwards I was taken to the Governor's room and introduced to the Wester Hailes management group; Mr Allan, Mr Whyte, etc. We discussed what my work would be. . . The atmosphere amongst the whole group was good and we were together in all that was being said. It was agreed that Malcolm Rifkind has been quite courageous in this as it's his

279

constituency, and after all he is the Minister responsible for prisons. Mr Allan stated that Rifkind has been solid in his support in this. So, in all it was a very good meeting and a sigh of relief all round. I am looking forward to starting work on Tuesday.

11th NOVEMBER '80

My Darling Sarah,

By now you'll have read or heard about today. I'm just back and it seems strange sitting in these stark surroundings after spending a day of freedom – from one extreme to another... Let me tell you about it. The morning started with two letters from you. I could tell you were down. Here I was reading your letters knowing that you are unaware of what is happening with me – sitting here waiting to go out. I was taken to the reception area and locked in what is nicknamed 'a dog box' – a small cupboard space approx. 3ft square. Once dressed in my own clothes I felt like superman. I seemed to smell and feel different. I was taken to the Governor's office where Laurence and Jack from W/Hailes were waiting. The Governor said no press were at the gate but if they got onto my being out sometime during the day and it became overbearing we should decide when to come back, all of which sounded sensible. What a momentous occasion, the first time I've been out of prison without a prison escort in thirteen years. How can I describe it to you? Can I tell you what it feels like to stand on the surface of Mars? No, I can't because I haven't experienced it. There was a feeling of nervousness and excitement in the Community Workshop but a definite friendliness. I was hungry as I'd given the prisoners at my table my prison breakfast knowing I was going out. They piled a big breakfast on me – lots of beautiful greasy goo... Laurence, Jack and I discussed the possibility of the press getting onto it. Laurence was nervous about Mr Hills, saying he may call me back to the prison if the press

280

do turn up. He said Hills had mentioned not having slept last night. No sooner had we finished when a girl from STV was on the phone. The local community cop came in and we had a chat. A local councillor came in saying The Express *had been onto him asking 'Is he not outraged at someone like me being near a primary school?'. Predictably* The Express *were the only negative ones. Lots of local people, men, women and children came in and talked to me. They were full of support. The work being done by the people here is impressive, it's thriving. Due to our caution I stayed in the building all day but there was more than enough for me to digest.*

24th NOVEMBER '80

I'm taken to Glasgow Sheriff Court on a mistaken identity trip. I told them prior to going (Tues. and again yesterday) that it wasn't me. While waiting a young guy approached and asked for my autograph — I declined trying not to offend him. I'm handcuffed and taken through to Glasgow in prison van with two prison staff as escort, what a waste of time. I'm apprehensive as I may lose the SEL. I think of Sarah and worry about how this will effect her. I got to court and immediately on seeing me the policeman said it's a mistake. It really is appalling this waste of money; one staff member brought in on overtime, a driver, a van and another staff member all for a mistake. A phone call could have cleared this up and I did protest enough to bring it to their attention beforehand. It was as though it suited them, even if it was a mistake.

PM: On return to Saughton it was early lock-up due to the POA meeting. I didn't take any lunch in anticipation of the SEL, hoping to get some decent food outside. The POA meeting went on past 2pm and I was pacing the cell floor worrying if I'd get out at all. These uncertainties were taking their toll. I was feeling drawn and tired with strain and desperately worried about Sarah, waiting on her own. My chest was tight, my guts knotted. It was almost 3pm when I was escorted to the reception area and locked in a small, claustrophobic 'dog box' to dress. I had a good laugh at this as an all-party penal reform group publicly condemned the dog boxes saying they should be abolished. I sat for some time waiting on the staff member coming for me. He eventually came and I was full of anger but having to fight this in order to get into good feelings so that we could enjoy our four hours. I told him we were over an hour late because of the POA meeting and he said he would speak to the Training Governor which he did, leaving me outside the door. My guess is that he was given a good warning as the last prisoner he took out returned drunk. On coming out of the office he told me that 25 minutes had been knocked off the 4 hour SEL. I was furious, but this regime doesn't allow me access to the Training Governor to question his decision. Here the fucker is, lopping off a precious 25 minutes of my contact with Sarah. By now I was sickened and yet trying desperately hard to keep my cool. The officer told me to call him Jimmy when outside and said normally he allows a guy one lager or two glasses of wine. He prefers telling me now so he doesn't have to do so in front of my visitor.

Outside The Gate: Sarah comes up from behind. She looks fantastic and yet I can see all the waiting and uncertainty has taken it out of her — she looks fragile. I love her so much and hate to see her being upset like this, particularly by a System that I despise. We question what car to take and this distresses Sarah as I feel she just wants to concentrate on being with me. We take our car and this eases me as I feel a sort of 'home ground' security about being in it. Our whole dialogue is inhibited due to this stranger sitting with us. I am aware of a constantly boiling anger in me. All our reactions and feelings are muted and we realise we are miles away from our usual spontaneous loving selves. However, we talk to the escort and bring him into things. We drive to our new flat. The owner is in and greets us. We walk around and I love it. For the first time our natural loving feelings emerge and overcome all the bad ones. Sarah and I examine the house in detail, inspecting every nook and cranny. We talked of ways the front room could be decorated. We stole an embrace in that front room. This is our future, our home. This is our life. We grudgingly left the flat.

Outside we bought some food and wine and went to a friend's house. We thought the escort would give us some privacy, but no. We ate and had a drink. The subject was prisons, prisons and more prisons. Eventually Sarah asked if he would give us some time on our own and he went into the next room. I could see that all Sarah wanted to do was cry. He left the room and she broke down. We embraced clinging to each other, both of us asking when this night-mare would end. When she cried she stifled it, afraid the escort would hear. I held her tight urging her to let it flow, telling her I love her, oh how I love her. I told her just how good it was for me to be able to support her at times like this and yet at the same time was aware that I was the source of all this misery. All I wanted was to make my wife happy, to be with her. I told her all of this, about the degredation of sitting having to whisper to each other with a strange man sitting behind the door probably listening to every word. I constantly felt intruded upon. It wasn't about sex or anything like that. This doesn't even enter it. Basically, it's about a man and his wife wanting to share some of their deep personal feelings for each other. Sitting there cheek to cheek I could feel her tears roll down my face. I love her, I deeply deeply love her. After a few minutes we got ourselves together and decided to leave these surroundings for a more public place.

In The Streets: It was beautiful walking hand in hand along the dark rainy streets. We discussed plans to move from Glasgow to Edinburgh, ways of decorating the flat, talked about our families and all the while the escort clung to our sides. He tells us how he has to hide his true personality in this job, how he would like to do more but can't. He tells of me being looked on as a 'hot potato', of varying staff views, good and bad. He talked of comments made by colleagues when it became known he was taking me out. Yes, it was courageous of him and we both acknowledged this.

Back at the Prison: It's difficult... Sarah and I have a few seconds on our own, express our love to each other; she reassures me she is together now after her cry. I know she is saying this for my benefit and me going back in wants to believe it. We part with all the poignant melodrama of a B movie.

Inside: The gates clang a desperate doom-laden noise behind me. The prison interior is dark, like some Dickensian scene. Inside, the reception area is well-lit. One prisoner is cleaning his boots; he's just returned from one day a week out to college. He has a wound on the back of his head and tells me that on leaving the prison this morning at 7.45, he was running for a bus when he collapsed after a paralysing pain in his side. His head crashed on the ground cutting it badly. Rather than return to the prison he got on the bus and went to college, then to hospital where he had four stitches put in the wound. He said there was no way he would have returned to the prison before his due time. One of the reception passmen (prisoner) told us the staff were taking industrial action starting tomorrow but didn't know what or how a work-to-rule would affect the prison.

On returning to the Hall the Principal Officer sent for me to say that as a result of Industrial Action I wouldn't be going out to work tomorrow. He had no idea how long it would last. I felt numb. He asked how my SEL went and I told him it was stressful. He then pulled out a newspaper with a photo of 'Birth', a sculpture of mine and asked what it meant. I told him. He then told me he wrote a poem called Birth. He has two adopted kids and then his wife fell pregnant. He explained in detail the full impact of this event, closed his eyes putting a clenched fist in 'thinker' style to his forehead and recited it. He then explained how he watched some bullies taunt another inoffensive prisoner and was so angered that he wrote a poem about it, which he again recited. I explained to him that he was known as a bastard amongst the prisoners. He said he was a 'book man'.

284

I think of Sarah and worry, I wonder and ask myself how she is coping... I lay in torment through the night, exhausted but not being able to sleep. I do feel empty and flat.

25th NOVEMBER '80

I should be looking forward to going out today but am not. Prisoners see the dispute in different ways. At slop out time (6am) some are delighted to be off work so as to get some extra sleep. I understand what they mean. At the same time I want out. Others hate the idea of being confined in their cells because of the tension between them and their cell mates. In this early morning period there is a rush for hot water which tends to run out quickly. We are locked in till breakfast time.

In the dining hall prisoners are surprised the work-to-rule is preventing me getting out to work. They seem angry about it. At the table ex-doctor Ghia approaches me to say he went in front of the Visiting Committee yesterday to complain about being kept in the mailbags for eleven months. I sympathise with him and give support. He leaves and this arouses dialogue at the table. My table mates talk about the way some medical staff seem to resent the doc. because he let the side down. There is also a strong racial element in it all. He has been assaulted, harassed and picked on by staff and prisoners. Most prisoners, distrustful of the prison medical doctors and staff, approach the doc. for a second opinion which he invariably gives. This has caused him great difficulties with the medical staff who have warned him about it. There seems to be a euphoric atmosphere in the dining hall due to the dispute but really it's about the change of routine.

I asked the guys at my table about the tension in a shared cell, turning it to masturbation. There is a false bravado by all three saying they don't care about their partners, they just do it. But, as the talk continued and got more serious one admits to waiting till his partner has gone to sleep — he listens for the heavy breathing. Another has arranged the beds so that his partners bed looks the other way. He can turn the radio up... Each admits to experiencing high tension in other areas, the stench of doing the toilet or just wanting to be alone.

Back in my cell I sit dreaming, expressing some of what I feel in the form of sketching. Here I am locked up in a solitary situation again. It all comes flooding back, all the old memories of the past. As the morning goes on staff come in with mail; letters from Sarah from the weekend. I'm wondering how she is, how she will take this industrial dispute. I'm supposed to be at two meetings in Wester Hailes this morning. I asked prison staff to ask Mr Whyte to deliver my written material for these meetings. Staff seem to be trying to lessen the load by having reasonable attitudes.

26th NOVEMBER '80

This morning it was the same old rush for hot water. The strong stench of urine and excrement filled the air as we slopped out. As we stood at the sinks shaving, the medical officer came into the toilet area with a prisoner carrying the medication box. He gave prisoners treatment as we stood there. Owly (one-eyed table mate) told me he approached the nurse officer last night to ask for something for chest pains and was told 'Fuck off'. Those of us at the table have been trying to persuade Owly to report sick as he hasn't been eating his food. At the breakfast table we discussed how each spent the time; studying, playing chess, reading. One said my name was mentioned in relation to the dispute when it came on the radio.

Later a senior officer who is on the local POA committee told me that he wants me to know that this action isn't anything personal, that staff aren't wondering ways that Boyle can be done dirty. I said I appreciated this. He was very critical of the Governor saying he is always away to Round Table meetings or similar ones. He said they are interested in getting the prisoners their recreation and have made this known to a 'mole'. The Governor will have to approach them about it. They will consent. I told him they should refuse to accept prisoners into the prison but he backed off this. I have spent the time writing to Sarah. The W/Hailes people have told her about the dispute. I worry about her as all these knocks are putting her in a vulnerable spot. I find myself being affected by it as the door keeps opening and closing in my face. I'm more vulnerable because of Sarah, as I keep thinking the system is putting us both through so much that she won't be able to take much more. Perhaps I'm underestimating Sarah's strength and endurance. Someone sent me in a Butlins holiday camp brochure. It's obviously someone trying to be snide.

27th NOVEMBER '80

6:20am... I realise that rather than waken at my usual 5.30, I am sleeping on till the door is unlocked. This is so unlike me but there is a creeping sense of 'What does it matter?' — I've got to fight this. There is a real air of depression. I can smell the strong stench of urine and excrement... prisoners bodies and cells smell of stale sweat. I go out and wash but don't shave, even though I usually do every morning. Thursday is laundry day. It's great to change my under-wear, shirt and socks. One change per week and I really enjoy it. The medic goes into the toilet areas as usual to distribute medicine. A staff member goes to the small wooden mailbox, opens the flap and takes out the mail. He comes to the toilet area where there is a small table, puts the letters down and begins censoring them. I have written one to Sarah. My eyes keep straying towards him as he reads letter after letter. Watching this I feel as though part of me is being raped:

> *My Darling Sarah,*
> *The long drawn-out hours take their toll in the form of mental depression which affects me physically also. It's like being a helpless pawn in a giant game of chess; there's nothing more de-moralising than the feeling of being picked up and slammed down whenever and however it suits the person in control. At moments like this one can only fall back on one's inner resources with a little help*

287

*from you. At this moment some mail has just come in
from you so I'll leave this to read how you
are...Well, where do I start? I plummet at the way all
of this has hit you; stop, start, spurt, torn apart and
yes, I know what you mean about the part inside
wanting to break down and scream at not being able
to take any more. I can't help asking, what the hell
am I doing bringing you through all of this? There is
this feeling of living a schizophrenic existence; this
raw bleeding part in me wants to howl and scream at
the pain of it all, and the exterior facade that presents
an unruffled face. Oh yes, Jimmy copes with it well. I
feel like the Hulk and want to throw the walls aside.*

Mid-morning

A letter from Sarah just as I am writing to her. Oh Fuck! It
tears me apart to the point where I find it difficult to read
her letter. This has hit her so hard just as I knew it would.
She went to the Third Eye Centre and broke down with
Chris; and I am bleeding profusely inside, raging at this
impotent and helpless situation. SARAH... why did you
let them see this? I start writing to her but have to stop. I lie
on top of the bedboards feeling painfully contorted. I can't
keep still and yet I'm so fucking tired and weary. I just can't
take any more of this. It's pushing me to the limits and yet I
know there is an iron part of me that is solid and won't be
moved — that will push through it. The pain I feel is
incredible. Why did I marry Sarah and pull her into all of
this? It's bad enough coming through this on my own
without her having to endure it. I want to cry at the
moment, feel all the tears welling up but they aren't
coming. I won't let these bastards see it's getting to me. I
won't!

I've just done a good hard work-out and feel so much
better...

Evening

Prisoners are now openly stating they want the dispute
over as soon as possible. Staff are saying they are losing
money — overtime etc. One prisoner told me a member of

staff came into his cell and told him he could go under the covers of his bed as long as he didn't take his clothes off. We had a laugh at this.

There is a good letter in *The Guardian* about my being sent here. This also brings me to the heart of the matter. My continuing imprisonment is nothing more than a vengeful act. My stay in here is futile and has nothing to do with my learning to adjust to life outside.

28th NOVEMBER '80

This morning I wakened very early feeling extremely cold. I had a headache. My body is sore with lying down. Last night a guy told me he is getting headaches due to being enclosed in a small space all the time. This is what I feel as I write this. I lay in bed till the light was switched on. There are four giant cockroaches on my floor so I jump naked out of bed, grap a shoe and smash them. I lift a bit of cardboard and scoop them up and toss them into the piss pot. I hate this place! Everything in here gets to me. The door is unlocked for slop-out and I manage to get some hot water, have a nice wash and shave.

There was an article in yesterdays *Guardian* by Jill Tweedie, on the way crime is reported in the press and she has cleverly related this to women in Holloway. I wanted to send this to Sarah. This meant my having to acknowledge the censor who, until now I've tried to wipe from my mind. I felt terrible going to him with my letter and article asking if I could send it out. He is a young guy of no more than twenty four. He says he has no objection but when it gets to Security they may not allow it. At this point I discover our letters are read twice. I gave him the letter and article and slopped out. On looking down I can see him reading my letter and a senior officer the article. I am not ashamed of the love I express in my letters to Sarah. I am consoled by telling myself they are just a shower of insensitive bastards. On coming into my cell I kiss the photo of Sarah. I whispered loudly so I could hear, 'I love you'. It's dark outside as I sit here feeling very cold. I'm hoping the rumour of the dispute ending today is true but I'm not building up my hopes. I've got to keep some sort of balance. It's depressing to think of another day locked in here.

Last night I curled naked in the sleeping bag made out of blankets and hugged myself. I masturbated to Sarah, imagining her in different poses. It was beautifully erotic and warm, in sharp contrast to the cold outside the blankets. I love the way I am able to fall back on the richness of my inner world for comfort and love. Bed is a very attractive place to be as I can pull the blankets over my head and crawl into the total darkness. I write me a poem:

Horizontal Shuffle

Grind your goddam pelvic rhythm
as your muscles flex their
erotic collusion with your man
in the horizontal shuffle

Feel him snake his flesh with
slippery smoothness deep into your
cavern with its silky walls
and frictionised motion

Cry your guttural sounds as he
utters his moans in that
mutual primitive chorus
of the horizontal shuffle

Toss back your head as you twist
to thrust a wet tongue through lips
into his throat with
passionate hunger.

Tense your body in expectation
as he probes your throbbing need
to explode into fragments of glitter
that climax the horizontal shuffle

Sparkle with joyful convulsion as
you jerk uncontrollably into
those soaring skies of infinite
distance and beauty.

Grunt your pleasure as he spurts
his sperm of milky fluid to mix
with your juice while peaking
in your horizontal shuffle.

29th NOVEMBER '80

This morning I lay in bed listening to the footsteps of the
night patrol clicking off the stone floor. It rang a metallic
sound throughout the hall. I felt so restless and thought of
how in the past I would have blown up at this stage or
rebelled in some way or other that would have resulted in
me being punished. Life has been a series of instances like
this, of being unable to express myself and so irrationally
exploding and in this way labelling myself the baddie and
having got an additional sentence I still would have
savoured the immediate short-term gratification. One
never thought of the consequences. It was a case of live fast,
die young and have a good-looking corpse.

Breakfast:

At the table I told some of the guys about my angry
thoughts related to all this frustration and boredom... The
youngest responded immediately saying he has been
fantasising about taking cans of polish up to the roof and
setting the place on fire. Another says he wants to do a
bastard screw in. The oldest guy says his thoughts would
leave us standing. He said this in an angry manner, full of
aggression. He went on to say that he's seen guys in pure
torment because they've heard something about their
wives and it has nothing whatsoever to do with their wives
but the mind in prison distorts it all and the guy goes
through sheer hell.

30th NOVEMBER '80

This morning I wakened very early. It was extremely cold

as I lay in bed so I rubbed my body with my hands to keep myself warm. I thought of Sarah and imagined her lying in bed. I remembered our flat bedroom well and could vividly imagine her lying there.

At 7.30am the staff come on duty; a mass of footsteps can be heard. While lying here I hear the sound of the judas spyhole open to reveal a naked, probing eye to check that I'm still here.

Spoke to an old guy who said this lock up is making him angry. He has a bad heart condition. He said he put it to staff that if he is feeling this way, what must some of the younger guys feel like? He asked who would be blamed if a young guy grabbed a screw and threw him over the gallery? This old man is certainly feeling it. He had heart tablets in his hands as he spoke.

1st DECEMBER '80
On waking this morning I lie in the darkness listening to what sounds like an army of cockroaches walking the floor.

Speaking to a guy in the dining hall this morning he said he hasn't gone more than three months this sentence without a smoke of hash — he is in nine years. He said he was glad to be out of 'B' hall as there was too much heroin there and he could feel the temptation. He was into hard drugs before this sentence. On speaking to him and an ex-Peterhead prisoner they remarked that the hard drug scene has changed in recent years in the nick. At one time in prison it was all pills (barbiturates etc.) but now it's all hash that is on the go. They say that everyone, even the screws, are more tolerant of this. But, if it is pills they go mad searching everyone and everywhere knowing there is violence associated with them. On hash everyone is passive.

This morning it is very cold so I've put a blanket around me while I walk in a small circle on the floor. There have been moments when even my dreams have deserted me, leaving me to stare at the blankness of my situation.

2nd DECEMBER '80

On waking I thought of Sarah, telling her out loud I love her. It was 5.25am. I got up and did some loosening up exercises before going into my yoga.

The strike is over! Going out this morning was fantastic. I stood in the reception area speaking to two brothers serving life sentences who were going out to their Granny's funeral. I left and walked out the gate alone to jokes from staff, 'Is this allowed?' Turning into the main road I could feel the energy soaring in me. How do I contain this when walking normally along the road? I find myself wanting to run, to sort of take-off. It is magnificent seeing cars and buses again.

10th DECEMBER '80

My Darling Sarah,

I had an interview with the Governor today. We discussed the possibility of getting transferred to the Training For Freedom Hostel and his view is that the matter is for the Parole Board and Department to decide. The view is that I am here like any other prisoner. It seems that there will be no move to the TFF Hostel till next November. Twelve months prior to release. When I quoted the part in George Younger's letter about 'Individual programmes to suit the needs of the individual' he told me this was only within the established programme set-up.

24th DECEMBER '80

My Darling Sarah,

Christmas Day rings hollow in here as we are all caught in the dilemma of wanting to be with our loved ones and yet trying not to be openly dispirited. I found it amusing to see an Assistant Governor appear at breakfast time – something unheard of.

For one young guy it was a tragic day as his Mum, Dad and brother were burned to death in a fire earlier this morning. This has made the rest of us count our blessings. Generally a sadness hangs over the place and no amount of pretence or acting will eliminate this. I wakened first thing, thought of you and wished you a Merry Christmas. The day passed quickly enough and now at 4.50pm we have been locked up till tomorrow morning. I've done some images of Christmas in prison in my sketchbook, and lost myself in this for a while...

Boxing Day: *Hope your day has gone well. I'm locked up and shutting out all the emotions of the occasion but keeping myself intact and together. I see everyone here struggling through what is obviously a difficult period for them.*

3rd JANUARY '81

Although very tired when I wakened this morning it was a great feeling knowing I'd be going out again. I stepped out of the gate and it was cold but sunny. I felt deliriously happy. I find that I'm unable to walk along the street. I have to run. This personifies what I feel inside. My thought process is like a newsreel out of control with everything going at high speed. I feel my physical freedom to the full; taking in the sky, the road, the horizon, feel the air, take a deep breath of it and run, run, run...

At the workshop I had a coffee with Laurence and he brought me up to date on things. We are joined by others from the one-parent family group and Mick, who fills me in on various activities...

Tonight I returned to the prison after a full day of community activities. Here the tension lies in me like a dead-weight. I feel it tight and taut. It's a far cry from my feelings earlier today. I feel stretched and strained sitting in my bare cell dressed in prison uniform. I feel like Cinderella at the stroke of twelve. Two tangerines sit forlornly on the bed reminding me that I was outside. What am I doing here?

8th JANUARY '81

BOYLE WAS THE BOSS (*Daily Record* front page)

Amazing attack by former Scots prison minister.

A former Government Minister in charge of Scotland's prisons yesterday launched an astonishing attack on Jimmy Boyle and the way he 'ran' Barlinnie's controversial Special Unit.

MP Harry Ewing said: 'Boyle was running the place. He imposed his personality on the unit'. The MP for Falkirk, Stirling and Grangemouth was speaking to Rotarians in his home town of Leven, Fife.

He also alleged that a bid to put another 'hard man' into the Special Unit beside Boyle failed... because convicted killer Boyle did not like anyone else with a strong personality. And after an incident with Boyle, the other prisoner was taken back to Peterhead Prison after only six weeks.

On conditions in the Unit, Mr Ewing who was junior Minister responsible for prisons in the Labour Government said: 'It has a rarified atmosphere. It is an unreal world where Boyle had made a bust of Nicholas Fairbairn, now Solicitor General, in appreciation of him defending him on a number of occasions.' Mr Ewing told the Rotarians that lifer Boyle, now in Saughton Prison, Edinburgh, and being prepared for freedom, could not stand another prisoner being introduced into the Special Unit.

He went on: 'Boyle was running the place and imposed his personality on the Unit. I wanted to see another prisoner with a similar personality introduced. One man was there for six weeks before he had to be removed.' Mr Ewing said the controversy about Boyle would spring up again next month when STV screen a film about him. 'It is his case that will be put in the film. I want to put the case of those looking after the 4999 other prisoners in the system who are liable to be painted black.'

But a spokesman for the Scottish Office said they had no record of anyone who had been removed because of a personality clash with Boyle.

And last night Dr Sarah Boyle, who married Boyle in

1980, also denied the 'hard man' incident. She said: 'I think I know the Special Unit's history as well as anyone and I don't know what Mr Ewing is talking about.'

An STV spokesman said: 'We must let the Boyle film speak for itself. Mr Ewing has accepted an invitation to discuss it the night after it is screened.'

Later last night Mr Ewing said attempts by the Scottish Office to deny the incident were 'Ridiculous.' He added: 'They know it is true and if they continue to suggest I am a liar I will reveal the name of the prisoner I'm talking about. I feel that too much eulogizing of Boyle can happen and it should be contained.'

> *Darling Sarah,*
>
> *Harry Ewing splashed all over the front page of the Record. What a pathetic little man he is. Although I was angry at the whole untruthful content there is a funny side to it. The idea of me doing a portrait of Nicky Fairbairn is hilarious. I am sure that even he must recognise there are limits to my artistic talents!*

9th JANUARY '80
EWING RAPPED OVER BOYLE

Former Prisons Minister Harry Ewing, at the centre of the latest controversy over the Barlinnie Special Unit, came under fire yesterday.

Attack No 1 was launched by the present Home Affairs Minister Malcolm Rifkind. He described as 'extra-ordinary' Mr Ewing's claims that convicted killert Jimmy Boyle ran the Unit when he was a prisoner there.

Attack No 2 came from one of Mr Ewing's own colleagues when he was a Labour Junior Minister in the Scottish Office. MP Neil Carmichael claimed that during the period Mr Ewing was the Minister responsible for the Special Unit, he only spent 20 minutes there...'

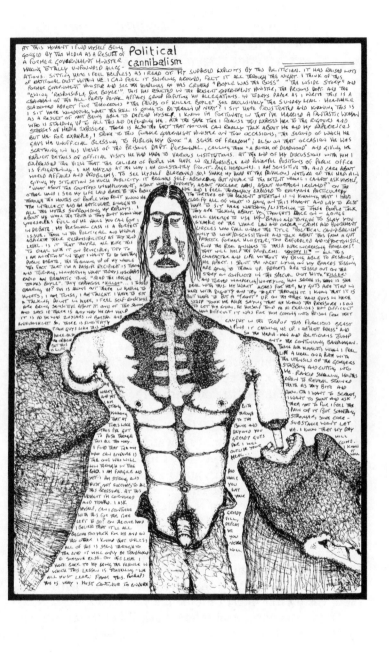

My Darling Sarah,
I was pleased at Malcolm Rifkind's reply today as it certainly places it all at the feet of Harry Ewing who is being shown for what he is, a political opportunist of the worst kind... I'm delighted that our lawyers are going for him...

21st JANUARY '81

In the workshop a phone message for me to call Sarah... She is feeling ill. I find myself torn apart to an extent that I've never experienced before. My most vulnerable spot has been hit. Sarah is badly upset as her legs have gone numb. She suspects multiple sclerosis. I can't take this fucking situation which keeps us apart. Robert drove me to our house. I cast caution to the wind — fuck them all. Holding Sarah I take her in the car to hospital. Conspicuously, I pull a cap over my eyes and a scarf round the lower part of my face. I know I can get into serious trouble for taking my wife to hospital. I find it difficult to comprehend these rules. All I'm doing is what any normal husband would. If at the end of the day it falls apart and they do me then fuck it. I know Sarah is feeling all the worse for being ill as it exposes us to this sort of danger. Both of us are trying hard to be protective and at the same time attend to our needs. I can at least take satisfaction from the fact that just being there gave her a great lift. It was a soul destroying job having to drop her at the front door of the hospital and watch Robert help her in. I sat watching her stumble and it burned its image deep into me. I felt a traitor and coward for leaving her. I felt as though I was running out on Sarah, who has stood up and defended me against all and sundry. The anguish in me was terrible. Robert, was unable to understand why I couldn't go in. The people in the workshop were very sensitive when I returned. Some of them eventually went to the hospital to see her. I spent the rest of the day ploughing my way through my work. Sarah called four hours later saying that she had had exhaustive tests and it is a viral infection of some sort.

There was pure relief in me. I asked her to take it easy,

stay in the flat and I would be across. I did, taking some food and champagne with me. it was great to be with her and in our house together. We drank the wine and had some food. I was constantly aware of the rules I was breaking in all this but was intent on supporting Sarah, but keeping in mind the danger of what we were doing. It was lovely lying on the floor together and letting Sarah cry; oh how this got to me. I guess I just held her but was aware that our time here was very short. Eventually I had to wrench myself away. It was difficult, very difficult.

I felt stunned and exhausted by the time I arrived back at the prison. The jangling of keys, the slamming of doors, the shouts of: 'Boyle back from Wester Hailes' rang in my ears. I stumbled across the yard to my cell feeling numb. . . I now sit here locked in with all the anger, frustration and weariness of my situation. I can only think of Sarah alone in the flat knowing she will be feeling even worse than I am. I have to leave this pen down to curl up on my wooden bed boards and moan at the mental stress I feel. . .

22nd JANUARY '81 (6.23am)
I've slept in snatches throughout the night feeling tense and torn. I love Sarah so much and the thought of her being ill and alone is getting to me. There is also a part that nags me for putting her through this. Little shits like Harry Ewing put tremendous pressure on us both when making statements about me. A sad little man trying to make political capital out of me — Christ, he must be hard up!
6.59am. I burst out into the main prison drive and the streets like a high velocity bullet. I ran towards my work, past people and traffic. I passed a 'For Hire' taxi and was tempted to jump on it and head for home to Sarah but again found myself caught in a dilemma, trying not to be irresponsible, trying to strike some sort of balance, trying not to take too much of a chance. I hate this fucking authority and its inhuman rules, and myself for being so subservient to them. I had to run past two telephone booths as they were within sight of the prison and I'm not allowed to use them. Eventually I reached a 'safe' phone

booth and spoke to Sarah. She sounded weak and tired. I awakened her; I implored her to stay in bed today... I told her I love her, told her again and again...

I bulldozed my way through various meetings except one. This young girl wants to see her father who was committed to the State Hospital when she was five months old — she is now seventeen years of age. He was committed for rape and murder. She wants to see him as her life has been a living nightmare. Her mother is an alcoholic but remarried and had two children to a military man. He beat the shit out of them all... Speaking to her seemed to help me in relation to my own situation. This place is filled with tragedies. There must be some way of dealing with them.

24th JANUARY '81
Somehow it all seems to be caving in. I received a letter from Sarah that seems to mirror my thoughts and feelings:

> *My Darling Jimmy,*
>   *As I write this I realise you'll probably be worried about me knowing that I'm not well at the moment. Tonight I sat here with the core of pain boring through me, feeling just terrible about the whole situation – and more than the sickness itself, just sick inside about it all. It got so bad that I really couldn't do anything else at all but groan in agony, feeling to the full my present futility and helplessness; no, even more, what it must be doing to you if it's affecting me as much as this. But, you reach a point where you just have to turn around and find something positive to focus on – pull together, make the effort, start up again and face it, whatever it is. And I must say I'm no clearer about this, just that this numbness continues...*

A voice calls for Governor's inspection and the sound of footsteps can be heard as each door is unlocked and slammed closed. Mine opens and I stand casually giving the impression that I'm only going along with this because

300

I have no option thus any participation is reluctant and minimal. 'Good Morning?' the female Assistant Governor asks. I say 'Okay,' and there is an embarrassed and awkward pause and at least she has the decency not to pretend to be inspecting my cell and moves on as the door is closed by one of her entourage.

25th JANUARY '81
The sun is shining as I sit on top of my bed writing this; the sound of a bird can be heard singing. Someone in the cell block is playing the guitar and singing. Looking out of my prison window I can see over the fence to small plots of land where people grow vegetables and flowers. I wonder if they ever think of the prisoners vegetating in here? This morning after breakfast I can see guys all spick and span, faces shaved, clothes pressed, shoes polished for church and chapel. Clearly, for the majority it is an avenue for in-creasing their chances of parole, for the few others religion is something they have grasped onto. One can be sceptical and say they are all at it for parole but I have spoken to a few who have really grasped it to satisfy a deep need — remorse?

I noticed two assistant governors sitting in the office used by the officers and drinking tea. They are tryint to be seen as 'one of the boys'. These guys have entered the prison service by the 'open competition' and find them-selves in a prison setting. I suppose in principle this is seen as healthy but in practice it runs into problems. It's here they come up against case-hardened prison officers who have lots of experience. Most of these assistant governors are young guys who haven't really matured yet and are out of their depth in here. In my experience they tend to spend the first few years ingratiating themselved with staff who are threatened by outsiders coming in. As outsiders they tend ot over-compensate and this isn't only the junior governors who are guilty of this — social workers, priests, ministers and teachers etc...

8th FEBRUARY '81

My Darling Sarah,

I didn't send you the usual letter this morning as I've been presented with 'another' problem – wait for it! I was taken in front of the Governor and one of his assistants and told that my Wester Hailes community project was 'suspended'. This is because I watched a preview of A Sense of Freedom.

I've already told you about the paranoia in the Prisons Department over the film. Well, it exists in the workshop to some extent. The view taken there is that in taking me on they are in the front line for criticism so asked if they could have a preview. I was approached by Laurence to arrange this and did. My view was that the people who had taken me on should have a look at it – this is the least I could do! The film was sent up by John McKenzie in video form and shown to us. Later in conversation to two assistant governors Laurence mentioned it. They took it back to the Governor and now I'm in trouble... Further to all this, though it isn't a major factor, there is the insidious process of censorship. Why shouldn't I see the film? This then takes us back to the origins of the book and how it was handled at that stage. They say that no official confirmation was given in writing but there was more than enough oral encouragement away back in the good old days.

10th FEBRUARY '81
BOYLE LOSES FREEDOM (front page *Scottish Daily Express*)

Killer Jimmy Boyle has lost his freedom to work outside prison. Prison bosses imposed the ban after Boyle was caught grabbing a sneak preview of his TV life story.

Until now Boyle, who is in Saughton Prison, has had licence to spend two days a week working as a helper at Wester Hailes community centre. Last night MPs were asking for a full statement by the Prisons Department about events at the centre last Friday.

It appears that film producer Jeremy Issacs, now boss of ITV's Channel Four travelled up from London with a copy of the TV documentary *A Sense of Freedom* which tells Boyle's story and is to be shown on Scottish Television. . .

GET BACK INSIDE! (*Daily Record*)
KILLER JIMMY BOYLE. . .

> *My Darling Sarah,*
> *Well, it's been a day filled with drama and fiction that will far outweigh the film itself. It's reached such a level that I'm beginning to believe I shot the projectionist! Who would believe that such headlines could be made from someone seeing a film. . .*

15th FEBRUARY '81

Tonight I was sitting in the TV room when I was called out. The officer told me that Mr Hills wanted to see me. Walking up the passage I was nervous, wondering what he wanted to see me about; in that short walk my fantasies ran wild; it could be something wrong with Sarah, bad news about my future release. . . Whatever, I prepared myself.

On going into the assistant governor's room he — Mr Hills — was taking off his watch and placing it on the desk in front of him. He told me I could walk out if I wanted to. He said he was looking for my help as tomorrow he was going to the preview of this film with a panel of people and would like to talk it over with me. He seemed extremely nervous and edgy. It must have taken a lot for him to see me.

He then told me he was angry at Issacs stopping the film where he had, why had he done this if he was supposed to be a friend? It would have made his job tomorrow easier if they had shown more of what came after, he said. He thought Jeremy Issacs was just stirring it up. I told him I doubted this very much and that if he himself wasn't so defensive about it then it wouldn't be so bad. Mr Hills then went on to declare that the penal system does do good. I told him if he wanted to get specific about this then just outside the door all his staff were clustered in a cell-like office and prisoners were in their cells, that they all had one thing in common — boredom. I reminded him that this was the best that Edinburgh as a Training Prison had to offer. He readily agreed to this, accepting it as true.

We then had a discussion on the penal system and I told him that every time someone from officialdom talks about it they rarely make constructive criticism. I said its the same old repetitive stuff.

All of this was extremely puzzling to me but one thing for sure, Mr Hills is nervous about tomrrow.

18th FEBRUARY '81
> *My Darling Sarah,*
>
> *Well, I'll give you reactions I've had from the film. Two prison officers said they thought it was a really good movie, one recommending it to win an award, the other saying he was surprised the time passed so quickly. Another was witty, 'Going through all that when all you wanted was a knife to open your parcel'. Those who spoke openly to me about it suggested mixed reactions amongst the other staff, something that is inevitable.*

19th FEBRUARY '81
> *My Darling Sarah,*
>
> *It was tremendous to get your letter today reading your account of things. I've been getting some mixed feedback on the Discussion programme last night. It seems to have been a disappointment. The favourable comments reserved for Wattie's contributions. I understand Mr Hills kept a low profile.*

20th FEBRUARY '81
This morning Mr Hills sent for me. I went in front of him and his Deputy Governor and was told I'd be resuming my two days as Wester Hailes, starting on Tuesday. He warned that one more slip and it would be taken away from me altogether. He said he would put it straight to the Prisons Department and Secretary of State.

24th FEBRUARY '81

Acclimatising to the outside world is becoming increasingly difficult as time goes on and I enter new areas. I feel very guarded and defensive and at the same time I'm putting up a front. It's difficult to explain this as it's all so complex and multi-layered. I went a walk with Laurence this morning and explained some of what was going on. I now fully recognise that one can't be locked in a closed institution and not feel to the full what I'm experiencing now.

When I'm with people on the outside I'm tense, feeling as though my guts are tied in a knot. The people around me are what I believe to be the very ordinary, salt-of-the-earth kind that I come from. They aren't armchair revolutionaries but simply people who have got off their arses and done something about their particular area and working together to improve it.

17th APRIL '81

*Dear Mr Harper, (*my lawyer*)*

Thank you for your letter of 6th February ref; JRH/RP regarding your client Mr James Boyle and comments that I am reported as having made regarding Mr Boyle when he was an inmate in the Barlinnie Special Unit...

Dealing first of all with the reported quotes to the effect that Mr Boyle 'ran' Barlinnie Special Unit and that he attempted to deny the entry to the Unit of another 'Hard man'. I have twice since the report of my speech made it quite clear that I said neither of these things.

What I said was that 'Boyle has a strong personality and in any small group, whether it be a small class at school, a small political group or as in this case a small group of prisoners it was relatively easy for that strong personality to manifest itself'.

That statement was made in the context of an argument being advanced in my speech that the Unit was too small and ought to be made bigger and it was

305

*in the same context that I related the story of the
prisoner (who I did not name) who was transferred to
the Unit and because of an incident had to be sent
back to his original prison.*

*Never at any time did I say that Boyle attempted to
prevent the man being brought to the Unit in the first
place and indeed I was aware that the Unit as a whole
had made representations to have the man kept in the
Unit even after the incident to which I refer.*

*In this part of my address I was arguing that had
the Unit been larger with more prisoners, say up to
fifteen, the possibility of two men coming into
conflict is reduced because of the number of other
men with whom the other prisoner may enjoy more in
common.*

*As I indicated at the beginning of my letter I have
dealt with this twice already, once on Radio Clyde in
the presence of Mrs Boyle who agreed that Mr Boyle
had a strong personality and the other occasion when
I clarified this matter on the S.T.V. programme the
evening after the screening of* A Sense of Freedom.

I do hope that both points are now fully cleared up.

*Turning to the reported statement to the effect that
Mr Boyle had made a bust of Nicholas Fairbairn in
appreciation of defending him. I have to tell you that
the first part of the report is correct. i.e. 'that Mr
Boyle made a bust of Nicholas Fairbairn', but the
second part is not correct and is again a case of a
reporter combining two entirely different parts of my
address. When it was pointed out to me by Mrs Boyle
that Mr Boyle had not in fact made a bust of Mr
Fairbairn I immediately apologised and asked
her personally to convey my apologies to her husband.*

*I again in response to your letter make it clear that
I accept that the bust I saw when I visited the Unit on
one of my visits was not in fact that of Mr Fairbairn
and I again apologise for any embarrassment this
may have caused Mr Boyle...'*

25th APRIL '81

After my run round the football field today I spoke to Jinksy, a lifer just four years into his sentence. He is seeing the prison psychiatrist. Jinksy told me he's read a magazine giving schizophrenic symptoms and told me that everyone of them fit him to a 'T'. I told him he is at a critical stage in his sentence and it could be this. He said it isn't this. He went on to tell me how Sarah is brainy and how he would like to write out what he is feeling for me to give her. He said he could answer any questions Sarah wrote out and he would do this truthfully. He said he doesn't want to go to the doctor here as he can't stand marching in and trying to talk while standing to attention. He is also afraid of getting largactil and other crappy drugs.

7th MAY '81

This morning when walking through 'B' Hall on my way to the reception to go out to Wester Hailes I met Jinksy. He was standing in the toilet area stripped to the waist. He told me not to contact his parents to say he cut his wrists. He had sent word through with another prisoner asking me to do this. I asked him how he felt, realising that it would be difficult for him to 'save face'. His right wrist was badly cut with two lines of stitches. Clearly he had made a serious attempt. I left him with the words, 'Stay strong, fight it.'

I met a Principal Officer who told me he had been to see *Jinksy (earlier in the week I had spoken to him about Jinksy asking if he would recommend him for the Special Unit). He told me Jinksy would be returned to his old Hall. He said he doubts if he will be put on a disciplinary report as they intend to waive this incident. I was puzzled at this and asked what he meant. He told me that anyone doing this is usually charged with causing self-inflicted wounds.

There are moments in here when thinking makes me shudder!

9th MAY '81

I have a shower then lie on top of my bed till 2pm. A voice

---

*Jinksy eventually hung himself in his cell.

shouts 'Visits'. Going down to the Hall desk I join others.

Two of us are taken along the corridor to the other side of the prison. We sit in a small side room. There are eleven prisoners in all. Looking round their faces there is tension as some wonder if their visitors will come. If they don't it usually means having to trudge back along the corridor — a humiliating experience. It means having to make excuses to their escort and prisoner mates as to why their visitor didn't turn up. A member of staff comes to the door with visiting slips in his hand and calls out the names. I am first and walk to the door to be searched. I walk into the visit room with my jacket on my arm. The room is vast with tables and chairs spread over it. Prison officers stand against the wall watching. I see Sarah sitting at one of the tables and walk over. My stomach is churning and I want privacy. I lean over and kiss her. 'Happy Birthday,' she says. Sitting at the table we hold hands tightly and look at each other. We talk about this and that, we look, smile, occasionally kiss...

Around us prisoners sit with their families. Children race all over the room with toys...

A voice shouts 'Time up' after an hour. This is hard and yet it is a relief. We embrace and tell each other of our love. We hug each other tightly before parting. We trudge back along the corridor after yet another search. Sunlight streams through gaps in the enclosed space. I think of Sarah entering her car in the car park. I look around me and feel like weeping.

24th JUNE '81

I was sitting speaking to young Robert this morning. He talked about being home on an SEL. He was in a terrible state and shattered by it. I asked him why this was. He replied that he felt so distant from his family and finds it difficult to speak to them. We talked about him being away from them for five and a half years and how it will never be the same again. He was filled with anger and resentment.

He said he had befriended a guy in prison and he was at his house when he went home. He said he had more in common with this guy than with his family. We talked about this and what prison does to people. In the afternoon Robert came in looking much better. He said the talk we had this morning had done him a power of good... No one at an official level tries to help these guys understand what they are going to come up against at a domestic and social level when released. No wonder many of them fall at the first hurdle.

28th JUNE '81
Big Humph, a prisoner, approached me this evening. He wants to see the Inspector of Prisons to lodge a complaint. He was scheduled to go on his SEL two weeks ago but it was cancelled. I asked him why.

He said on the Hall Notice Board it states that prisoners going on SELs must save £1 from their weekly prison earnings and have it transferred to their personal cash property before going. The night before his SEL he was informed that he was twenty six pence short. He told the officer that he had this much credit on his wages card so would he transfer it. He was told it was too late. As a result his family expecting him home the following day were disappointed. No one informed them...

10th JULY '81
(Stolen time): This is my first summer in open space for fourteen years. Leaving the prison in the morning I walked along a small lane. Birds were singing and chirping but the thickness of the greenery amazed me. I've walked this path in the winter when it's bare but the change of seasons has put splendid clothes on it.

Today I went right out into the country and seaside. Sarah was with me and so it was lovely sharing this experience together. The sun shone brightly in North Berwick. Again, the rolling laid-back countryside was stunning. It seemed to go on forever. On a quiet beach I undressed putting on my swimming trunks and like a puppy rushed into the water. It was cold, very cold. Sarah watched, laughing. I waded in smelling the tang of the salt, feeling the hardness of the water, the softness of the sand. I plunged into the shallows. Only the icy water could have matched the intensity of my feelings I had to be as extreme as the experience.

Together we ran across the sand leaving our footprints embedded. Sarah found a jellyfish. We watched as the waves lapped it further onto the beach. My first jellyfish in fourteen years. He was no ordinary jellyfish, he was special! Together we walked to a point in the distance, a soft green downy part that allowed us to lie down. Sarah snuggled up to me, we kissed, we embraced and looked into the distance as the sun cast a beautiful light on the water. it was so peaceful.

To think that all of this will be accessible to me in the freedom of my lifetime, to imagine the rest of my life looking at this natural beauty.

12th JULY '81

The guy who smashed his cell furniture the other week didn't do it as a result of a direct domestic problem. This is what I first heard. Having probed to find out why, as he seemed such a stable guy, I was informed he wasn't right after his SEL. Apparently he has told guys close to him that being out was a pure 'wind up'. Like most guys he went out with the expectation that all would be well once he was back with his family. In fact it hit him like a ton of bricks that he had changed. He had been living on memories of all those years, keeping it alive, reminding himself what it was before he came in, but time had passed.

Now, having heard this a few times I've brought the subject up with a few guys and am surprised to find quite a lot aren't taking SELs even though they have been eligible for years. I asked why and they all reply that it means going round having to ask screws only to be rejected; and then going home for a few hours. They couldn't handle this they said. It would be too much for them. This flies in the face of the assumption that guys will do anything to get out of prison for a few hours.

Another guy went home on his SEL last week to find that

his family didn't come to meet him. This was a bitter disappointment. The member of staff took him for a meal.

The pain that is locked up in this building where I sit can be felt. Behind each cell door is someone aching like an open wound. Each is just a human being needing to be treated as such. This dinosaur of a system is tearing them apart emotionally. What do I mean by this?

I can perhaps illustrate this by giving insight to my feelings at this moment. I have this tight knotted feeling in my stomach, this jealousy in my heart that my wife is with someone else. I pick up small things said during the week and let them magnify out of all proportion in here. I know that when out during the week and stealing time with her she will alleviate these feelings in me. We will have the good fortune of being able to talk about it. The reason I feel this is because sitting here locked in this cell I feel totally devalued. I therefore wonder why anyone could possibly love me or stay with me. It strikes at the very root of my potency. I want to be with her badly but can't. So, I distort this feeling of wanting to be with her onto her wanting to be with me and seeking a substitute. It is completely irrational but stems from being locked in this small cell with my thoughts. What I have that the others don't is the ability to articulate it, to write it out and to meet Sarah mid-week. They don't and it is for these reasons that guys smash up their cells, explode violently, attempt or succeed in suicide.

14th JULY '81
Arriving back in prison tonight after my day at Wester Hailes, the duty Chief Officer was waiting at the gate. He told me the step-father of my son called to say James is causing problems — not serious — but was about to be put into a place of care.

He said that normally he wouldn't tell someone news like this at this time of night but I'm a pretty level headed type and he knows I can cope with it. He spoke to the Assistant Governor who told him I have access to a phone at my work so can phone from there tomorrow.

16th JULY '81

This morning I called John, my son's step-father. He explained to me that James is going from bad to worse, that he is glue-sniffing and lately he's had to be carried home suspected of taking heroin. He is only fifteen years old. He said police suspected this and know that heroin is being 'pushed' from the local community centre in the Gorbals and that lots of young girls are taking it.

John said the situation has reached a critical stage and he would like to talk to me about it and we agreed to meet. He came to Edinburgh. One of the problems is that James is put on a pedestal because he is my son. His pals treat him as a hard man but he isn't. All James really knows about me is what he reads, hears and sees in the film. He's really confused as to who and what his father is. The social worker, his mother, and John all agree that I am the only hope for the boy. John wanted to give James over to me this afternoon but I had to explain my circumstances.

18th JULY '81

The Governor and his Assistant are not at all happy about the situation concerning James. It is clear they don't want me participating extensively in helping the boy. They have stated that I cannot assume any responsibility for the boy in my present situation. Also, that my access to him must be very limited. All of us are quite shocked at this... I hate being in a position where I have to ask them. I made this clear to them.

25th OCTOBER '81

This morning the clocks were turned back to signify the end of summertime. For some it meant an extra hour in bed. For me it was an extra hour pacing the floor.

Although I still have a year to go in prison this is my last night locked in a traditional cell. Tomorrow I will be allowed five days Home Leave and then go on to what is officially called Training For Freedom. Moving from this rigid penal system I go to a more relaxed setting. However, I am realistic enough to know it is a continuance of my futile confinement. What is momentous is my having five days away with Sarah.

When I wakened the cell was dark. Getting out of bed I put on my trousers and looked out of the window. Frost covered the grass outside. It was cold. I walked up and down the floor. Pacing this floor I carried — wrapped in this body of mine — a messy paradox of human emotion. On the one hand there is the pleasure-filled adrenalin of expectation of being outside, on the other there is a fearful anxiety about a last minute hitch preventing it. Even with barely twenty-four hours to go I raise the wearying question, 'Am I ever going to make it'.

Walking in this space I told myself it was coming to an end. There are two hours till this door is unlocked. Being in this space means I don't have the basic freedom to switch off the light, go to the toilet, or have a drink of fresh water. After today all of this will be changed. With this perspective I can't help but get vivid images of tomorrow night when tasting freedom with Sarah. I will be able to go for a walk, shop, switch on the TV, walk in the rain, open the door and go into the street... As though to act as a balance part of me intrudes to remind me not to be too confident as nothing has happened yet.

I am so distrustful of the authorities. I feel there is still a chance they may want to get back at me. I know they don't like the way I have challenged the system. They don't like to see me leaving a winner. At the same time I don't want to dwell on these negative feelings; I've had enough of those in my lifetime. With these powerful emotions in my mind and body I am having to ease the see-sawing of their movements; and yet I know there is a part of me colluding with this. There is a part of me wanting to experience all the emotional trauma of this situation so that I have *lived* it. This moment in time has been a long time coming so I want to taste it to the full — the good and the bad.

26th OCTOBER '81
Stepping across the gate into Sarah's arms. We embrace and kiss. So lovely to touch in legitimate time. We waste no

313

time jumping in the car and heading into the distance.

Accumulated thoughts: I am wondering what it will be like to sleep together, having known each other for four years and been married almost two. Up the long winding roads the scenery was spectacular. Sitting there with Sarah at my side, the prison far behind and the wonders of the Scottish Highlands all around me I felt stunned with pleasure... How can I possibly explain this experience to anyone after fourteen years in prison. Every fibre was open and alert to this vast mountain scenery. Finally we reached our caravan situated high up on the hillside with a wide and full view of the valley. It was getting quite dark though still enough light for us to see our view from the caravan. Sheep were all around us. We looked down the valley to a spattering of cottages and farmhouses. The visual images are overwhelming. The night was spent in a small double bed with me always aware of Sarah next to me. I was restless. It will take some getting used to after fourteen years of sleeping alone... It's the first time in years I've slept on a mattress.

27th OCTOBER '81
Here we are with each other throughout the day and seeing each other as we waken in the morning. It's gonna take some time for us to adjust to... mind you we made the most of it.

Outside I am greeted by snow-capped mountains, jagged skylines and paintbox splashes of Autumn colouring. Nearby there are rushing streams and rivers... As I write this I'm still tired and not really able to express fully all the thoughts and feelings which were racing through me all night. This freedom is so precious that I'm scared to sleep in case I miss any of it. I was full of stresses and strains from the sudden change in my situation.

29th OCTOBER '81
In the morning I was up early and out exploring the land-scape with all my senses. Sarah by my side was monitoring, a stable influence and steady hand to my almost uncon-

trollable desire for more. It was thrilling to stand in the silent morning and look to the distance without any man-made structure obstructing the view as in prison. The ever-changing light here is so dramatic; one can imagine any aspiring film technician being inspired by nature's ability to create the most powerful theatrical setting in this land-scape.

There are moments when Sarah and I speak but lots of the time is spent in silence, in just being with each other.

30th OCTOBER '81

Sarah brought me to the prison gate and we parted. . . I was swallowed up by the surrounding wall. Back in here again, it felt as though I had never been away. This place has a way of crushing one's good feelings. The Training For Freedom hostel is secluded in a corner of the prison. On entering the voice shoued, 'Boyle for TFF'. I walked to a small door that was opened by a uniformed prison officer. He escorted me to the small building. He is the duty officer and has a colleague who shares hostel duty with him.

He tells me the Governor has left orders that I've to remain in the prison till such times as I start my work on Monday. He apologises saying he would have let me out on the three hours church parole on Sunday but for some reason the Governor has stated that I've not to go out. In taking my particulars I told him that come Monday I start a community job at Wester Hailes and will be employed by them. He informs me that I will have to bring my weekly wage to him or his colleague who will give me weekly expenses and £3 pocket money. Another £3 will go into my savings for release.

He tells me that each week I'll be given twelve hours free time and every third weekend I'll get forty-eight hours home leave. Each Sunday morning we get three hours Church parole!

Upstairs, blazoned in red print behind the door, was a notice warning all prisoners not to drink alcohol when out on parole. It says this will be considered a breach of the hostel rules and liable to punishment.

Some of the other guys come to greet me. I know them from the old system. They show me to my bed in a dormitory. It is filthy. There are approximately twelve beds. We sit speaking and they tell me what a dump it is. One describes this particular part of the sentence as 'running the gauntlet'. He expands on this saying that if a few minutes late on returning, or smelling of drink, you get thrown in the punishment cells. He described one occasion when it happened to him. He arrived back after a couple of pints but took some mints to cover the smell. They took him to the prison medical officer to verify he had been drinking. He said he hasn't had as much as a wine gum. They took him to the punishment cells and kept him there overnight. In the morning he went before the Governor and was found guilty. They told me how on occasions they've been in a pub and a prison officer has walked in and they've all ducked under the table. One said if any of them are with a girl it is embarrassing.

When talking about their work, one or two described how the prison is tied to two industries, the Fruitmarket, which those working there describe as 'brutal exploitation' and another place where guys do some painting which is considered okay. They say that I am fortunate to be working in the Community. There is another guy doing similar work and one other working in a hospital.

They get their food from the main prison kitchen. They can bring in odd bits and pieces. One of the guys took me to his room. I asked him about this and he informed me that one gets promoted to one of these six small rooms from the dormitory. The door is left unlocked but there is a heavy grill on the window. He told me we can all sit in a small room watching TV and have an electric kettle to make coffee and tea. We are locked in this second floor together from 9.30pm to the following morning.

2nd NOVEMBER '81
First day out from TFF but wasn't allowed out till 9.45am. It's great to see everyone again. They all wanted to know how the five days went. I could tell they were very pleased

for us. We have made so many good friends here that it's magic to be back with them. In a way they are our point of sanity with this system we are having to deal with. I spent the day putting myself about, particularly among the younger people. Now that I have more time I can connect to them at a deeper level.

16th NOVEMBER '81
This morning I was taken from the hostel to the social work unit in the prison. The social worker sat as though not knowing what to do. It soon became apparent that he had no papers or anything on me. I explained to him how this is the first social worker I've had in fourteen years. He said this is most unusual as one normally gets a social work report when the Parole Application is being compiled, and that contact is essential when someone is going onto TFF. He said how difficult it will be to get a social worker who can cope with me on a supervisory basis. I asked him the procedure for selecting one. He said its a team decision in the Office catchment area where my home is. I told him that I hoped they picked someone reasonable as an idiot would be pointless. He said perhaps I could bring an idiot on.

23rd NOVEMBER '81
This morning the social worker came across again. He informed me that he has passed my request for a social worker on to my local office. He said they feel it is a long way off therefore will take some time. I said it was immaterial to me. He's a rather placid guy and carries keys to lock and unlock doors. In many ways he seems like a prison officer, the better type perhaps. I find this sort of meeting has little value. There is a piece in *The Scotsman* quoting the prison governor, Mr Hills: 'While people must be controlled in custody they must also be given the freedom to respond and to be treated decently. To achieve that state of affairs, a prison must demonstrate a reasonable justice, recognise the formal rights of a prisoner, and have contact with and be involved with the community'.

5th DECEMBER '81

On returning from work this afternoon I met with the prison officer on duty. He said I may be in trouble. I asked what for and he replied that I shoudn't be working on a Saturday. He walked me to the Governor's office telling me to keep my cool.

The Training Governor was with an assistant governor. The former asked what I was doing working on a Saturday? I asked what he meant as I've been working every Saturday morning since coming onto TFF. He then told me my maximum hours of work are fifty per week. He said I have to work within these hours. He said he has been onto Mr Hills, who has instructed that I haven't to go out. I reminded him that I have twelve hours free time and have arranged to meet my wife shortly.

He said it has been specifically laid down that I don't work at the weekends. I told him that I haven't been told this and pulled out my licence:

1) You will obey such instructions as you may receive from the Governor with regard to the hours which you may be absent from the prison each day: *09.45 hrs – 21.00 hrs.*

I was asked to leave the room, the prison officer escorting me to do likewise. Some minutes later I was called back in and told that Mr Hills has instructed (on the phone from his home) that I write in my own handwriting what I thought my working hours to be. He also instructed that I won't be going anywhere till my employer is contacted.

I wrote:

> *Dear Sir,*
> *The agreement in which I was out was as per Parole Licence. The licence states that I will be absent from the prison each day: 09.45 hrs. – 21.00 hurs. I have been asked to write this statement and I have no idea what I am really expected to write.*
>
> *J. Boyle*

On returning to the Governor's office the Training Governor told me I will get my twelve hours this weekend but I won't be going to work on Monday or Tuesday till this matter is cleared up.

I spoke to the duty hostel officer who told me the whole thing is being blown out of all proportion because it is Jimmy Boyle. He said some of the other prisoners are going out in hours far in excess of mine. He told me of one of the guys is going off to Celtic Park today and is off somewhere else tomorrow. He said the staff he has spoken to are saying that I have been pretty good, causing no problems for them.

We talked for a bit and he said he's read my history on file, that the early years were bad but in the past ten years I have been faultless. He said one of the problems about here is that the Governor is insisting that I am the same as any other prisoner when I'm not. He notices this with basic Parole Forms as mine are more restrictive than everyone elses. I have a different one from everyone else in the hostel.

10th DECEMBER '81
There's been considerable upheaval over the Xmas Leave for us all on TFF. I was told the dates had come through 24th — 27th Dec. This is only four days whereas in other hostels it's five days. We were informed that all paroles stop between 1st — 4th January. There are no local paroles either (twelve hours are local paroles). I said the rules in this place could be sold as antuques.

We intend taking the matter to the Visiting Committee.

15th DECEMBER '81
This morning the prison officer told me the Training Governor wanted to see me, and then Mr Hills would see me. I was to stay in from work.

The passman (cleaner) prisoner told me that the Training Governor was upset at me yesterday. When doing his inspection of the Hostel he noticed some pennies and a broken watch on top of my locker and stated I shouldn't be leaving 'valuables' lying around. I counted the pennies;

they amounted to 37 pence. The watch was valued at four quid! Surely this isn't why he wants to see me?

Another prisoner informed me that my Trust Fund (set up through royalties from *A Sense of Freedom*) was on TV last night. It gave a good account of the people who have benefitted from it. I was pleased to hear this.

by 11am I was an hour late for work and asked the prison officer when the Governors were going to see me. He went to the phone and returned embarrassed saying: a) The Training Governor isn't on duty today and b) Mr Hills has left. The staff member remarked, 'They couldn't organise a piss up in a brewery'.

19th DECEMBER '81
This morning I sat waiting for the Governor to see me. All the while I was conscious of a drug meeting I had to organise in the community. I sat around till 10.45am, got my jacket and asked a prison officer painting the hostel to let me out. The duty hostel officer came in then. He said the Training Governor has instructed that I stay in till he completes the Governor's Orderly Room. I asked the officer to phone my work and say I won't make the meeting. I sat till 11.40am and was taken to the Governor's office. The Training Governor said Mr Hills wasn't present but he understood I had asked to see him. I stood there feeling extremely angry. There is no sensitivity to the work I am doing outside or the people waiting for me there. This is nothing but gross discourtesy and completely irresponsible.

Putting my best face on I explained yes, I wanted to ask why our Christmes leave had been cut from five to three days. The Training Governor was quite friendly in his attitude saying he doesn't understand why it is so restricted. He asked the duty hostel officer who said it is normal procedure. I explained to him how in Perth Prison the hostel people there are getting from the 24th — 28th. On top of this our local twelve hour parole is restricted from 30th Dec. to 4th Jan. He said he would take it up with Mr Hills. He said he personally thinks it absurd. He mentioned Northern Ireland saying people get out all the time over this period.

22nd DECEMBER '81
The Assistant Governor has been over seeing the guys individually to tell them they can have their Christmas Leave extended to the 29th if they want. It will mean bringing one of their forty eight paroles forward. I told him I would take it but it is disgraceful we have to use our ordinary paroles to make up the extension.

24th DECEMBER '81
This morning started with me writing a petition to the Secretary of State for Scotland to complain about the shortage of Christmas leave for prisoners on the TFF. I have asked that the Inspector of Prisons review the situation in the hostel as there seems some confusion as to whether it is a hostel or part of the prison. When I returned to the prison after work the duty officer was disagreeing about the time on our Licences. It stated 2pm and he though it should be 3.30pm. We all felt like tearing his head off. He kept us to the last minute before signing it. I queried mine which said I should return at 6pm on the 27th instead of the 29th. He said I would have to stay back while he checked it with the Governor. This further enraged the prisoners who thought he was 'winding me up'.

Still dressed in my working clothes I walked into the rain wearing my wellies. Sarah was there with Laurence. He drove us to the airport and we flew to London. Heathrow is magic, all nationalities melting into this one pot. The weather here isn't so bad so I look out of place in my wellies. My freedom is such that this means nothing to me.

We arrive and go to Peter McDougalls. . . Jeremy, John McKenzie, some actors and acresses are there. . . It's great. We celebrate the coming of Christmas. Sarah and I go off to St Martin-in-the-Fields in Trafalgar Square for mass. The singing and spirit of Christmas is soaking into me. My first one on the outside. . .

321

CHRISTMAS DAY '81

The spiritual quality of the night before combined with waking beside Sarah gave this Christmas morning a very special imprint. Sleepily we smiled and kissed each other. Our being together at nights still doesn't have natural fluency simply because we are in an on/off situation. This didn't detract from what we felt now.

Both of us got dressed, made breakfast then sat with our presents and some champagne. We toasted this special day. If I had a dream it would be this moment in freedom with Sarah.

Opening our gifts was such fun. I had some lovely presents; a jumper, some books and a lovely collage of us. Sarah was equally delighted with her presents from me.

We visited her Dad, who greeted us with warm hugs and kisses. he said to me, 'At long last we've met.' This is something both of us were looking forward to. The atmosphere in the house couldn't have been better. His wit and intellect were sharp, his recall quite amazing. He did not look a man of seventy-eight. I remember this man from every time I went to the movies. As film censor, his name would be scribbled on the certificate.

1st JANUARY '82

I sat with George in his small room in the hostel. He completes his life sentence in July. He spoke with strong anger and conviction when he said he couldn't do to anyone what the authorities have done to him; put him away for all these years for something he did when only a sixteen year old boy. Although he couldn't articulate this too well he was in effect saying that society allows people to live in sub-standard conditions. In doing so they have to live by a different set of values from the more affluent sections. But, when kids like George get caught up in gangs and someone dies as in George's case then the full weight of the authorities falls on him. The same authorities turn a blind eye to all the other equally horrific problems of his lifestyle which are not labelled 'criminal'. This is the world he was born into. There is a burning resentment in him as he speaks.

322

During our conversation he remarked that both of us have done our time differently. He tells me he has played the system and never got on the wrong side of the screws or Governors. He doesn't mind falling out with the odd screw but not anyone higher up as that could harm his chances of freedom. He said that I have beaten the system by taking them on and he loves this.

George began to open up and tell me ways that he has beaten them. He explained how as a Young Offender they were allowed parcels at Christmas time. On his way out of the Xmas visit with his parcel he stuck a lump of cannabis under his tongue and when reaching the screws the junior looked to the senior to ask if he should search. The senior replied, 'It's only wee George and he's okay; let him through.'

George pointed to a small bottle of aftershave on his table and explained to me that when returning to the prison tonight he stole it out of a drunk man's pocket. He says he knows he is taking a risk and that his freedom is at stake but he wants to tell himself that they haven't changed him. He talked about his work at a local hospital and resents the fact that the Governor has initiated this to make a name for himself as a liberal humanitarian. George says this is all part of the prison game. He said when the Governor is mentioned its always in a good light. George says they should judge him on what is happening on the inside.

Another prisoner joined us. We continued this dialogue and it was good. The Bells rang us into 1982. I kissed my marriage ring and silently wished Sarah a Happy New Year. The three of us wished each other all the best. I excused myself from them and sat reading a letter Sarah had given me to open at the New Year.

15th JANUARY '82

I returned to the prison tonight and spent some time speaking to George and another prisoner. We discussed the problems of adjusting to society after a long time away. Both of them agreed that the Hostel is good in that it does give them a chance to sort themselves out although they both think that it should be done long before this.

They discuss the gap between them, their families and friends. They both talk at length and in some depth about the difficulties of adjusting to outside life and the particular frustration of having to deal with Governors who only see prisoner's problems in the context of them wanting extra hours outside.

25th JANUARY '82

The duty officer informed me that I must return to the prison at 3pm to go in front of the Visiting Committee. I lay thinking of the V.C. and decided if I go in with a heavy staff escort surrounding me them I will withdraw from the proceedings and take my case elsewhere. Another prisoner told me this happened to him recently.

When I got there I was made to stand outside the Governor's office. Wattie, a prisoner at my table when in C Hall was surrounded by prison staff. He was waiting to go in. He looked pale and shaken. I remembered the last time I saw him he was full of tension waiting on a reply from the Parole Board. He has since slashed a prisoner for no apparent reason. He seemed to be in deep trouble now. He told me he is waiting to go to the High Court for it. I felt for him.

Another life prisoner came out from the Visiting Committee. He had been complaining about only being able to hand out three handicraft objects a year. He won and this was increased to six a year.

I walked in without an escort. Governor Hills sat at the top of the table with two male members of the Visiting Committee. A female member sat nearby. The Chief Officer was present.

I explained that I had written a petition asking the new Chief Inspector of Prisons to look into the Training For Freedom hostel. I was asking them to forward this onto him. I explained that I wanted him to look into the whole running of the TFF hostel, the social and employment matters. Mr Hills fumbled about in his desk for my original petition. He said he didn't have a copy. He stated that he understands the new Inspector of Prisons doesn't look into individual cases. I said there was absolutely nothing in the rule book about what this man does, therefore, I could only recall his original appointment and thought he said he would look into individual cases. Mr Hills again fumbled around looking for something on this man's brief. He stated that I could see the Departmental Inspector of Prisons. I said the significant difference between them was, my request was for the one who is 'independent'. It turned out that Mr Hills had nothing on this man's brief. The Chairman of the V.C. agreed that the Governor should get his information to him and he would let me know...

I returned to Wester Hailes and my work.

7th MARCH '82

The weekend with Sarah has softened me. I feel warm and relaxed, my mind at ease with the world. The experience of being together, lying on the bed in each others arms, the closeness, the love... ahh the love. Such beauty in our shared experience! All of this comes to an end as I return to prison. The Gate with its studded bolts of rusted metal remind me of rotting teeth in a gaping mouth. The rancid stench, the fear, the acute pain of having to step over the threshold grips me like an iron fist. I walk into the darkness of its throat and feel as though I've been swallowed up. My being here has reduced the flame of our love.

A guard stands looking at me. His eyes are empty, his face expressionless. The neat black moustache sits stiffly on his tight, thin lips. No word is exchanged between us. He stretches a boney hand to take my licence. I walk past him and the door slams closed behind me. The crunch of the keys, the grating of metal grind into my eardrums. I feel a lump of defeat fall heavily within me. The flame, the flame of our love flickers to counter all that surrounds me.

Other prisoners are clustered in the television room. They are locked into it as television is a necessary drug to escape the present situation. I leave them to sit in my small cell. I will get through this experience, I will.

325

8th MARCH '82

This morning I went down to go for my usual run around the small compound immediately surrounding the hostel. The duty officer informs me that as from today no hostel prisoner will be allowed outside this door unescorted. The reason for this is that the Chief Officer suspects drugs have been smuggled into the prison through the hostel. I explained that I appreciate their concern about drugs but I need my morning run. I reminded him that I abhor the use of drugs and feel that this restriction on the hostel prisoners is in no way going to prevent drugs getting into the prison. I also reminded him that my two years in the main prison have let me see how extensively durgs are used by prisoners. He acknowledged this saying in his experience this prison has been particularly bad for it over the past three or four years. He then told me there are plans to secure our windows so drugs cannot be thrown over the wall to a nearby working party in the main prison. I told him that I find all of this pretty incredulous and would like to see the Governor about it. There is no doubt that the drugs problem in the main prison has reached an alarming level.

10th MARCH '82

Billy is the new prisoner. He has just come from five days Home Leave. He told me the five days blew his head. He said he has done some community work in Dungavel, in a Children's Home. He said unlike other prisoners he didn't have regular outside visitors so had no idea what to expect outside.

He was thrown onto the streets with a tenner and hadn't a clue what to do, he could have been a raving loony for all they knew. He said they told him to report to Saughton and this hostel for TFF. He has never been in Edinburgh before; he comes from Glasgow.

27th MARCH '82

The prisoner passman approached me to say that Billy is acting strange and resisting any friendliness. He mentioned

Billy having been in Carstairs State Hospital and so maybe his behaviour is related to his 'illness'. I said I would have a chat with him as a few guys have mentioned this to me recently.

I approached Billy and asked how he was doing. I presented a very friendly face and was warm towards him. He was tight and remarked that he was okay. I asked if things were difficult and he replied he was okay. His wall of resistance was fighting off my wave of friendliness. He walked away not wanting to take it any further.

28th MARCH '82 (12.30am)
I left the TV room shortly after 10pm to go to my bed. Billy followed me and asked to speak to me. He remarked very seriously that he knows what is going on in here and what we are doing to him. I said that I know he is going through a bad time. I invited him in to sit down and closed the door. He then told me his food is being tampered with and that he will cause trouble if it happens again. I couldn't quite believe my ears. I asked him to explain and he said he was in agony as someone had put something into his food. He then told me that today he had seriously considered smashing a broken bottle into my face. I could see this guy was frighteningly disturbed. I looked him straight in the eyee and told him in a stern tone of voice not to think I'm a mug because I talk in gentle tones. He immediately pulled back from his frightening stance.

I then asked him what it was all about. Billy then told me everything has been going haywire since he arrived here. He said he was out for a drink on Wednesday and that night after he had eaten his food in the hostel he started sweating and feeling bad. He said it could only have been the food. He then told me that this was the same pattern as Perth, prior to his smashing a bottle into a screw's face. He said he had it all sussed out and as I was a very influential person I must know about it. He said today when I asked if he was having a hard time that this confirmed it. I then explained to him why I had done this. I told him I have done the same for others having problems here.

Billy said he walks to work in the morning with that bastard (another prisoner) so could blow him away no bother. He mentioned George as another little bastard and another prisoner. He said he thinks it is these three who are putting the passmen prisoners up to it. Billy said he could get a mob through to do anyone and he wouldn't need to lift a finger. I told him that I am not in the least impressed or intimidated by this talk. I said I really don't know him but that what he says makes me not want to trust him. He said he went through to Glasgow today and told his brother this. He drove him back through here and contacted an ex-prisoner.

The ex-prisoner told them I wouldn't do anything like that, 'Jimmy would rather do you a good turn than a bad one.' This is why he came to speak to me tonight. He said that he is going off his head in this place. I told him it's going to be very difficult for me to change his mind but I want to tell him that the other guys here are only interested in getting their time done and getting out. They are not into poisoning food. I told him they wouldn't even jeopardise their provisional release dates by complaining when the Governor cut short their Christmas leaves. So, there's no chance of them considering poisoning his food.

I asked him what had happened in Perth. He told me he got into conflict with a group of prisoners, 'the poison' he kept calling it. He said they kept 'winding him up' but when the screw did it he stuck the bottle in his face. Two detectives charged him and he was sent to Carstairs State Hospital without going to trial. He had served six and a half years of his sentence. The day after he was in Carstairs he felt great away from that 'poison in Perth'. The man in Carstairs stated he would like him to stay there a few years and as he is just starting a life sentence he will have some years to do anyway. Billy says he was quite happy to do this as it kept him away from the poison. He told me his brother will come to the prison tomorrow morning at church parole time with the ex-prisoner I know. He would like us all to have a talk and sort this thing out.

I told him that if we are going to talk then I have to be

straight and tell him this is all in his head. I reminded him that prior to talking to me I was the one putting everyone else up to poisoning him. This has now shifted from me to the other three guys. Billy replied saying it must be one of them. I told him he should speak to them in the way he is to me. He was quick to reject this saying he would never speak to anyone about the food being tampered with. I reminded him that these guys only want to do their time and get out. He said that is all he wants to do...

The common denominator between the Perth incident and what he feels here is his taking drugs (in Perth) and drink here. He said he won't touch drink again and will see this never happens. If the food is tampered with after this then he will go for someone. I advised him to buy his own food as I don't eat here but not for the same reasons as him; after fourteen years of eating prison food I don't want another drop. I sat for over two hours with Bill and finally told him I was going to bed. He left. By the end of our conversation he became easier, laughing and so on, so I hope this has a good effect on him. Clearly, he benefited from speaking to someone. At the same time what emerged is that this guy is badly disturbed and showed to me quite definite signs of blowing up. I know that I will put a chair in front of my door just in case. I do not trust this guy. He kept saying he will not get caught if he strikes. By this I take it he will do it when people are in their beds. I will take personal precautions.

28th MARCH '82 (7.43am)
I wakened from a tense sleep, looking at the chair against the door and immediately criticised myself for being selfish and perhaps melodramatic. The former because other guys slept open and unknown of the danger of the troubled Billy in their midst. On thinking about the melodramatic part I consider this not to be the case. I can see Billy will be an unpredictable and dangerous quality.

Later:
On the Church parole I walked with Billy, in front of the

others, to where his brother's car sat. I asked them to move to a spot where we could watch for Sarah coming to pick me up, away from the prying eyes of the prison.

I spoke to them briefly saying Billy and I had a talk last night, mentioning his feelings etc. I cautioned them on his paranoia saying the guys in the hostel wouldn't consider poisoning his food. I outlined to them the danger of Billy's condition and how there may be a guy come into the hostel who will react to his paranoia and though Billy may be the victor in that he'll physically beat the guy with the broken bottle, ultimately he will be the loser as he will do many more years inside. Surely he hasn't come this far in his sentence for this to happen? Billy asked pointedly why it is he feels better now. I replied its because he has had the opportunity to speak about it and not keep it pent-up in his own head. A problem shared is a problem helped.

Sarah came along and we hailed her. She turned her car to stop behind us. I left them to join her. The ex-prisoner followed us and with a straight face said the wee guy (Billy) is bonkers...

Sarah and I went for a walk in one of Edinburgh's natural walkways and discussed all of this. She thought it appalling that someone in Billy's condition should be left like this. Sarah said if there weren't so many complications she would write a letter to the medical side condemning them for this. She suggested that if Billy's behaviour deteriorates then I should speak to the prison psychiatrist. The complications referred to are related to Billy's release date as this would simply be taken away from him and only set him back further. We agreed that I give him some support meantime but monitor the situation very carefully.

29th MARCH '82
This morning I did my exercises and was having a shower when the prison passman remarked that Billy was in a bad state. It seems he has made it known that people had better not mess him around or he will crash an iron bar over their heads. The passman said he spoke to guys who were in Perth with Billy and they say he is much worse. The picture

emerging is that everyone in the hostel is afraid that Billy will crack-up while they are sleeping and do one of them an injury. The passman said he keeps a chair behind his door to prevent anyone getting in. The guys sleeping next to him in the dormitory are afraid. What is amazing here is that these guys despite their fears won't go to the authorities. They would rather live with Billy. It isn't that they are afraid of being caught 'grassing', simply that to do so would be to harm him — his provisional release date would be taken away from him. The authorities would react in a punitive and inhumane way and most know Billy wouldn't survive this.

I stood at the door waiting to get out at 10.30am as I had lots of work on. The only way I would get through it was on a well-disciplined schedule. The duty staff officer told me the Governor wanted to see me. Eventually I was called to the office and the Governor spoke to me. He said the police wanted to speak to me about two youngsters who had absconded from List 'D' School. He asked me about it. I informed him that two youngsters approached me led by one of their older brothers. I was told they had run away from this institution and they were looking for advice. I advised them to return and do their time. I thought that by running away they were leaving themselves open to further offences and court appearances. In my experience this usually led to Borstal and then prison. They agreed to return. I called the head of the School and he agreed to come and pick them up. I would have taken them to the meeting place with the head of the school myself but I had other commitments. The elder brother agreed to go with them.

Within a few minutes two uniformed policemen came in. The senior, a Chief Inspector, did most of the talking. He said depending what way I answered his questions there was a possibility of charges being made against me. The charge being, harbouring two List 'D' absconders. He then told me that he understood I knew the whereabouts of the two youngsters and did from last Tuesday. I informed him of what I had told the Governor. The policeman then told

331

me that the youngsters, including their brother, had become involved in a serious fight with the police resulting in injuries to his men. Apparently the police tried to arrest them at the place where they were meeting the head of the school and wouldn't believe them when they said they were handing themselves in. He asked if I had ever thought of calling the police and I told him no, not in order to deceive them but the head of the school was handling it.

The inspector in telling of the damage they have done to his men and police vehicles said he has known the brothers for four years and knows more about them than I ever could. He was rather dull and authoritarian with no understanding of the pressures on youngsters living in these areas. He did, however, accept my story. It was well supported by the head of the school.

31st MARCH '82

This morning on leaving the hostel the duty officer mentioned Billy to me. He said he had spoken to him but that Billy expressed difficulty when out shopping. This seemed to alleviate the anxieties of the duty officer. He took the view that it is a difficult period of adjustment. I could suss that he was groping in my direction. I asked him why Billy had been sent to Carstairs. He said it was a fixation, more an obsession and persecution complex that others were trying to poison him. I remarked that Billy has stopped eating. The officer's face fell. He said with some trepidation, that he hopes it isn't returning again. He said the assistant governor had asked how Billy is doing.

Billy is now bringing in fish suppers to eat at night. He doesn't eat in the place...

My visit to the local childrens hostel was the highlight of their day to most of the kids. A good percentage asked me if I knew their Dads either in Perth, Saughton or Peterhead prisons. Their Dads or uncles all knew me and were good fighters. My heart goes out to these babes, what chance have they got in life...

16th APRIL '82
This morning the talk in the Hostel centred round two things: 1) George being seen in a pub last night. A prison officer saw him. George was taken aside by the duty officer on return and told next time he would be put in the solitary cells. 2) Another prisoner was given the sack at the Fruit-market because of bad communications between the prison and his boss. The prison are going to try and get him reinstated.

26th APRIL '82
This morning the senior social worker collected me from the TFF hostel. We sat in his office. He said he didn't know why he had brought me across as he has nothing to tell me. I asked him if there had been any progress on getting me a social work supervisor yet? He replied that it is a bit soon yet and no-one ever has one this soon. I told him this is inconsistent with the facts as other guys have theirs. He said this is true but normally for those having problems... He hoped that I would have one within the next month. I told him I don't want any last minute hitches.

We then sat speaking in a stilted way. He asked me how I would handle the amount of publicity I'm likely to face when released. I told him that I have no fears. He said there would be good publicity but how would I handle it if someone wanted to have a go at me. I told him I didn't understand. He said some of my old enemies. I told him that I usually see some of my old friends when visiting my family in the Gorbals. To date they've tried to smother me in kindness.

I moved him from this to talking about the TFF and why the Social Work Unit are not more involved there as some guys are really struggling. I knew I had hit a bull's eye with this. He readily acknowledged the failure in this area. He said the TFF Hostel is badly needing re-vamped as it is run on criteria that are long out of date and irrelevant to today's situation. He said he had to be careful about tackling this as 'they' would accuse him of 'airy fairy' ideas. He said change is slow in coming, sighting the example of an assistant governor he knew who has twelve years in the system who said he never has enough time to tackle new issues. His work is basically geared to keeping the present rusting system going along. He said these guys are so swamped in other things that their priorities are other things. Innovation is low in their priority. I gave him another example of many assistant governors who had come into the Unit while working in Barlinnie main prison. They largely complained of being treated as glorified message boys and given little responsibility.

He then talked about Mr Hills saying that most of his time is taken up in trying to educate the public about prisons and in making offenders more acceptable to the community. He said he can hardly fault this as it is a job needing to be done. I said the problem is that his energy is geared to this at the expense of the internal running of the prison. He agreed.

He said he would push to get me a social worker. I asked him what sort of restrictions are liable to be placed on me when released. He said they are standard and advised me to ask what the conditions of release would be around September. He said he didn't know whether I would have any special conditions and gave a wry smile. This smile is about his knowing they have already given me a special licence of conditions on TFF. I asked him what restrictions there would be on travel. He said they aren't too happy at ex-prisoners travelling overseas in case they cause diplomatic hassle. I looked at him saying this hardly applies to guys like me. Perhaps ex-President Nixon's men but not me as I am hardly known outside Scotland. He said I am very modest, that I am an international figure.

Listening to guys like him makes me want to puke. In all probability this guy looks on himself as pretty progressive whereas I see him as a wisened thirty eight year old bureaucrat upholding the system. He is the definition of social control in the long-running debate of Care/Control within social work. Back in the hostel I was told the Training Governor wanted to see me... I told him about the senior social worker and his statement about a social worker only being necessary at the end of my sentence. Both of them (escorting hostel officer) disagreed with this saying it's much better if I have a social worker early on. The Training Governor said a social worker would ideally be given prior to the five days Home Leave. The officer made a pertinent observation that I am the only one in the Hostel without a social work supervisor.

5th MAY '82
The war between Britain and Argentina is beginning to result in high casualties. I want to record my feelings about this. First, I would prefer for there to be no conflict (military) whatsoever.

What I find interesting within me is that a strong part wants to see Britain being defeated and humiliated. Obviously this would result in a high loss of life. I am trying to be honest with what is going on inside me as this contradiction is difficult to work out. Perhaps it relates to my past, and the fact that the Junta is being accused of having no consideration for human rights in their country. Whilst this may be true there is this deep part of me that wants people to know that there is a gross negligence of human rights in this country. I think this is the thread of discontent in me. I am firmly behind Tony Benn and his supporters in their uncompromising stance to call a halt to the violence in the South Atlantic. The thought of two right wing leaders in Britain and Argentina clinging to their political lives by sending people to be killed is nauseating. Equally, to see the saturation coverage the media is spouting on a KILL, KILL, KILL basis is nauseating. At this moment of writing I have the vivid image of young boys in their teens now reduced to dead bodies and thrown about by the heaving seas with no future left. They are but memories to their relatives, cut off from their future prematurely. In thinking about the conflict I am forcing myself to look at the personal side of it in this way. I don't want to be told through the lifeless monotone of a Ministry of Defence Spokesman who sits there devoid of all emotion, sombre in his account of the affair, all of which is

335

calculated to reduce public reaction. I want to lower myself into the freezing cold water and feel the reality of these young lives; dying, so we are told, in a cause of principle.

There can be no victors in this affair now that a life has been lost. The fact that hundreds have not been killed renders it a tragedy without due cause or reason. I want to register my protest at this war and say that I condemn it, totally and unequivocally.

17th MAY '82

This morning George returned from a few days leave to visit his dying father in Crewe. We talked about it. He said his father is near to death and all the family are down there with him. George described moments when at the bedside he humourously told his father to hold on for two weeks till he is out. George said he has always dreaded losing someone when he is in prison. It hasn't happened yet. The prison authorities have told him he can have another few days at his father's bedside. George said he approached the Governor to ask the Parole Board to release him two weeks early but the governor refused.

At the Quarry hut (where I work) I watched two young guys play pool. We talked about Argentina. One was filled with exhultation as he watched the news on the TV. He talked with full anger and conviction saying we should blow these Argie bastards out of the island. He said we have the power to crush these bastards and should do so. Heatedly he remarked that he would go and fight in a minute. On this issue he was excessively patriotic. He told me he would vote for Margaret Thatcher now as she is the right leader to deal with this. He called Labour a bunch of weak bastards as they want to talk and bring back the Task Force. This youngster said he keeps all the newspaper clippings on the war and videotapes all the TV items on it. He said any soldier or military man must expect to die if he joins up. He repeated that he would join to fight for his country. He said this is the greatest thing ever to happen in his lifetime as it has brought everybody together to fight these bastards.

This is the frightening part of this situation. I meet so many like him. The anger and aggression in his voice is frightening. Ironically, his present situation is terrible. Along with his imprisonment, his wife and child have been thrown out of the house. They are virtually homeless. I find it difficult to comprehend that this young guy talks so patriotically about his country and the need to fight and die for it when it can't even provide him with the basic protection for his wife and child — a roof over their heads. As though to reinforce the distorted influences in his life, although homeless, he has a TV and video recorder which is a pretty expensive commodity!

18th MAY '82
...This morning I was introduced to my social work supervisor.

19th MAY '82
On going into the Hostel kitchen two new instructions were on the wall "No unauthorised cooking allowed" and "All meals must be eaten in the dining hall"....

21st MAY '82
Wattie, who previously worked in the Fruit market and was subsequently sacked when the prison dentist kept him back from work for dental treatment, is still unemployed. The prison admit negligence in not informing the Fruit market, which means no blame can be laid at the feet of Wattie.

However, the duty officers in the Hostel are far from happy at him hanging around all day. No-one has approached him to ask about another job or would consider letting him go out and search for one. In fact, noises are being made that he be taken back to 'closed conditions'. In response to this Wattie is saying he doesn't care what happens so long as 'they' don't touch his release date.

Last week he was growing a beard and had a few days' growth. The duty officer told him to get it off as he hasn't had permission from the Governor to grow one. Wattie said he was thinking of taking it off anyway. He said this rather than confront the officer knowing that it is deliberate pressure being put on him.

23rd MAY '82

On entering the prison gates tonight I was taken aside by the Assistant Governor who then walked with me to the Hostel. He informed me that there had been some trouble in the Hostel as money had been stolen and staff were in searching the place. They have left my cell closed till I returned from local parole leave. He said if the money is found in my cell I won't be in trouble as it was stolen during the period I was out. At this point I thought one of the prisoners had their money stolen.

On entering the Hostel all the prisoners were congregated in the kitchen area while staff searched. One of them told me that all the prisoners' expenses — £150, had been stolen from the office.

When the prisoners were together I made my views clear by stating that whoever did it must be a nutcase, putting his life on the line for a measly £150. Also that it will mean a severe tightening up of the place and perhaps someone being made a scapegoat. The worrying thing is that some staff are going round saying 'the party is over'. They are clearly implying there will be repercussions. When on our own some of the prisoners stated that it was great that someone had done the bastards. I broke this vicious circle of hate breedig hate by letting them know that some innocent person could fall victim to a retaliatory measure. Some of the guys found the strength to give alternative views. Others, of course, carried on with their anti-authority hatred.

24th MAY '82

One of the guys told me that staff found two knives when searching the Hostel for the stolen cash. This has raised lots of anxiety in the place. Those prisoners in the Hostel, when it went missing, have been kept off work. The Governor came in and spoke to them saying that investigations are continuing and they will be kept in till such times as they are cleared. Most of them suss they will get out tomorrow.

What worries me is that Billy is now back eating prison food as he is one of those being kept in. . . .

25th MAY '82
Tonight I spoke to the Governor after having arranged to meet him earlier. I explained to him that I was concerned about an issue in the Hostel but was apprehensive about speaking to him as prison authorities tend to be punitive in approach.

I explained in detail the problems surrounding Billy, saying he needed help. After listening he agreed. He told me that he didn't know about the knives being found in the Hostel. He said he was pleased that we had spoken so frankly as we do have a duty to the community outside and Billy could do a lot of damage to someone. I told him I had spoken to Peter Whatmore about it, that I called him to ask what was the right thing to do. Mr Hills said he was 'surprised' as Whatmore hadn't said a word to him. I told him the problem for me speaking truthfully to him is that he starts pointing the finger at Peter Whatmore or people like him. I explained how everyone in the Hostel realised how precious a provisional release date was and as a result they were protective of Billy. I mentioned how guys are lying in fear at nights, and the passman, with the chair against the door. Mr. Hills said morale must be low if the staff aren't picking this up.

I returned to the hut wondering, have I done the right thing, what way will he respond to this? On the one hand I don't want Billy doing any more damage and on the other he can't be allowed to do something and end up in a worse situation. If that happened they would say it was his own fault, that he was given every bit of support and help when in fact he wasn't. He would be the real victim.

1st JUNE '82
I went in front of the Deputy Governor on request this

morning, I explained that I had been refused permission to run in the Edinburgh Marathon and wanted to know why? He said the reason is that Younger's Brewery is sponsoring the competition and this alone should be enough to deter me from running. I replied this was a poor excuse for stopping me. He said that in discussions they felt it would be embarrassing if on coming through the tape I was offered a drink. He said they had refused five other 'D' categories for the same reason. I told him this was unacceptable though I would have to go along with it. He asked if I had been in Skye during my last weekend home. I told him I was. He asked what I was doing there? I replied that I didn't see any reason for not being there. He said I should know better. I asked what he meant. He said this distance is unacceptable. I reminded him that I have been in Dunbar and in Glasgow in other weekends home. He said they were acceptable distances but if anything had happened in Skye I could have been in trouble. I told him I was more likely to be in trouble if something happened in Glasgow!

I explained to him that we are getting into a ridiculous stage with all of this. He replied that this is embarassing to the Governor and I could at least phone the Governor and say where I am. I told him this is a new rule he is making up. He said it isn't a new rule and went on to say other prisoners can do what they want in this respect as they won't be recognised by people. Also, I should know better!

All of this was discussed with me made to stand in front of him whilst his henchmen stood at his side. I felt a deep anger in me. I felt that in being treated this way it is difficult to maintain any good feelings towards these people.

7th JUNE '82
This morning I enquired about bringing my bicycle into the prison when I returned from work but was told it wouldn't be allowed. I was told that on a previous occasion when a prisoner tried this he was given two reasons: 1) It could be used as a means of transport for someone escaping. 2) It could be a security risk. I was incredulous at this, though

found the former extremely funny. I have this image of someone stopping to haul my bike over the wall in order to cycle to freedom...

14th JUNE '82
This morning the remaining prisoner working in the Fruit-market was sacked. It seems his boss was upset at him arriving in three minutes late...

9th JULY '82
Free from the prison Sarah and I zoomed home to complete our packing before heading to the airport. The hustle and bustle of people moving around, the tannoy system alerting us to which passengers were leaving at what time. This is magic! Soon Sarah and I will be completely free to go to those far-off places... Getting our tickets we checked in. Passing machines that sift the gun-men from the innocent passengers we waited with the other shuttlers. It was crowded with people drinking and talking. Sarah whispered in my ear, 'George Younger is over there'. Looking across the room I could see the Secretary of State for Scotland with his wife. I felt an excitement and knew this was good luck. Looking across the room I could see this little man standing there away from the trappings of office and asked myself, what is this all about? He would be jostled and pushed like everyone else on the way to the plane. At the same time I was aware that the hand holding the drink could sign my freedom tomorrow. As we stood there I could see one or two businessmen approach him to introduce themselves, perhaps putting in a good — grovellers — word for the Government and their benevolence to industry, rightly or wrongly. It was all so sycophantic. The flight passengers were called and we walked to the plane. As we approached his seat he looked up and smiled. We occupied the seats immediately behind which I'm sure must have made him feel uncomfortable. He turned to talk to me about the weather and how 'muggy' it was, saying it was more so in London. I introduced him to Sarah and then we settled in. He sat reading

341

the *Daily Mail* as I read *Confessions of a Justified Sinner*. I couldn't help thinking of how, from the prison situation I am in, access to the Secretary of State for Scotland is non-existent as there are layers and layers of bureaucracy. And yet, here I am sitting here beside him... The flight was quick though bumpy. While waiting to leave the plane he took the initiative in asking Sarah about mutual friends. His wife joined in. We eventually parted with him wishing us a pleasant weekend...

14th JULY '82
This morning a prison officer came into the Hostel to escort me back into the prison as I was to have 'mug shots' taken. I had to sit before a screen while the lights flashed my profile. I felt queasy about this though didn't allow myself to be taken down by it. Afterwards, while waiting on the officer, I looked in another room to see two guys playing chess. On looking closer the chess men were all askew. Both men were stoned out of their heads. One of them eventually looked my way. I could see immediately that he was gone. He tried to speak to me but couldn't. He approached giving me a postcard to post for him. He was too far gone for me to caution. I looked in to where the staff sat and they were sitting quite the thing. There is such a division between staff and prisoners that they just don't see this guy stoned. Perhaps this is one of the good reasons for keeping the dividing line...

20th JULY '82
Billy and another prisoner due for release have been told they can have their three days Home Leave any time between now and when they are released in September.

28th AUGUST '82
Tam, serving 10 years for seriously assaulting his wife came onto TFF last week. He is a first offender and has served four years of his sentence. He comes from a small village, so Edinburgh is a strange new world to him. Today was his first six hour parole since arriving here. He wants to use six

today and six tomorrow as his wife has come down to join him. They are having a go at making it up. She has paid an extortionate sum to get a flat for the weekend. Rates are at a premium due to the Edinburgh Festival. They spent a nice six hours with each other and left the flat to return to the prison on time. However, not knowing Edinburgh they took a wrong turn and ended up in the opposite direction. Eventually they arrived at the prison gate 20 minutes late. On entering Tam was immediately taken to task by the officer and told he was on a disciplinary report and would go before the Governor on Monday. This, in effect, meant that Tam would not see his wife on his remaining six hour parole tomorrow. He was shattered. He asked John, another TFF prisoner, to speak to his wife when she came to meet him in the morning.

29th AUGUST '82
On going out for our three hour church parole Sarah was waiting. We passed John waiting for Tam's wife to arrive. I told Sarah about it and as I did so Tam's wife passed us beaming with happiness on her way to the prison. It really is disgraceful. There was no consideration given to Tam's wife, her position or the financial outlay to see her husband. . . I spoke to John afterwards. He said Tam's wife was terribly angry and left on her own in this city with no opportunity to speak to her husband.

30th AUGUST '82
Tam is downstairs as I write this. He said staff are going to forget the incident and not put him in front of the Governor. He is relieved at this. I am appalled by it. The person most affected and harmed is Tam's wife and through the dynamics of the prison game the prison staff are making themselves goodies by not going through with the disciplinary report when the real damage has been done.

31st AUGUST '82
This morning on going downstairs I noticed one of the

343

three guys scheduled to be released tomorrow as he stood at the cooker. I could see at a glance the full depth of the despair he is feeling. Despite this he is trying to keep up a front. These three guys are expecting to go out tomorrow but no governor has come to speak to them. It is an atrocious state of affiars. On going out to work I bumped into Malcolm Rifkind (Local MP and Under-Secretary of State) as he was being shown round the workshop. He came across and we shook hands. He asked how things have been here and I told him it has been an invaluable placement for me. I told him I had nine weeks to go before being released. He was pleased to hear this. He asked if I would be leaving the Community Workshop in November? I told him yes, that Sarah and I want a break but we have made many friends here so will keep our ties with the place. He asked what I was intending to do on release? I explained that Sarah and I intended opening a Centre here in Edinburgh. It will be a place offering support to ex-prisoners and mental patients on release. Also, it will be a place were we will campaign for change inside these institutions. He said this is needed... Back in the Hostel two of the three due to be released were told they would be released on the 7th Sept. They were shattered. Billy, who was one of them, has his family coming to meet him at the gate in the morning. The third was told there is no date for his release yet. It may come in the second or third week of the month. The cruelty of doing this to guys who expected to be released tomorrow is crushing to all of us. These people are playing with our minds.

7th SEPTEMBER '82
(6.30am) All night I've been restless. Inside me the adrenalin has been pumping, making me aware of something bigger and more important than sleep. Outside my door — across the narrow corridor — I can hear the muffled sounds of movement. I feel a wrenching pain inside. I'd have preferred to have slept. Footsteps and whispered voices can be heard with more muffled activity. The morning light is dull outside the window. My day will

come. A stab of fear objects to this confident thought — as real as the walls around me. My head tells me to be careful, to live for the moment, but my drum-beating heart wants to disregard it and make merry with wild anticipation. The muffled sounds now slip through my window. They are outside. I don't know what will become of Billy in the future but I am in dread for him. They sneak out and through the gate. All of this with regard to those of us left behind. They know what it feels like. Lying here I imagine their stifled joy. Pulling the blankets over my head I try to blank the pain of my confinement and the joy of their freedom. The mainstreet of my mind projects images of them crossing the threshold to freedom. I can see them shake hands with glowing faces as they walk down the prison driveway. Freedom when it comes will be held precious by me.

1st OCTOBER '82

The Governor asked me to return to the prison at 2.30pm. He was most amiable saying he wanted to write a final report on me. He said he doesn't want to get caught up in the conflict of my being sent here. He prefers to ask how this particular period here went. He wanted to know about my Community placement. I told him the Wester Hailes people and the work was demanding but rewarding as I had made many friends there. He asked if this sort of work would be of benefit to other prisoners. I said yes. He said he feels the scope of my placement may have been too loose. I said it was difficult for me working with many other peoples' problems and handling a lot of responsibility only to return here to be treated like a child. He said he would never take any one on such a lengthy programme again as he doesn't believe it is good.

He asked about the TFF Hostel. I told him the weekend leaves are atrocious, that after such a long period of confinement the simple example of getting used to sharing a bed with someone is in itself a traumatic experience. That once every three weeks is disruptive. He replied that having to live on three different levels must be difficult. I

345

commented on the 9.30pm deadline saying the return time while trying to establish a social life was difficult. Most people only begin their evening entertainment then. He replied that this is becuase the Hostel is within the prison walls. In all, this meeting was amiable and the best I've had with the Governor. In answer to my enquiries he said they had been given an assurance by the Department that my Licence will be through early and he sees no problems with my getting out on 1st November.

9th OCTOBER '82

Last night I went to bed feeling tired and hoping for a good sleep. Three times during the night I wakened — the cold image of steel bars illuminated by the lights stabbed their impression into my consciousness. Each time I hoped for immediate sleep. The 'gate fever' has me gripped in its nightmare fist. It's bad enough coping with it in daytime without doing a nightshift!

Leaving the prison into the dull grey Edinburgh morning I felt good at being outside. Heading into the city centre I walked through the west end full of the agonies of my 'gate fever'. Here I am with three weeks to go and having to drag myself through days that seem to span a week of time. I am very suspicious and paranoid in case someone tries to do something and prevent my release. I have this image of a monster-sized accusing finger pointing my way. My time is dragging. In marathon terms, I've hit the wall.

As I walked along the street wrapped up in a heavy jacket and trying to alleviate the anxieties in my head I recognised something familiar about the small, dapper figure coming my way. He was an old man, smartly dressed with a pink, well-cared for face. He looked at me with puzzled recognition. I suppose both of us were used to being recognised in the streets. At nose distance and almost upon each other we reached out to shake hands smilingly. It was Lord Cameron! He recognised who I was. Extraordinary! Both of us startled, automatically shook hands and began blustering amiably before saying goodbye. I was shocked. Here is this man who sentenced me to spend the past fifteen years of my life in prison and we meet on the street like this. What powerful force of destiny places me in bizarre situations like this? It's incredible to think I am in the throes of anguish while walking the streets, that sleeplessness and pressures of impending release are biting into me at the moment he appears. Looking back on it I feel this is the sort of experience one could easily imagine. Inside me when speaking to him I felt a deep tension and anger at the old bastard for having subjected me to this. Another reasoning part sees him as a minute part of the 'system', whilst a small vocal noise cried from deep inside 'Aye, but it's what he represents'. I couldn't help but wonder, where has he been these past fifteen years? I don't know any other prisoner who has come up against the extremes I have on the way to freedom.

20th OCTOBER '82
I returned to the prison early to meet with an assistant governor. He came into the TFF Hostel and spoke to me in the office there.

I was informed that the papers he was carrying were my Conditions of Licence — my release papers. The tension in my entire body was tremendous. I have waited fifteen years to sign these and for many of those years thinking that I would never do so.

The A.G. sat down and began to read out the conditions. I wasn't really listening "... your supervisor ...". He ran through each of these conditions with a speed and flatness that vastly underplayed their significance to me sitting opposite. I was shaking with excitement. Having completed them he went on to say, "Good luck for your future", in a voice as unfeeling and as mechanised as when he read out the conditions. He had at least six copies of the Licence which I had to sign and date. They already had the signature of R.C. Allan. The papers said I would be released on 1st November.

I took six of my local twelve-hour parole hours to get out and see Sarah. We shared this wonderful moment together. It was infectious and such a relief to know the exact date. I am still trying to contain it though as there are ten slow days to go.

Almost on cue, and with uncanny timing, two journalists arrived on our doorstep to ask for an interview. They wanted an Exclusive. We informed them that an official gag is on me till I'm released. I am not allowed to talk to the media till after the 1st Nov.

1.20am: The 'gate fever' has hit me. Sitting here wide awake I find it difficult to sleep. Almost neurotically I worry that something will go wrong over the next ten days and I won't be released. I know all of this is irrational but the adrenalin surging through my body at this moment is difficult to control. I haven't met one person approaching release who hasn't been subjected to this.

25th OCTOBER '82

The tension is mounting and I feel it with one week to go. Last night I slept pretty soundly, this being a result of my arduous physical exercise routine. Instead of the feelings in me being joyous and bubbling with happiness I am filled with anxiety. I look round at the walls containing me and know I distrust them so much. I have had to contend with them over the past fifteen years and have become so conditioned to living with them that I cannot imagine life without them.

In a physical sense I am experiencing severe pains of tension in my neck and back. These are symptoms of the situation. Yesterday I felt myself break free from this acute pain when I went for a lengthy run. I could feel all the tension evaporate. It was as though the 'burn' from the run channelled the energy. There is no doubt that throughout the coming week I'll have to push myself into these hard physical areas to ensure my being worn out. I have to ward off the wakeful darkness of the nights. I know that ultimately I can cope with it as I've shown over the years. However, I do know what *the feeling of confinement* is like in the silence of night. I would prefer not to have this.

348

27th OCTOBER '82

The stress is considerable ... The night-time hours are particularly hard as the silence of night cuts a wedge deep into me. Flashing thoughts collide in my head as the final day approaches. It is these newly released thoughts that knock me punch-drunk and cross-eyed through these final days.... I leave the prison for work aware that these hours on the outside are bliss from the dreaded 'gate fever'. There are many distractions on the outside, away from the self-penetration of being alone in a cell....

31st OCTOBER '82

The last day! How can I possibly trust it to be? *Every* morning for the past 15 years I've wakened to these surroundings. This morning is no different except for the underlying feeling of excitement.

I am gaining first-hand experience of the process of freedom. Inside I am aware that many things are going on. There is a part that wants to be joyous about it all but another seemingly stronger part stopping this as something may go wrong at the last minute. This is a sort of 'defence mechanism' that has taken me through less joyful experiences. If I were to go over the top with good feeling and it went wrong then I would be devastated. Recovery would be very difficult. What could go wrong now? I have experienced enough to know that the prison authorities are capable of anything. I distrust them considerably.

Sitting here at this moment I can say there isn't lots of good feeling in me. Many people would find this hard to believe but it's exactly my experience as I sit here. I am filled with stress and strain in these last hours. I know that this time tomorrow having stepped across the ugly prison doorstep for the last time I can afford to let my feelings go.

Having said that I am aware that there is massive media interest in my release. So, immediately I'll be on stage. For the first time I'll be free to speak to them. These past years they have followed my life and I haven't been able to say anything. The gag will be off. However, the point of it is that their presence will be an intrusion in my feelings. An intrusion in something Sarah and I would like to share ourselves.

I know life for us both will take some adjusting to. We have lived an unreal married life for so long. My fifteen years have been spent in prison surroundings therefore dominated by a strict order and authority. It will take some getting used to on the outside.

There are two other guys here in the Hostel going out the same time as me. They too are fraught with all the same anxieties. They are two brothers and will vanish into anonymity. The others remaining must feel as I have in the past. The whole thing about confinement is that one is always under the control of someone else. As a result there is uncertainty and dread as anything one may want to do must first be looked at through the eye of authority so inevitably one doesn't have any choice. It is little wonder that many prisoners on release head straight for drugs or drink. It must be a reaction to the whole process of confinement but particularly the last strenuous days. The freedom to do what has been for so long forbidden must be such a powerful force. The tendency to go for drugs or drink has a double attraction in that it immediately reduces all the tensions one has been living under. The authorities are so strict on the inside that it is also looked on as a real symbol of freedom. The sad thing is that lots of guys lose control when under the influence and are no sooner out than in.

There has to be change in all of this. The authorities must be more civilised in their approach. I know that I have a lot going for me on release, just in having a stable relationship and home. The anxieties I experience do not have the sharp edge of despair that others will have. Most are going out to the unknown. Most have no-one or nothing to go out to.

Church Parole: In the house Sarah and I have breakfast. Sarah is feeling it very much. She says she too has 'gate fever'. She cried and we held each other. Matters weren't helped much by a phone-in programme. Two calls commenting on my release state their opinions about it.

One guy says he knows of hundreds of enemies going to do me in. He advises I take a plane out of the country. The latter is a woman I've helped recently. She says I'm a magic guy. We both laugh at this.

1st NOVEMBER '82

12.01 am: Sitting here awake I am feeling okay. I will rest for the day ahead as it will be heavy going. I find it hard to grasp that this is my last night in a prison cell.

With freedom, Sarah and I will have an opportunity to work at our marriage and relationship. Another aspect to be attended to once the 'media circus' is over will be my exploring the pain of my confinement. Locked inside me is a tremendous amount of pain which I've had to hold in over the years. It will take many years for me to untie the knots inside. In Sarah I couldn't have a better partner to share this with.

5.45 am: ... getting dressed I was told by the duty officer that the media are lining the drive in front of the prison. Looking out the small window I could see across the barbed wire fence. They were assembling.

I was taken with the two others due to be released into the reception areas. We signed our release papers and collected our personal belongings. The brothers agreed to stay behind while the media caught hold of me. They preferred the anonymity.

I was taken to the gate where I waited for Sarah. These were the longest minutes of all. The gate officer said Mr Hills had called to say he was coming in. I stood on edge. Mr Hills drove in the gate. He didn't look at me. He didn't speak. Sarah arrived. Mr Hills gave the signal and the duty officer opened the gate. I stepped over to Freedom.